Assessing
Career
Development

Edited by
JOHN D. KRUMBOLTZ
Stanford University
and
DANIEL A. HAMEL
Harvard University

MAYFIELD PUBLISHING COMPANY

Library of Congress Catalog Card Number: 81-84697
International Standard Book Number: 0-87484-552-1

Manfactured in the United States of America
Mayfield Publishing Company
285 Hamilton Avenue
Palo Alto, California 94301

Sponsoring editor: Charles Murphy
Manuscript editor: Suzanne Lipsett
Designer: Judith Winthrop
Production manager: Cathy Willkie
Compositor: Boyer & Brass
Printer and binder: Bookcrafters

Contents

PART FIVE

FUTURE DIRECTIONS: FUNDING AND RESEARCH   225

APPENDIX

Preface

We are born and we die. We have no choice at all about the first event and relatively little choice about the final one. However, in the period between the two we are able to exercise some power about the way our time is spent.

A career can be thought of as the sum total of the ways in which a person has chosen to spend a lifetime. Obituary columns present case histories of careers. The time the deceased spent raising a family is represented by a list of the surviving children. The time spent in educational activities is represented by the mention of schools attended and academic honors received. The time spent at work is represented by positions held and major occupational accomplishments. Time spent in community activities is represented by organizational and religious memberships. An obituary, then, is a summary of the selected activities thought to represent the most important ways in which a person has spent time.

Those of us who are not yet dead can therefore influence our careers and our lives by choosing the ways in which we spend our time. Some will argue that many people have no choice, that the events of their life are predetermined by such factors as race, sex, geographical locale, and parents' socioeconomic class, and that alternatives are therefore nonexistent. Environmental factors certainly exert a powerful influence on people's lives, but each person can still choose whether or not to acquiesce to such factors. If indeed there were no alternatives to the conditions into which we are born, then the subject of this book, career development, would have no significance. Careers would unfold as preordained, people would have no control over their career direction, and career education and counseling would be superfluous. However, we do not believe significant career events are inevitable. We think individuals have a great deal more power to influence the directions of their own careers than they may suspect.

One could conceive of a lifetime as an almost infinite series of moment-to-moment decisions about how to spend the next second, minute, or hour. If the decision making that affected careers merely involved decisions about the next minute, it would not be important. However, some of our decisions affect not just the next minute but considerably longer periods of time. For example, the decision to enroll in a particular course of study—say, world history rather than biology in the tenth grade—would certainly influence the way one spent at least an hour a day for the ensuing academic year and the decision about which, if any, college to attend would have a profound influence on the way one spent as much as four years of one's life. A marriage decision could influence greatly the way one spent much of the rest of one's life. Decisions about occupational activities have profound implications not only for the ways one spends working time but for determining one's economic level, types of home, neighborhood, friends and associates, and the quality of one's leisure time. Career decisions, affecting as they do many aspects of an individual's life, are vitally important.

Most people realize that decisions about spending future time are crucial. They worry about making good choices but are not sure what the best choices are or how to go about making them. Many people need help in making career decisions, and the fields of vocational counseling and career education have developed in response to this need.

Career education is basically an attempt to help people gain the knowledge and develop the skills and attitudes needed to make important decisions about spending future time in ways that are most beneficial to them and to their society. The objective of career education sounds simple, but in fact it is complex. Profound philosophical questions arise about the relative values of the individual and society. Practical questions arise about the specific knowledge, skills, and attitudes desirable for particular individuals. Basic questions arise about the nature of a good decision and the process needed to arrive at it.

Finally, there are questions of whether career guidance and education achieve their intended effect. Do the people who receive career education benefit in any way? Do they really make better career decisions? Are the benefits they receive different from those intended by the designers of career education programs? Are they harmed in any way by attempts to help? How can we tell whether career education is working?

This last series of questions is the focus of this book. The volume represents an attempt to cast light on the issues involved in measuring the outcomes of career education and the career development it is designed to produce. As Bailey points out in chapter 1, career education as a formal program is relatively new, although the basic ideas behind it could probably be traced to antiquity, since people had to make career decisions long before the notion of career education was devised.

It is important that we find effective ways of measuring career development and the outcomes of career education, for the only way we can determine that our good intentions are attained is by assessing their impact on the intended beneficiaries. If those we hope to aid do not benefit, our efforts have been wasted and we had best devote our time and money to more productive activities. If our efforts are only partially beneficial, we may diagnose strengths and weaknesses to improve our effectiveness. In the unlikely event that we discover our efforts achieve all their intended benefits, we can more confidently advocate the expansion of the program to others not yet served by it. Whatever the results of our assessment, they will have important implications for the future of career education and the guiding of people through the career development process. Although definitive answers remain elusive, the authors represented in this volume bring into sharp focus the major issues confronting evaluation efforts and offer practical recommendations for making immediate progress and achieving long-range solutions.

The contents of the book reflect the broad range of experience and expertise represented by the contributors. The first chapter, by Bailey, paints a broad overview of the origins of the career development and career education movements. The various conceptualizations and their implications for implementation create an agenda for the subsequent focus on assessment and evaluation. Another early chapter, by Borow, examines several of the major theories of career development and suggests how these models of vocational behavior are linked to guidance practice, research, and assessment efforts.

Next, in part II, several measurement specialists take a close look at some technical requirements in vocational assessment. By defining the nature and extent of current problems, these experts provide us with insights into the technical issues that must be resolved. Among the topics addressed here are guidelines for establishing the validity and reliability of career development instruments, procedures for constructing suitable measures, and the relationship between certain career development instruments and conventional measures of abilities and academic achievement.

In part III, another group of authors discusses their recommendations for some alternative ways of viewing the assessment of career development outcomes. Performance testing, simulation devices, and the use of item domains are among some novel approaches that hold great promise.

Of great relevance to many are the practical problems of career education evaluators, discussed in part IV. Psychologists and educators are often called upon to address concerns "in the field," removed from the ivory tower of theory and conceptualization. Covered in this section are the practical difficulties encountered by evaluators attempting to build adequate measures, select a battery of instruments appropriate for evaluating a given program, and assess the implementation of a comprehensive career education program. These accounts are filled with rich, and, at times, humorous anecdotes that should provide inspiration for those seeking creative solutions to measurement problems in career development.

Finally, in part V, the outlook for assessing outcomes of career development receives attention from authors concerned about both funding opportunities and research priorities. These concluding chapters contain descriptions of specific resources and practical suggestions for achieving progress in assessing career development.

The volume concludes with an annotated bibliography of presently available career education measures. Strategies and techniques for improving the quality of career education evaluation are emphasized throughout. This emphasis has great salience for guidance practitioners, administrators, local and state curriculum planners, educational researchers, and others who must deal with the constant presence of accountability demands.

A few words are in order here regarding what this book is *not* about. Readers looking for a "how to do it" manual will probably be disappointed. Although several contributors discuss specific evaluation methods and most make concrete proposals for improving assessment efforts, the focus is not methodological. Nor is the book a state-of-the-art summary of major evaluation studies. Again, several chapters report the outcomes of studies designed to assess particular aspects of the career development process, but the coverage is representative rather than comprehensive.

The scope of the volume is broad and the material is intended to be provocative as well as informative. The individual authors are experts on the evolution of the career education movement, career development theory, practical assessment problems in the field, technical issues in developing adequate measures, and alternative ways to conduct assessment. Thus, this collection of papers suggests a set of priorities for the field as a whole.

The difficulties of improving our evaluation of career development outcomes should not deter us from the task. Career education and career development are important things to be evaluating. An incredible amount of human suffering and wasted potential is attributable to faulty career development and planning. Yet despite our awareness of the career development difficulties of vast numbers of people and the millions of dollars spent on career education programs, we lack the evidence needed to decide what learning experiences are most beneficial to students who are seeking a range of career development competencies.

Good evaluation techniques will yield dependable answers to these questions. Poor evaluations could yield answers that lead us to take inappropriate actions. The purpose of this book is to assess our current means of measuring the outcomes of career education and career development and to point out ways to improve the assessment and research process. Career education itself is a new field, and the measurement of its outcomes is newer still. We hope that writing about ways to improve assessment will help everyone in career education be more effective.

Acknowledgments

This book was inspired by the National Conference on Testing Issues in Career Development held in Washington, D.C., in May 1978. Robert Wise and Judy Shoemaker of the National Institute of Education, sponsor of the conference, were instrumental in planning and conducting this meeting. Professor Robert Calfee of Stanford University played a key role in organizing the conference, contacting participants, and urging us to ask participants to contribute papers for a volume on assessing career development outcomes.

We are also grateful for the ideas and suggestions of many individuals who responded to our questions about topics to be covered at the conference. Among those who contributed especially useful recommendations were Reg Corder, John Crites, H. B. Gelatt, John Holland, G. Brian Jones, Martin Katz, Arthur Kroll, Anita Mitchell, Roger Myers, and Linda Pfister. In addition, conference participants who did not contribute chapters to the volume but who shared their expertise with others during the conference sessions were Walter Adams, Robert Calfee, Dean Nafziger, Terry Newell, Alice Scates, Hollie Thomas, and Jerry Walker. Their creativity and concerns are reflected in the scope of this volume.

Work on this book was greatly facilitated by the Advanced Study Center at the National Center for Research in Vocational Education, Ohio State University, where John Krumboltz held a fellowship. Cindy Cheely, Suzette Martin, and Mildred Cabrera were extremely helpful in working on parts of the manuscript. James Watkins and Robert Campbell helped to create a scholarly working atmosphere. Credit also goes to Robert E. Taylor, for having the foresight and initiative to establish the Advanced Study Center.

Finally, colleagues in the Office of Career Development at the Harvard Business School, where Daniel Hamel is a staff psychologist, were most helpful. Sandy Berke transformed wretched scrawl into comprehensible text, and Pat Light provided much support and encouragement.

PART ONE
HISTORICAL AND THEORETICAL BACKGROUNDS

To understand the problems and possibilities associated with assessing career development outcomes, we need to answer a number of questions, both historical and theoretical. How did career development become an important concept in American education? How was funding linked to evaluation provisions? What is the relationship between traditional vocational education and career education? How do the knowledge and theory in vocational psychology and guidance relate to the recent clamor for outcome evaluations of career development programs and career education curricula? The first two chapters of this volume provide a context in which some of the technical and practical issues addressed in subsequent sections can be explored.

In chapter 1, Bailey traces the evolution of the career education concept and discusses the federal government's role in funding and implementing career education programs. By citing key national conferences, legislative initiatives, and various definitions proposed in the professional literature and elsewhere, he traces the development of career education as a widespread and widely heralded phenomenon. In discussing national implementation strategies, he

1

describes specific budget allocations and guidelines for using past and future appropriations.

One of Bailey's most valuable contributions is the creation of a typology based on what he perceives to be some common orientations to the implementation and assessment of career education. These orientations—career education viewed as a subject, an instructional strategy, a developmental process, and a curriculum concept—have significantly different emphases and utilize different kinds of measuring tools. His discussion is more illustrative than comprehensive, but will certainly stimulate further efforts to understand and integrate varying orientations to assessment.

Chapter 2, by Borow, completes the historical and theoretical background. Borow's long and distinguished career of helping others to understand the career-development process is brought to bear forcefully on his subject matter here. He clarifies the conditions and forces that influenced the origins of the vocational guidance movement earlier in this century, and then takes a critical look at attempts to build theories on career development phenomena, suggesting some criteria that any adequate theory must satisfy (for instance, does a particular theory lead to improved clinical or measurement technology or help us solve practical problems?).

Borow also describes and discusses a sampling of four prominent career development theories. Readers hoping for more exhaustive treatment of these and other theories should look elsewhere. Borow's intent is to cite some specific examples of the present state of the art. His commentary about unifying precepts, methodological problems, limitations of scope, and problems of practical application represents a most useful critique. Even better, Borow synthesizes the implications of his critical analysis to suggest a dozen or so strategies and guidelines for making career development theories more rigorous and useful to practitioners.

This initial section is intended to provide a useful perspective for readers evaluating the descriptions and recommendations in subsequent chapters. It reflects our belief that new initiatives in the assessment and evaluation areas should be guided by a full awareness of the philosophical, historical, economic, and theoretical factors that have shaped present-day concern about career development outcomes.

1

The relationship of career development and career education to assessment and evaluation

LARRY J. BAILEY

Southern Illinois University

This volume is a collection of essays primarily concerned with assessment and evaluation issues in relation to two broad concepts—career education and career development. The concepts are dealt with from several different perspectives. One author deals with major theories of career development. Another deals with measuring the process of career development. A third deals with the evaluation of career education programs using career development measures. Confusing? Perhaps so to one who does not fully appreciate the similarities and differences between the two concepts of career education and career development. Most professionals in education understand one or the other concept better than they do both.

This article was written mindful of Super's observation that "when the concepts of career development are more widely understood, and when its methods and materials are more visible and are put to use in the curriculum, career education will indeed have come of age" (1976, p. 42). To illustrate how career development concepts began to merge with vocationally oriented programs and practices in the late 1960s, the paper begins with a brief historical review of the origin of career education as a federal initiative. Next, the emergence of career education as a major national education priority is discussed. Then, to make obvious how different orientations toward career education are reflected in theory and practice, evolution of the career education movement from 1972 to the present is summarized. Finally, approaches to implementation and assessment that are indicative of different conceptions of the purpose of career education are identified and discussed.

THE RECENT HISTORY OF
CAREER EDUCATION

The historical, philosophical, psychological, social, and economic foundations of learning about and preparing for work are rich and varied. A number of writers (for example, Bailey and Stadt [1973], Hansen [1977], Herr [1976], Marland [1974], Olson [1975], O'Toole [1975], and Super [1976]) have documented different aspects of these bodies of literature. The recent phenomenon referred to by some as the "career education movement" has been variously influenced by these several fundamental areas. During its incubation period and formative years, however, the career education movement was shaped much less by theory than by practical motives and perceived (albeit, legitimate) needs.

The Role of the
Federal Government

A major precursor of the 1971 career education movement initiated by the U.S. Office of Education was what Mangum (1968) referred to as a "reorientation in the nature of vocational education." This phrase was used to characterize the Vocational Education Act of 1963, which represented the first basic reconsideration of vocational education since the 1917 Smith-Hughes Act. The intent of the 1963 legislation was no less than a reorientation of the traditional emphasis from filling the requirements of the labor market to meeting the needs of people. The high level of unemployment among untrained and inexperienced youth was the immediate motivation for the act. Less well recognized but implicit in the act was the growing need for more comprehensive approaches to preparation for work. Involved was the recognition that any dichotomy between academic and vocational education is outmoded, that all acceptable education must be relevant, and that adaptability to change is as important as initial preparation. It was toward these principles that the act was groping. In fact, it approached them more closely in intent than in achievement.

One feature of the Vocational Education Act was the provision for an external assessment to be conducted at the end of five years. This assessment was completed in late 1967 by the president-appointed Advisory Council on Vocational Education. Important to the present discussion is the fact that the Advisory Council continued and elaborated the philosophical "reorientation" begun in 1963. Among the principles of learning about and preparing for work that the council endorsed were the following:

1. Occupational preparation should begin in the elementary schools with a realistic picture of the world of work. Its fundamental purposes should be to familiarize the student with his world and to provide him with the intellectual tools and rational habits of thought to play a satisfying role in it.

2. In junior high school economic orientation and occupational preparation should reach a more sophisticated state with study by all students of the economic and industrial system by which goods and services are produced and distributed. The objective should be exposure to the full range of occupational choices which will be available at a later point and full knowledge of the relative advantages and requirements of each.

3. Occupational preparation should become more specific in high school, though preparation should not be limited to a specific occupation. Given the uncertainties of a changing economy and the limited experiences upon which vocational choices must be made, instruction should be built around significant families of occupations or industries which promise expanding opportunities.

4. Occupational education should be based on a spiral curriculum which treats concepts at higher and higher levels of complexity as the student moves through the program. Vocational preparation should be used to make general education concrete and understandable; general education should point up the vocational implications of all education. Curriculum materials should be prepared for both general and vocational education to emphasize these relationships [Mangum, 1968, pp. 49 – 50].

Virtually all the recommendations of the Advisory Council on Vocational Education were incorporated into a new law passed in 1968, called the Amendments to the Vocational Education Act of 1963. The principles described above regarding learning about and preparing for work were incorporated into "Part D—Exemplary Programs and Projects." The purpose of this part was to "stimulate, through federal financial support, new ways to create a bridge between school and earning a living for young people. . . ." (PL 90 – 576, p. 17).

The National Conference on
Exemplary Programs and Projects
After passage of the 1968 amendments, the United States Office of Education (USOE) sought to maximize utilization of the funds allocated under Part D. To that end, USOE sponsored nine regional and one national conference. Eight consultants presented papers at the national conference held in Atlanta, Georgia, in March 1969. Papers by Herr (1969) and Gysbers (1969) were especially significant.

The more important of the two papers in terms of influence on the evolution of career education was Herr's. He maintained that the concept of developmental tasks and knowledge of career development theory and principles should be used as the organizing structure of a systems approach to education from kindergarten through higher education. Herr advocated a system of education that would develop directly and systematically students' attitudes and knowledge of self, educational and occupational alternatives, and decision-making abilities relating to vocational identity and choice.

Herr abstracted the major theories of career development and gave broad prescriptions for centering career development in the curriculum. Above all, he argued for appropriate experiences at each level of education—for example, "Because of the importance of early childhood experiences in the family, the school and community, intervention in career development needs to begin during the first decade of life" (Herr, 1968, p. 8). Throughout, he emphasized the significance of characteristics of individuals—the very thing that was causing vocational education leaders to refocus thinking and programming. For example, Herr states, "In sum . . . the emphases attendant to guidance and aspects of education which have vocational implications have shifted from a Parsonian model of matching men and jobs to a model more committed to the clarification of those aspects of self—e.g., interests, capacities, values—which need development for a lifelong process of planning and decision making" (Herr, 1969, p. 8). Herr was astute in tying his ideas to the behavioral objectives approach, which was much in vogue, and to the structure and terminology of vocational education. He was also careful to underscore his theme:

> One of the operational goals critical to implementing the Exemplary Programs and Projects Section of the Vocational Education Act relates to the need to design behavioral descriptions which would encompass the characteristics of career development, placing these at appropriate developmental levels, and wedding them to educational strategies which will facilitate them [Herr, 1969, p. 18].

No one has expressed more succinctly the integration of career development theory, the behavioral approach to educational programming, and the reorientation of vocational education. With this relationship clarified, the foundation was laid for the emergence of career education.

Beginning in fiscal year 1970, USOE awarded the first of two rounds of pilot projects supported by a total of $47 million of Part D funds. Each round was thirty-six months in duration, with sixty-six projects in the first round and fifty-eight projects in the second round (Jezierski, 1978). This nationwide network of "Vocational Exemplary Projects" was already in place at the time Sidney P. Marland became Commissioner of Education.

"Career Education Now"

On February 10, 1970, U.S. Commissioner of Education, James E. Allen, delivered an address before the Annual Convention of the National Association of Secondary School Principals. In a little known milestone in the evolution of career education, it appears that Allen coined the term career education: "It is the renewed awareness of the university of the basic human and social need for competence that is generating not only increased emphasis today on *career education* but a whole new concept of its character and its place in the total educational enterprise" (Allen, 1970, p. 5, emphasis added).

A year later, Allen's successor, Sidney P. Marland, elevated the concept to the level of a national education priority in his famous "Career Education Now" speech (Marland, 1971). Marland opened his speech with a condemnation of administrators who had relegated vocational education to second-class status. Then he launched an attack on general education, suggesting that schools be rid of it and arguing that useful knowledge is superior to general knowledge. He next proposed that a universal goal of American education be preparation for useful and rewarding employment. Marland spoke of lifelong learning, humanness, occupational exploration, new leadership for the states, true and complete reform of the high school, emphasis on new vocational fields, cooperation with business, labor-leadership development, and state-plan innovation. The "idea" he advocated (which he readily admits was not new) soon became a "movement."

The Development Era:
1971 – 1974

Marland's remarks were iterated in numerous speeches and articles throughout 1971 and 1972. His role, however, was not confined to speech making. Under Marland's leadership, a dual strategy evolved at the federal level (High, 1976). One arm of the strategy was to assist and encourage innovations and pilot projects of the type that had already begun with Part D vocational education funds. Marland exercised his discretionary authority to obligate various additional funds for career education. Principal among these was $18 million from vocational education Part C research and development monies.

The second arm of this strategy, undertaken in conjunction with the National Institute of Education, called for carefully planned, systematic research and development. Specifically, this meant the development of four different delivery systems, referred to as (1) the school-based model, (2) the employer-based model, (3) the home/community-based model, and (4) the rural/residential-based model (Rieder, 1974).

State-level efforts in career education were occurring simultaneously with federal-level ones. By 1974, (1) five states had enacted specific career education legislation, (2) twenty-five state legislatures had appropriated specific funds for career education, (3) forty-two states and territories had designated a state-level Coordinator of Career Education, and (4) thirty states had established official state definitions of career education. Countless other activities were occurring at local education levels and in colleges and universities.

During the period 1971 – 1974, career education was also the subject of dozens of texts and hundreds of journal articles, speeches, monographs, research reports, and the like. More than a hundred commercial publishing companies introduced new instructional materials. A wide range of professional associations adopted resolutions and policy statements supporting career education. A number of large corporations such as General Motors and General Electric became active partners in career education implementation. A myriad of other business, labor, professional, and community groups supported career-education initiatives. See Herr (1976) and Hoyt (1977) for good summaries of these various efforts.

A New Definition and New Legislation in 1974

Two major events occurred in 1974 that helped to bring about consensus on a definition of career education, consolidation of responsibility for leadership with USOE, and authorization of federal funds specifically earmarked for career education. On August 21, 1974, the president signed the Education Amendments of 1974. Section 406 of the act contained five provisions for career education: (1) establishment of an Office of Career Education within USOE, (2) establishment of a National Advisory Council for Career Education, (3) a mandate for a nationwide survey and assessment of the status of career education, (4) authorization for funds for demonstration grants and exemplary career education models and programs, and (5) authorization grants for state planning.

The total authorization for Section 406 was $15 million for each fiscal year ending prior to July 1, 1978, although Congress actually appropriated only $10 million. The bulk of monies appropriated through fiscal year 1978 were for projects related to five designated categories:

Category 1: Activities designed to effect incremental improvements in K – 12 career education programs.

Category 2: Activities designed to demonstrate the most effective methods and techniques in career education in such settings as the senior high school, the community college, adult and community education agencies, and institutions of higher education.

Category 3: Activities designed to demonstrate the most effective methods and techniques in career education for such special segments of the population as handicapped, gifted and talented, minority and low-income youth, and to reduce sex stereotyping in career choices.

Category 4: Activities designed to demonstrate the most effective methods and techniques for the training and retraining of persons for conducting career education programs.

Category 5: Activities designed to communicate career-education philosophy, methods, program activities, and evaluation results to career education practitioners and to the general public.

Whereas passage of Section 406 of the Education Amendments of 1974 represented the first congressional endorsement of career education, another event represented the first official USOE endorsement of career education. When Commissioner Marland established career education as a priority of the Office of Education, he emphasized the importance of *not* having an official definition. This decision has been variously praised and condemned. Both camps can provide convincing arguments to support their points of view. Re-gardless of the ultimate wisdom of Marland's position, dozens of definitions for career education emerged to fill the void.

In order to assess the degree of consensus regarding career education, a draft paper was prepared by USOE in February 1974 along with a study guide designed to elicit responses to specific statements contained in the draft document. Responses to the paper and study guide were solicited primarily from three groups: (1) "mini-conference" participants, (2) State Department of Education personnel, and (3) national leaders.

Analysis of the responses by these three groups indicated a high degree of consensus on the nineteen statements and questions contained in the study guide. Further, the degree of consensus did not differ greatly in either degree or direction among the three groups. The apparent agreement evidenced from the responses convinced USOE that the final policy statement should not differ greatly from the original version. The consensus draft, entitled *An Introduction to Career Education: A Policy Paper of the U.S. Office of Education* (Hoyt, 1975), was officially adopted by USOE in November 1974. The official definition and nine learner outcomes for career education follow:

> Career education is the totality of experiences through which one learns about and prepares to engage in work as part of her or his way of life.

Learner Outcomes for Career Education:

1. Competent in the basic academic skills required for adaptability in our rapidly changing society.
2. Equipped with good work habits.
3. Capable of choosing and who have chosen a personally meaningful set of work values that foster in them a desire to work.
4. Equipped with career decision-making skills, job-hunting skills, and job-getting skills.
5. Equipped with vocational personal skills at a level that will allow them to gain entry into and attain a degree of success in the occupational society.
6. Equipped with career decisions based on the widest possible set of data concerning themselves and their educational-vocational opportunities.
7. Aware of means available to them for continuing and recurrent education once they have left the formal system of schooling.
8. Successful in being placed in a paid occupation, in further education, or in a vocation consistent with their current career education.
9. Successful in incorporating work values into their total personal value structure in such a way that they are able to choose what, for them, is a desirable lifestyle.

Toward National Implementation

As career education continued to evolve after 1974, strengthened by the infusion of federal monies for demonstration projects and state planning, efforts were made to formulate additional new legislation. Under the leadership of the National Advisory Council for Career Education (NACCE), a proposal was advanced for federal assistance (NACCE, 1975) to move career education beyond the demonstration mode to nationwide implementation. Despite opposition from the Carter administration (related more to inflation fighting than philosophical disagreement), Congress eventually passed and the president signed into law on December 13, 1977 the Career Education Incentive Act. A summary of the law follows:

Purpose

> . . . to assist States and local educational agencies and institutions of post secondary education, including collaborative arrangements with the appropriate agencies and organizations, in making education as preparation for work, and as a means of relating work values to other life roles and choices (such as family life), a major goal of all who teach and all who learn . . .

Authorizations

> $ 50,000,000 for FY 1979
> $100,000,000 for FY 1980
> $100,000,000 for FY 1981
> $ 50,000,000 for FY 1982
> $ 25,000,000 for FY 1983

Use of Funds

1. Employing State agency personnel to administer and coordinate programs
2. Providing State leadership for career education (directly or through contract)
   A. conducting inservice institutes
   B. training local career education coordinators
   C. collecting, evaluating, and disseminating career education materials
   D. conducting statewide needs assessments and evaluations
   E. conducting statewide leadership conferences
   F. engaging in collaborative relationships with other agencies of State government and with public agencies and private organizations representing business, labor, industry and the professions and organizations representing the handicapped, minority groups, women, and older Americans
   G. promoting the adaption of teacher-training curricula
3. Making payments to local educational agencies for comprehensive programs including
   A. instilling career education concepts and approaches in the classroom
   B. developing and implementing comprehensive career guidance, counseling, placement, and follow-up services
   C. developing and implementing collaborative relationships with organizations representing the handicapped, minority groups and women
   D. developing and implementing work experiences for students whose primary purpose is career exploration
   E. training of local career education coordinators
   F. providing inservice education for educational personnel
   G. conducting institutes for members of boards of local educational agencies
   H. purchasing instructional materials and supplies
   I. establishing and operating community career education councils
   J. establishing and operating career education resource centers

      K. adapting, reviewing, and revising local plans
      L. conducting needs assessments and evaluations
  4. Reviewing and revising the State plan

Post-Secondary Educational Demonstration Projects

      Commissioner is authorized to arrange grants or contracts to institutions of higher education for the conduct of demonstration projects which—

  1. May have national significance in promoting the field of career education in post-secondary programs
  2. Have unusual promise of promoting post-secondary career guidance and counseling programs, particularly those designed to overcome bias and stereotyping on account of race, sex, age, economic status, or handicap
  3. Show promise of strengthening career guidance, counseling, placement, and follow-up services.

      At this writing, appropriations for the act are likely to be much less than the authorization levels. Regardless of how much Congress appropriates, the conclusion is justified that career education is well on its way to becoming institutionalized within the form and substance of American education.

DIFFERENT ORIENTATIONS
TOWARD CAREER EDUCATION

      Contrary to the views of some critics, career education owes much of its strength to the fact that it encompasses a "totality of experiences through which one learns about and prepares to engage in work." Its roots are grounded in many disciplines (for example, philosophy, psychology, literature) and many applied fields (such as guidance and counseling and vocational education). Its goals are advocated for all learners, including males and females, WASPs and ethnic minorities, college and non-college-bound students, preschool- through retirement-age people, and average individuals and those with handicapping conditions. Career education encourages new linkages and partnership among education, business, labor, industry, and other community groups. It has been labeled a fad, an idea, a concept, a process, a program, a subject, a curriculum, and by some all of education.

      It is not the purpose of this paper to advocate or criticize a particular view of career education. Rather, this discussion is designed to acknowledge that a number of thoughtful people perceive career education differently. Any attempt to assess career development and career education must take into account such differences. Aware of the limitation of any categorial system (Bailey and Stadt, 1973, pp. 219–223), I have attempted to provide an objective summary of the more common orientations toward career education and to illustrate how the role of assessment is perceived within each (see Table 1-1). A discussion of these orientations follows.

TABLE 1-1
COMMON ORIENTATIONS TO IMPLEMENTATION AND
ASSESSMENT OF CAREER EDUCATION

ORIENTATION	EMPHASIS	INSTRUMENTATION (EXAMPLES)
1. As a subject	Focus is on the teaching of occupational information and related facts and figures about industries, job-training requirements, and salary levels.	The Test of Occupational Knowledge Career Awareness Inventory
2. As an instructional strategy	Work-related topics, activities, and materials are infused into the conventional curriculum to help develop basic academic skills.	California Achievement Test; Iowa Test of Basic Skills; Metropolitan Achievement Test
3. As a developmental process	Focus is on facilitating career development through individual and group guidance activities.	Career Maturity Inventory; Work Values Inventory
4. As a curriculum concept	A comprehensive curriculum-based approach that often incorporates the three previous categories (e.g., Life Centered Career Education Curriculum). Competencies are stated as outcomes of instruction. Mastery learning is emphasized.	Traditional psychometric techniques are considered to have limited usefulness. Assessment is criterion-referenced. Formative evaluation is predominate.

Note: These four orientations are illustrative but not necessarily exhaustive categories.

As a Subject

Some practitioners in the vocational education and guidance and counseling fields have long advocated the teaching of *occupational information*. One textbook widely used in preservice education programs presents the point of view "that we need to help the classroom teacher incorporate occupational information into the traditional subject-matter areas" (Norris 1963, Foreword). Suggestions for teaching occupational information typically include field trips, use of songs, resource speakers, scrapbooks, bulletin boards, and the like.

This traditional approach is still practiced today in some career education programs. Assessment is usually not a concern of teachers who use this approach, since the "means" very often are used as the "ends." However, such instruments as The Test of Occupational Knowledge (McSherry and O'Hara, 1966) and the Career Awareness Inventory (Fadale, 1974) seem to be based on a subject-matter orientation.

As an Instructional Strategy

One of the learner outcomes for career education stated in the USOE policy paper on career education is, "Competent in the basic academic skills required for adaptability in our rapidly changing society." While listed as an outcome, in practice career education is usually used as a means that is, an instructional strategy) to accomplish the "end" of teaching basic academic skills. The official position of the Council of Chief State School Officers reflects this orientation: "Career education is essentially an instructional strategy, aimed at improving education outcomes by relating teaching and learning activities to the concept of career development . . ." (Jesser, 1978).

Bonnet (1978) summarized a number of projects that have used this so-called "infusion approach" to career education. The assessment of basic academic skills usually involves the use of standardized tests of cognitive achievement (for example, the California Achievement Test, Iowa Test of Basic Skills, Metropolitan Achievement Test).

As a Developmental Process

This third approach has its origin in the guidance and counseling field. Practitioners in guidance and counseling have been influenced by two broad classes of theories emanating from vocational psychology (Super, 1969). One approach, referred to as the *occupational model,* developed between the early 1900s to about 1950. Commonly referred to as *trait-and-factor theory,* this approach was the forerunner of all modern theories of career choice. Historically, this approach has dictated much of the practice of vocational guidance because of its simplicity and ease of implementation. This was made obvious in 1937, when the National Vocational Guidance Association (1937) defined the major components of vocational guidance as the study of individuals, the study of occupations, and counseling. Although characteristically a method of vocational guidance, the trait-and-factor rationale has often been used to justify the teaching of occupational information (see Table 1-1 and the related discussion above).

During the early 1950s, alternative theories of vocational behavior began to emerge. Super (1969) characterized these theories as the *career model* of vocational counseling. The distinguishing feature of this approach is the emphasis on development (originally called vocational development, but now called career development) throughout the lifespan rather than the more static trait-and-factor emphasis on occupational choice.

Theories of career development continued to evolve throughout the 1950s, and vocational psychologists during this time put in a great deal of effort to define and measure the process of career development (that is, vocational maturity). As theory building and research evolved in vocational psychology, principles of career development and practices for facilitating them began to be taught in counselor-education departments. When new generations of practicing counselors moved into elementary and secondary schools, the nature and practice of career guidance began to shift away from testing students, surveying occupational information, and matching people and jobs to helping students develop self-awareness and self-knowledge, identify their interests and abilities, clarify their values, and learn decision-making skills. It was this type of orientation that prompted Professor Herr (among others) to link career-development principles and practices with vocational education.

When career education became a national priority in 1971, it was only natural that practitioners with a career guidance background would perceive career education in this fashion. Thus, career education programs oriented toward career development have tended to emphasize "affective" (for example, self-awareness, sense of agency, work attitudes) and "process" (for example, decision making and values clarification) types of learning outcomes. Similarly, approaches to assessment often utilize those instruments developed by vocational psychologists to diagnose and measure vocational maturity and related factors of career development. Commonly used instruments include the Career Maturity Inventory (Crites, 1978), the Work Values Inventory (Super, 1968), and the Assessment of Career Development (American College Testing Program, 1974).

As a Curriculum Concept

The second orientation in Table 1-1 represents the view that career education is a means to an end. The first and third orientations listed are different approaches to achieving career development concepts, attitudes, and skills through career education. Orientations 1 and 3 can be thought of as *parts* of a more comprehensive curriculum-based approach to career education. This fourth type of orientation to career education is used to represent broad, comprehensive models and approaches to career education. Such curriculum models for career education often incorporate orientations 1, 2, and 3 into a single approach. A good example is Brolin's (1978) Life Centered Career Education

Curriculum. This approach, based on the career development model of Gysbers and Moore from the University of Missouri, was developed specifically for special education but is generalizable to all learners.

Life-career development is described as a concept in which *life* includes all aspects of a person's growth and development over the lifespan; *career* implies many settings, many roles, and many events; and *development* means that people are continually changing and becoming (Gysbers and Moore, 1973). This broad curriculum view of career education organizes twenty-two student competencies into three primary categories: daily-living skills, personal-social skills, and occupational guidance and preparation. Instruction to develop academic competencies is seen as supportive to skills in these three categories.

Assessment in the life-centered approach is criterion referenced. Formative evaluation methods are used to determine the extent to which students demonstrate "competency" in relation to the stated learning task. Traditional psychometric techniques are considered to have limited usefulness in evaluating student achievement. "Although many objectives can be evaluated by commercially available tests, it is doubtful that any test or battery will adequately evaluate all objectives" (Brolin, 1978, p. 150).

SUMMARY AND IMPLICATIONS

The present paper was written to summarize the recent history and to describe four common approaches to career education. The objectives were (1) to demonstrate how different historical events have influenced different conceptions of career education and (2) to point out similarities and differences between career development and career education. The discussion was intended to be informative and not theoretical or prescriptive. I hope it has provided the background the reader needs to comprehend more fully the issues, problems, and approaches discussed in this volume.

The remaining papers in this volume address issues, problems, and methods related to assessing career development and evaluating career education. These papers represent a step toward the development of a broader agenda for assessment and evaluation. This step is inevitable given the dynamic and evolutionary nature of career development and career education.

REFERENCES

ALLEN, J. A. *Competence for all as the goal for secondary education.* Address given at the Annual Convention of the National Association of Secondary School Principals, Washington, D.C., February 10, 1970.

AMERICAN COLLEGE TESTING PROGRAM. *Assessment of career development.* Boston: Houghton Mifflin, 1974.

BAILEY, L. J., AND STADT, R. W.   *Career education: New approaches to human development.* Bloomington, Ill.: McKnight, 1973.

BONNET, D. G.   *A synthesis of results and programmatic recommendations emerging from career education evaluations in 1975 – 76.* Washington, D.C.: U.S. Government Printing Office, 1978.

BROLIN, D. E. (Ed.)   *Life centered career education: A competency based approach.* Reston, Va.: Council for Exceptional Children, 1978.

CRITES, J. O.   *Career maturity inventory.* Monterey, Calif.: CTB/McGraw-Hill, 1978.

FADALE, L. M.   *Career awareness inventory.* Ithaca, N.Y.: Cornell Institute for Research and Development in Occupational Education, August 1973.

GYSBERS, N. C.   *Elements of a model for promoting career development in elementary and junior high school.* Paper presented at the National Conference on Exemplary Programs and Projects, Atlanta, Ga., March 1969. (ERIC Document Reproduction Service No. ED 045 860)

GYSBERS, N., and MOORE, E.   Career conscious individual model. *Life career development: A model.* Columbia, Mo.: University of Missouri, 1973.

HANSEN, L. S.   *An examination of the definitions and concepts of career education.* Washington, D.C.: U.S. Office of Education, June 1977.

HERR, E. L.   *Unifying an entire system of education around a career development theme.* Paper presented at the National Conference on Exemplary Programs and Projects, Atlanta, Ga., March 1969. (ERIC Document Reproduction Service No. ED 045 860)

HERR, E. L.   *The emerging history of career education: A summary view.* Washington, D.C.: U.S. Office of Education, 1976. (ERIC Document Reproduction Service No. ED 122 011)

HIGH, S. C.   Career education: A national overview. *School Science and Mathematics Journal,* 1976, 76(4), 276 – 284.

HOYT, K. B.   *An introduction to career education: A policy paper of the U.S. Office of Education.* Washington, D.C.: U.S. Office of Education, 1977.

HOYT, K. B.   Community resources for career education. *Occupational Outlook Quarterly, 21*(2), 10 – 21.

JESSER, D. L.   Career education today: The greening of a reform movement. *The College Board Review,* 1978, No. 108, 11 – 15.

JEZIERSKI, K.   *Index of interim, supplemental, and final reports from career education pilot projects supported under part c and part d of public law 90–576.* Washington. D.C.: U.S. Government Printing Office, May 1978.

McSHERRY, J. P., and O'HARA, R. P.   *The test of occupational knowledge.* Copyright 1966 by J. P. McSherry and R. P. O'Hara.

MANGUM, G. L.   *Reorienting vocational education.* Ann Arbor, Mich.: Institute of Labor and Industrial Relations, 1968.

MARLAND, S. P.   *Career education now.* Address given at the Annual Convention of the National Association of Secondary School Principals, Houston, Texas, January 23, 1971.

MARLAND, S. P.   *Career education: A proposal for reform.* New York: McGraw-Hill, 1974.

NATIONAL ADVISORY COUNCIL FOR CAREER EDUCATION.   *Interim report with recommendations for legislation.* Washington, D.C.: U.S. Government Printing Office, 1975.

NATIONAL VOCATIONAL GUIDANCE ASSOCIATION.   Principles and practices of vocational guidance. *Occupations,* 1937, 15, 772 – 778.

OLSON, P. A.   *The liberal arts and career education: A look at the past and the future.* Washington, D.C.: U.S. Office of Education, June 1975. (ERIC Document Reproduction No. ED 113 487)

O'TOOLE, J.   *The reserve army of the underemployed.* Washington, D.C.: U.S. Office of Education, 1975. (ERIC Document Reproduction No. ED 109 509)

PUBLIC LAW 90 – 576,   *Amendments to the vocational education act of 1963.* October 16, 1968.

RIEDER, C. H.   Education and work: A NIE priority. *Journal of Research and Development in Education,* 1974, 7(3), 110 – 118.

SUPER, D. E.   Vocational development theory: Persons, positions, and processes. *The Counseling Psychologist,* 1969, *1*(1), 2 – 9.

SUPER, D. E.   *Work values inventory.* Boston: Houghton Mifflin, 1968.

SUPER, D. E.   *Career education and the meanings of work.* Washington, D.C.: U.S. Office of Education, June 1976. (ERIC Document Reproduction No. ED 128 593)

2

Career development theory and instrumental outcomes of career guidance: a critique

HENRY BOROW
University of Minnesota

The emergence of vocational guidance as a product of its times and as a response to the insistent social-reform pressures of early-twentieth-century America has been well documented (Brewer, 1942; Miller, 1964; Stephens, 1970). A sense of uncompromising pragmatism marked the beginnings of the movement, particularly as practitioners confronted the employment problems of out-of-school youth, rural migrants, and European immigrants. The guidance of that era did not indulge itself in the luxury of theory.

As vocational guidance institutionalized itself within the schools and colleges during the 1920s and 1930s and took on a modest measure of respectability, it adopted an empirical rationale and an accompanying strategy. As a hybrid applied science—or, more correctly, as an emerging technology—vocational guidance lacked a knowledge discipline of its own and drew heavily on the principles and methods of the psychology of individual differences and the nascent field of psychometrics. The generalized research problem was articulated as the development, validation, and application of objective tests of work-relevant human traits and later, of methods of job analysis and worker-trait analysis for major occupational groups. The goal of practice was to help indi-

18

viduals make appropriate vocational choices (an aim that has remained virtually unaltered); the logic rested on the assumed merit of matching the individual's characteristics to job requirements; and the implementing method was the testing and profiling of each client's trait makeup.

There exist, as Cronbach has noted, two broad disciplines of applied psychology, one concerned with the measurement of psychological traits for practical purposes of prediction and classification, the other with the application of cause-and-effect relationships to the planned *change* of behavior. The first adopts a static view of human nature, assuming traits to be fixed, and deals chiefly with the effective distribution of human talents in society. This is essentially the approach that characterized the classical trait-measurement and choice-making model of vocational guidance. As promulgated and practiced by psychologists, if not always by teachers and counselors, its strategy was not readily distinguishable from that of the personnel-selection prediction model that surfaced in industry around the time of World War I (Viteles, 1932). In fact, the vocational-guidance systems advanced by two prominent psychologists nearly thirty years apart blueprinted the process as an exclusively predictive operation (Hull, 1928; Horst, 1956). Apart from its links to trait-measurement technology and differential psychology, conventional vocational guidance developed outside the mainstream of the behavioral sciences. It was conceptually anemic and basically atheoretical.

THE ROOTS OF THEORY MAKING

The slowness of broad conceptual schemes of occupational behavior to appear can be best understood within the *Zeitgeist* of early applied psychology. Behavior science was the last of the major knowledge disciplines to wean itself from the mother science of philosophy. The psychology of individual differences was itself a direct descendant of the experimentally based psychophysics of Wilhelm Wundt and was, from the outset, profoundly influenced by the same insistence on objective observation that characterized Wundt's laboratory in Leipzig. James McKeen Cattell, the young American who studied with Wundt, derived the first psychological tests from basic psychophysical measurement methodology, and thus laid the groundwork for the psychology of individual differences. Distrustful of the speculative and mentalistic modes of inquiry that characterized natural philosophy, and self-conscious about its status as an emerging empirical science, psychology, especially in its applied forms, ardently embraced empiricism as its epistemology and objective testing as its instrumentation. Fully aware of the necessity of quantifying its findings, differential psychology drew on the mathematical formulations of Karl Pearson, the illustrious British biometrician. The product-moment correlation, in particular, became a standard procedure in predicting objective performance outcomes from test scores.

Given this historical climate, we can better understand the conceptual sterility and narrow constraints of early forms of vocational guidance. Interestingly, a striking parallel was to be found in the pointedly mechanistic logic of applied-psychology research on personnel selection and worker efficiency in industry. It will be recalled that important psychodynamic factors of motivation and morale in worker performance and adjustment were largely ignored until the Western Electric Hawthorne studies were mounted in the mid-1930s.

Because the typical measures (psychological tests) used in career guidance to assist clients with suitable vocational decisions were expressly designed for straightforward prediction, they contributed little to the theoretical understanding of behavior in nontest situations (Loevinger, 1957). It is not surprising, therefore, that a career guidance technology that was preoccupied with the harmonious matching of personal-trait variables to occupational-trait requirements should have been theory-poor. Crites (1969) notes that exploratory inquiries into the developmental process by which interest patterns are formed and into the relationship between interest and self-concept began to appear in the 1940s. These papers may be said to mark the first systematic attempts to conceptualize the phenomena of career development and occupational choice.

By midcentury, theory construction was well under way. The decade between 1950 and 1960 witnessed the publication of more than a dozen theories of varying scope, general to specific, and derived from several behavior-science disciplines (psychology, psychoanalysis, economics, and cross-disciplinary). It is commonly accepted that the most influential of these earlier contributions were the theories offered by Ginzberg (1951) and his associates and by Super (1953). Ginzberg, an economist who has been a prolific writer in the area of human-resources policy and development, has since published only a few relatively minor papers on his theory of occupational choice, but his pioneering model continues to draw attention. Super, who, beginning in 1951, initiated the publication of a series of seminal journal papers on the subject, has been a prodigious contributor to research, theory, and application across a broad spectrum of career development problems. Although Super's (1942) avant-garde book, *The Dynamics of Vocational Adjustment,* had not presented a theory of career development or choice, it went well beyond conventional trait-measurement psychology in delineating occupational behavior and prefigured some of the elements of later theory making.

THE UTILITY AND CRITERIA
OF THEORY

It is a common misunderstanding that theory operates most prominently in those sciences that have chiefly "soft" data and numerous knowledge gaps in their structure. In fact, the best theories are to be found in such fields as physics, which have laboriously assembled large sets of dependable empirical propositions. The heart of sound theory resides in the scientific principles or lawful relationships that have been derived from controlled observation. In the absence of a logical matrix, however, such a posteriori laws would stand merely as an unordered collection of descriptive statements about events. The power of good theory is that it furnishes a nomological network that permits these propositions to be meaningfully interconnected and allows us to move beyond the description of phenomena into the realm of explanation. It does this by introducing hypothetical (theoretical) constructs, terms of understanding that connect the propositions of the theory in a systematic way. Moreover, theory is heuristic in suggesting promising new empirical probes that, if successful, introduce newly confirmed propositions into the theory network and extend the knowledge base. This procedure of deducing and testing hypotheses is coincidentally a method of revising and validating the theory itself.

The uses and advantages of theory may be summarized as follows:

1. Theory allows us to establish logical relations between propositions and thus to begin dealing with important questions of explanation or understanding.

2. The fertility of theory assists in the generation of promising hypotheses about relationships that can then be empirically tested and the confirmation or disconfirmation of which increases the dependability of our knowledge claims about the subject.

3. Because of its contributions to explanatory principles (for example, cause-and-effect relations), theory may suggest strategies for the application of knowledge to real-world problem solving. To illustrate, classical Freudian psychoanalysis was not only a theory of the origin of the neuroses but also an elaborate system, derived in significant part from the theory itself, for diagnosing and treating neurotic behavior. In like manner, any adequate and comprehensive theory of career development should potentially facilitate problem identification, selection of appropriate guidance-intervention modes, and the testing of guidance outcomes.

The foregoing remarks on the benefits derivable from theory making presupposes the adequacy of theory. Unfortunately, many theories, including those of career development, fail to meet the test of adequacy. One is reminded of John Gardner's *obiter dictum* to the effect that bad theory is like bad plumbing; neither holds water. Let us, then, review the criteria by which the merit of a theory, the reliance we may place on it, may be gauged. The desiderata enumerated here reflect Osipow's (1973) treatment but include several additional criteria. Since they are largely self-explanatory, the questions are presented with minimal elaboration.

- Does the theory incorporate a set of tested empirical propositions that are broadly descriptive of the behavioral events in the system? Stated differently, is there a set of relevant knowledge claims that have been verified by research?

- Are the propositions in the set logically related, consistent with one another, and not contradictory?

- Are the variables in the propositions operationally defined and are they logically tied to the hypothetical constructs?

- Do the hypothetical constructs lend themselves to construct validation? Are they represented by objective indicators or referents (for example, a choice-anxiety scale) which can be subjected to experimental scrutiny?
- Is the theory parsimonious? (That theory is best which requires the fewest a priori assumptions, that is, axioms or postulates. For example, an early theory to explain electrical activity violated the rule of parsimony by inventing the existence of a superflous element (ether) as a conductor.
- Does the theory possess generality? Does it integrate and explain across a broad domain of behavioral events or is it applicable only to a restricted range of phenomena or to specific subpopulations?
- How provocative or heuristic is the theory in generating pertinent questions for research? Is it a catalyst for the formation of new hypotheses that, when subjected to test, lead to an extension of the network of descriptive laws and, simultaneously, provide for partial validation and revision of theory?
- In the search for more efficacious methods of career guidance, does our particular career development theory matter? Does it set a course for the construction of an improved technology? These last questions tacitly affirm the principles, previously noted, that good theory potentially contributes to the solution of practical problems.

A SAMPLE OF CAREER DEVELOPMENT THEORIES

In the interval from 1950 to 1970, a spate of so-called theories were spawned. These systems varied with respect to their orienting disciplines, degrees of logical formalism, breadth (generality versus restrictiveness of application), and principal substantive focus (for example, occupational socialization processes; life stages; choice-making dynamics). Crites (1969) has attempted to bring a semblance of order to the multifarious theories by means of a two-dimensional typology. Along the orientation dimension, Crites subsumes systems that are (1) nonpsychological (for example, economic, cultural, social), (2) psychological (for example, trait measurement, developmental, psychoanalytic), and (3) general and not readily categorized by orienting discipline (for example, interdisciplinary, typological). With respect to the rubric of substantive focus (this writer's term), Crites dichotomizes theories into vocational choice and vocational-adjustment subsets. Although Crites' taxonomy is helpful in providing a macrolevel panorama of theory, its dimensional grossness necessitates an arbitrary cell placement of systems, some of which share a broader commonality of features than superficial inspection might suggest.

No attempt will be made here to present an exhaustive review of career development theories. Instead, four formal conceptualizations have been selected for brief description. Two of these, the developments by Ginzberg (1951) and Super (1953, 1963), are noteworthy both because they provided the early critical impetus to theory making about vocational-choice behavior and because they became influential prototypic models for the variant theories of others. The remaining two contributions, by Holland (1973, 1978) and Krumboltz, Mitchell, and Jones (1976, 1978), are significant because, in comparison with other systems, they yield reasonably well to translation into explicit strategies for career guidance. Readers who seek more detailed descriptions and critiques of career development theories should consult Osipow (1973).

Ginzberg's Theory

As originally developed and published, Ginzberg's conceptual account of the career choice-making process was actually the collaborative effort of an interdisciplinary team that included an economist (Ginzberg), a psychiatrist, a sociologist, and a psychologist (Ginzberg, et al., 1951). The product is more accurately termed a descriptive model than a theory of vocational choice behavior. Over the years since its first appearance, it has been almost exclusively identified with Ginzberg, the senior member of the project team. Ginzberg views the working out of a vocational choice as an orderly developmental process spanning chiefly the adolescent years. On interview data obtained from sixty-four subjects ranging from sixth graders to graduate students, Ginzberg's research team constructed a three-stage psychosocial scenario culminating in the specification of a delimited occupational goal. The *fantasy period,* extending to approximately age 11, is dominated by egocentric behavior, occupational preferences expressed by simple stereotypes, and exclusion of the personal qualifications and job-entry barriers that the objective world imposes. In the *tentative period,* ranging from age 11 to age 17, the youth introduces considerations of his or her own interests, capacities, and personal values in articulating the rationale for certain occupational preferences. Toward the end of the seventeenth year, a transition typically ensues leading to the *realistic period,* in which the individual attempts to synthesize an appropriate vocational plan from personal-trait factors and perceived real-world factors. The plan takes form through the realistic period substages of exploration (testing one's self in the environment), crystallization (readiness or commitment), and specification of choice. While Ginzberg initially explained the resolution of the complex choice-making task as a compromise with the demands and restrictions of reality, he later interpreted the motivational basis of career decision making as an attempt to optimize one's personal satisfaction. He also introduced somewhat more flexibility into his model by conceding that occupational choice behavior may extend well beyond the adolescent years and by assigning a more influential role to environmental and situational factors in choice. However, despite the constraints of reality, Ginzberg (1972) believes that "the individual remains the prime mover in the decision-making process" (p. 175).

Super's Theory

The theoretical formulations of Donald Super, which are generally viewed as constituting the most comprehensive model of career development, draw upon concepts of differential, developmental, and phenomenological psychology (Super, 1957, 1963). In Super's view, the self-concept operates both as a significant source of information about the individual's makeup and as a determiner of his or her maturing vocational identity. Although the processes by which occupational aspirations, preferences, and choices evolve are focal, Super's conceptualization of occupational behavior in pre-employed youth, more than most others, transcends decision making per se and broadens the account to include movement toward psychological autonomy, growth of occupational awareness, and acceptance of responsibility for one's life planning. Extensions and refinements of the system have been introduced from the findings of the Career Pattern Study, a long-term longitudinal research project initiated in 1951 at Columbia University Teachers' College (Super, et al., 1957).

Super and his associates have published two sets of overlapping "propositions" that delineate their career development model (Super, 1953; Super and Bachrach, 1957). In both instances the elements are to be seen less as a tightly woven set of logical postulates and empirical propositions in a formal theory and more as an overarching series of principles to stake out the domain of analysis and to guide research. Like Ginzberg's conceptualization, Super's is premised on career development as an ongoing, orderly, and predictable process. A life-stage structure is employed that is cast in the form of a series of vocational-developmental tasks (special instances of Havighurst's [1953] developmental tasks). It is assumed that these tasks are normal life-adjustment problems, imposed by the society, that must be encountered sequentially and mastered in the process of acquiring relevant coping behaviors and coming to terms with adult vocational roles. Examples within the crystallization of the vocational-preference-task complex (ages 14—18) are awareness of the need to use information resources and acquiring knowledge of such resources.

In the context of youth's vocational-developmental task learning, "self-concepts begin to form prior to adolescence, become clearer in adolescence, and are translated into occupational terms in adolescence" (Super and Bachrach, 1957). The formation and progressive clarification of the self-concept are shaped by one's social experiences and one's perceptions of the meaning of those experiences. Thus, reality considerations affecting career-related decisions assume increasing influence with age. Movement through the sequence of vocational-developmental tasks and toward satisfactory and satisfying status in the establishment stage of the individual's career history is represented by the summarizing concept of *vocational maturity* (Super, 1957). Crites (1973) states that this term "captures and conveys the concept of progressive change which underlies career awareness, exploration and decision making" (p. 1).

In identifying career development as a dynamic process, Super clearly implies that it must be understood in terms of psychological needs and motives. Thus, he interprets career development behavior as a time-extended effort to build and implement a self-concept. Although his formulation deals principally with those vocational developmental tasks that are encountered prior to full-time labor-force entry, he extends the relevance of this motivational principle to the work experience itself by proposing that "work and life satisfactions depend upon the extent to which an individual can implement his self-concept through his occupational role" (Super and Bachrach, 1957, pp. 118–120).

Super clearly sees implications in his model for revamping traditional practice. This linkage to theory is strongly indicated by his proposed redefinition of career guidance as "the process of helping a person to develop and accept an integrated and adequate picture of himself and of his role in the world of work, to test this concept against reality, and to convert it into a reality, with satisfaction to himself and benefit to society" (Super, 1957, p. 197). Yet it may be argued that, although Super's model effectively broadens the goals of career guidance, it affords only a gross mapping of an improved intervention methodology. Specifications for a counselor and career educator modus operandi remain relatively scant.

Holland's Theory

Holland (1973, 1978) has offered a systematic account of how occupational choices are made that is a contemporary version of the classical trait-measurement scheme. His conceptual model, however, is considerably more elaborate than the older Parsonian model and is buttressed by an impressive array of predictive and concurrent validity studies. Holland begins by constructing a personality typology based on differentiated item-resource clusters. Any of a number of instruments, including Holland's Vocational Preference Inventory, his more recently developed Self-Directed Search, and the Strong Campbell Interest Inventory, may be used to place any individual in the typology. The six-model personal orientations produced by this assessment approach are indicative, Holland believes, of distinctive personal coping styles. Individuals manifesting these varying styles tend to search out certain preferred environments, in particular harmonious or congruent occupational environments. Although he believes that each of the model personal orientations in his typology results from a wide set of cultural and personal experiences, Holland does not regard his formulation as essentially developmental, choosing to describe it as "a modern differentialist view" (Holland and Gottfredson, 1978, p. 151).

Holland's system also identifies six occupational environments that correspond closely in their features (working conditions and worker characteristics) to his model personal orientations or personality types. The six environments, operationally defined by means of ratings on Astin's (1963) Environmental Assessment Technique and by occupational codes, are generically titled *Realistic, Investigative, Social Conventional, Enterprising,* and *Artistic.* The system does not force categorical placement of scores into discrete personal orientations or occupational environments. Instead, a hexagonal arrangement is used to represent correspondence between personality types and occupational environments. An individual's profile may hypothetically place him or her at any point within the hexagon. The distance from or proximity to the geometric center of any environment indicates the degree of personal-environmental congruence. Holland's research suggests that the assessed orientations of students correspond in a fairly consistent manner to their curricular and occupational aspirations and choices and that these latter variables appear to find a good fit within the occupational-environment typology.

It is only in a loose sense that Holland's formulation can be labeled a theory. It is, instead, an empirically based system for matching selected constellations of personal attributes, including dispositions to prefer certain task-oriented environments over others, with limited sets of characteristics of curricular and occupational groups. As such, it provides one systematic way for students to undertake exploration of career options. Yet we need to remind ourselves that other empirically supported systems—for example, the Career Planning Program (American College Testing Program, 1974)—that do not claim allegiance to a formal theory, perform the same service and probably perform it just as effectively as Holland's Self-Directed Search technique. Finally, theory apart, the definitive vindication of any career planning device is to be sought in users' subsequent work histories. Such evidence, even short range, is lacking for Holland's system and others as well.

Krumboltz's Social-Learning Theory

The rational-empirical model of Krumboltz and his colleagues presents the shaping of career preferences and the acquisition of career decision-making response modes as problems in behavioral learning (Krumboltz, Mitchell, and Jones, 1976, 1978). The system identifies four broad types of influence on the genesis of career aspirations and decision-making skills. They are identified as (1) innate potentials and special abilities, (2) environmental conditions and events, (3) learning experiences, and (4) an assortment of means for cognizing and acting on the environment that fall under the generic term of *task-approach skills*. About the first group of influencers the theory says little except that they include natively endowed predispositions to profit differentially from learning situations. The environmental conditions relevant to the theory are those that operate to broaden or constrain the range of career-related options. Examples of such conditions are the number and nature of training opportunities within the individual's environment and the restrictive rules and laws governing job entry.

The preponderance of analytical details in the Krumboltz theory concerns the last two groups of influencers, learning experiences and task-approach skills. Learnings are of two kinds: (1) instrumental learning experiences (ILEs)—essentially instances of operant learning by which the individual acts on the environment, evoking a response to his or her response that either increases (positive reinforcement) or decreases (aversive control) the habit strength of the individual's particular behavior; and (2) associative learning experiences (ALEs)—mainly classical conditioning events and instances of learning from observation of behavior models by which attitudes are acquired having either positive or negative valences; for example, attitudes toward salespersons or mathematics.

Task approach skills (TASs) include "performance standards and values, work habits, perceptual and cognitive processes . . ., mental sets and emotional responses" (Krumboltz, Mitchell, and Jones, 1978, p. 107). They function both as influencers of the learning that occurs in arriving at a decision and as consequences or outcomes of such learning. Thus, in the context of vocational planning, task-approach skills may be said to include such career decision-making behaviors as value clarification, goal setting, information seeking, and weighing and selecting alternatives.

In the flux of their ongoing actions upon career decision making, the task-approach skills interact with another set of influencers called self-observation generalizations (SOGs). These are self-concepts, defined as implicit or explicit self-statements about one's status with reference to perceived standards of achievement. For example, a student might say, "I really think I can do OK in my shop course next term because I'm pretty good about fixing things around the house." Thus, in employing SOGs, Krumboltz's theory, while essentially a behavioral-psychology position, pointedly draws upon self-concept theory in explaining how career plans and decisions are developed. It may be noted that the theory is further hybridized by conjoining concepts from cognitive learning with those of behavioral learning (operant and classical conditioning and learning through observing models). The interplay among the various influencers here described eventuates in actions or behaviors by the individual that themselves bring social consequences (reinforcers) affecting the degree to which such behaviors are likely to become habitual.

Proceeding from the foregoing rationale, Krumboltz's social-learning theory generates a set of relatively broad-based propositions to explicate the processes of career planning and decision making. It then develops illustrative testable hypotheses about both positive and negative influences for each general proposition, the empirical confirmation of which would furnish partial validation of the theory. The following example, drawn from the exposition of the theory, patently indicates its emphasis on social learning as the basis of career development.

> *Proposition IIA3:* An individual is more likely to learn the cognitive and performance skills and emotional responses necessary for career planning, self-observing, goal setting and information seeking if that individual has access to people and other resources with the necessary information.
>
> *Illustrative Hypothesis:* Students in schools that set up procedures for making career information easily accessible in meaningful ways will develop CDM skills to a greater extent than will students in schools not providing such opportunities [Krumboltz, Mitchell, and Jones, 1978, p. 123].

Because it is anchored in social learning, Krumboltz's theory provides a framework for identifying and testing some of the career guidance assumptions and practices that have long been part of the conventional wisdom. That Krumboltz and his associates regard their theory as having important implications for counseling practice is seen in their concluding statement.

Career counseling is . . . a process of opening up new learning experiences and motivating a client to initiate career-relevant exploratory activities. The responsibilities of a career counselor, then, are as follows: (a) to help the client learn a rational sequence of career decision-making skills, (b) to help the client arrange an appropriate sequence of career-relevant exploratory-learning experiences and (c) to teach the client how to evaluate the personal consequences of those learning experiences [Krumboltz, Mitchell, and Jones, 1978, p. 127].

SOME UNIFYING PRECEPTS

Is it useful to speak of the various career development models and theory systems as a group? Do they possess shared assumptions and objectives? Comparative descriptions of theories in the literature have frequently drawn attention to their disparate characteristics. Nevertheless, the major career development conceptualizations can be shown to possess a set of more or less common organizing tenets and premises. A partial enumeration of such mutually embodied principles follows:

1. Psychosocial growth may be described as occurring within a series of life stages having cognitive, emotional, and social-development components. In contemporary industrial society, career development represents one highly significant type of psychosocial growth.

2. Occupational-choice behavior is not confined to a single, fixed decision but is best viewed as a time-extended process entailing a sequence of choice points that are mainly imposed by the culture. There is potentially a lawful or orderly movement within the evolving career pattern that is causally related to both the personal attributes and the life experiences of the individual. Because these influences are numerous and complex and because contingency factors (for example, economic changes) and chance factors are also operative, long-range predictions of occupational behavior and choice are likely to be hazardous.

3. Acquiring career-relevant competence involves confronting at each life stage a set of typical and necessary problem-solving experiences called vocational-developmental tasks. They bear a resemblance to, but are not identical to, Krumboltz's TASs. Mastery of vocational-developmental tasks enlarges the repertoire of coping skills and dispositions and provides the basis for the successful encounter of developmental tasks at the next life stage. The level of mastery (of skills, knowledge, self-understanding, attitudes) that an individual has achieved at any point in his or her career development is represented by the summarizing concept of *career maturity*. (Although the concepts of vocational-developmental tasks and career maturity do not conflict with Holland's theory, they occupy neither an important explicit nor implicit place in his theory since, as previously noted, Holland's formulations are not essentially developmental in character.)

4. The socialization process within which the vocational-developmental tasks are met provides access to occupational role models and social imitation and, further, the opportunity to engage in vocational-exploratory behavior and reality-testing experiences. Such exploratory and self-testing events bring consequences for the individual in the form of a social-support system; that is, feedback as encouragement, approval, denial, or disapproval.

5. The motivational wellsprings of career development, choice, and adjustment are to be found in the ongoing effort to build and clarify one's self-concept and, through it, to attain a stable and comfortable career identity. Accordingly, forming occupational preferences and making career choices over time may be understood as an attempt to implement the self-concept (Super, 1953; Super and Bachrach, 1957), to optimize personal satisfaction (Ginzberg, 1972), or to find congruence between one's needs and the conditions and rewards of the work environment (Holland, 1973; Lofquist and Dawis, 1969).

A CRITIQUE OF THEORY

The productive uses of theory in science have been noted earlier in this paper. Of course, whether theories bear fruit depends heavily upon their adequacy. Since their first appearance at midcentury, theory systems in career development have stimulated research on the development of occupational motives, have provided a thematic structure within which available knowledge might be synthesized and better integrated, and have forced an examination and clarification of the aims of career guidance. Such gains, however, have been of modest proportions and have been won only slowly. It is difficult to escape the conclusion that the net yield of thirty years of theory making has been somewhat disappointing. Much of the explanation would appear to reside in the flawed quality and dubious relevance of much of theory. The limitations of extant theoretical formulations fall into three categories: methodology, scope, and practicality. They will be briefly discussed.

Methodological Problems
POOR THEORY FORMULATION
The training of vocational and counseling psychologists, like that of other applied psychologists, slights metatheory, the logic of theory construction. Treatises on the development, analysis, and validation of career development models frequently offend the ground rules of theoretical discourse, and they lack the rigor that theory formulations require if they are to contribute to the organization of knowledge. Common failings include treating postulates as testable hypotheses and unconfirmed propositions as empirical laws.

NEGLECT OF EMPIRICAL DATA
Our theories betray a poverty of baseline data. Word pictures of the allegedly typical career-relevant behavior patterns of various youth-age cohorts and of the psychological import of such profiles have not generally been derived from carefully controlled and replicated observation or from adequate samples. It has seemed more tempting to weave a "theory" than to obtain hard evidence. It is a twist of irony that theory building, which has the potential virtue of spawning useful research, may sometimes act as an opiate that slakes the thirst for facts. Crites evidently agrees. In discussing what he calls "disadvantages and excesses of unbridled theory construction," he writes "theorizing may be the

single most obstructive factor to the production of solid empirical research" (Crites, 1969, p. 630).

WEAK PREDICTIVE ABILITY

Because they incorporate laws that define cause-and-effect relationships, good theories claim predictive power. Theory building in career development, however, has relied on an accretion of weak statistical laws that merely report the correspondence between, for example, scores on theory-poor interest inventories and the tendency to select certain academic majors. The result, as Crites has observed, is that the thrust of theories of career choice and work adjustment has been more descriptive than predictive of occupational behavior. What is sorely lacking in theory building are quantitative indicators with construct validity, such as, for example, tests that tap choice anxiety. The research use of such a scale, which might help us to interpret the high incidence of vocational indecision in late adolescence as a possible function of avoidance motivation, would make a serviceable contribution to the theory of career selection. The recent development of tests of career maturity may be a step toward such construct-valid instrumentation.

Problems of Scope Limitation
NARROW RANGE OF OUTCOME CRITERIA

Career-related behavior occupies a spacious and complex topical domain permitting access to a wide assortment of theory and research issues. It is dismaying, therefore, to discover that a disproportionate share of recently published research on career development theory remains preoccupied with the objective of predicting occupational choice. To illustrate, a large number of reported research studies focus on Holland's theory, and these are predominantly studies of statistical correspondence between subjects' personal-orientation typology scores and the occupational environments within which their major fields of academic study and stated vocational choices fall. On the positive side, two of the systems reviewed earlier in this paper (Super's and Krumboltz's) give prominent attention to vocational-choice process and to determinants of career decision-making skills acquisition. If researchers were to confirm their hypotheses and untested propositions on these themes, the effective scope of the theories would be broadened.

INCOMPLETENESS

Despite years of effort, present-day career development theories have evolved as partial theory only. They are miniature or segmented systems that track only portions of the terrain of occupational behavior. It is by no means uncommon for theories (in all disciplines) to be truncated and to exhibit gaps in their descriptive and explanatory networks. Moreover, some special theories are intentionally restricted in scope but remain useful for their particular purpose. Problems arise, however, when researchers and especially practitioners treat such theories as complete systems.

A LACK OF INTEGRATION WITH THE WORLD OF WORK

A common assumption of career development theories is that individuals who make realistic and appropriate vocational choices (as internally defined by the precepts of the theories) will exhibit significantly better adjustment to work (defined by the conventional criteria of employment status, job performance, job satisfaction, and career advancement). A few loosely controlled follow-up studies suggest this may be true. However, no studies exist that treat this assumption as a testable hypothesis derived from a comprehensive theory of work. One reason is the segmented and disjunctive nature of theory, a condition noted earlier. Career development theories still lack critical interface with theories of work-site adjustment such as those of Vroom (1964) and Lofquist and Dawis (1969). It may be hoped that theorists and researchers alike will profit from the attempts of Crites (1969) and Super and Hall (1978) to assemble and integrate career development data from both prework and work-site settings, including school-to-work transition, worker motivation, and job satisfaction.

Problems of Practical Application in Counseling
INADEQUATE THEORY-PRACTICE LINKS

Ausubel (1968) argues persuasively that the development of a good theory of learning does not guarantee the improvement of teaching. Effective instructional techniques, he notes, are derived from relevant principles of learning, but they "are not simple and direct applications of these principles." Correspondingly, even if we possess strong theories of career development, such theories would not be definitively prescriptive of a sound system for career guidance and counseling practice. The more explicit (and accurate) a theory is in specifying the connections between antecedent conditions of influence and consequent behavior-response patterns, the more directly the theory speaks to practice. The social-learning theory of Krumboltz et al. (1976, 1978), briefly described earlier, represents a significant stride in this direction. However, while pertinent theory may give direction to research on practice, the findings from which feed back to theory and fortify it, there must ultimately be developed a system of practice or technology based on research and policy that has roots in the formal theory but is distinct from it. In career guidance, such linkages between theory systems and systems of practice remain only a promise.

POOR ADAPTABILITY TO SPECIAL POPULATIONS

Career development theories are general theories. They rarely deal in a serious manner with the sociocultural conditions and developmental histories of subpopulations. It is, therefore, inappropriate to generalize from findings on heterogeneous population samples to the motives, outlooks, and coping behaviors of special groups, such as minorities and the severely socioeconomically disadvantaged. From a practical standpoint, it may be even more questionable to employ with such groups counseling goals and strategies that have grown out of career development conceptual models oriented to the general population.

AVOIDANCE OF MARKETPLACE REALITIES

Career development theories tacitly assume that the range of career options is broad and, further, that individuals who exhibit acceptable career maturity and acquire good career decision-making skills are able to exercise personal choices among these options toward the end of finding a self-fulfilling career. There is virtually no formal provision in the theories, however, for the effects of labor-market restrictions or of employers' economic priorities on the individual's quest for a satisfying occupational role. Counselors who operate within such an idealized theory framework may be guiding students toward disillusionment rather than self-fulfillment. The serious and growing disparity between high-level occupational aspirations and the realities of the labor market and the nation's occupational structure raises the disquieting possibility that much of existing career development theory is irrelevant to the problems and needs of youth. Warnath (1975) faults counselors for assuming "that the working world is just and is guided by rational principles." He charges that our theories fail to take note of the fact that "jobs . . . are designed to meet the needs of production and profit . . . and not to meet the personal needs of the people who fill those jobs."

WHERE ARE WE NOW?
THE STATUS OF THEORY MAKING

Reflection on the foregoing catalog of methodological, thematic, and pragmatic difficulties with career development theory nets a sober image. Too much of the aggregate effort in the theory realm has been of a speculative quality; too little has been committed to compiling a solid empirical track record. Moreover, the questions theorists have found most attractive for analysis may not be those that beset practitioners in the field.

It seems obvious that theory making has enjoyed only limited success with respect both to its internal logical integrity and its impact on the quality of research and practice in career guidance and personnel work in industry. Advances have occurred in the applied domain, but such gains have most often had their origins in exigencies and developments apart from formal theory. It is doubtful, for example, whether the current robust state of activity in computer-assisted career guidance, school-based career education, or the reduction in occupational-role sex typing can be attributed to any significant degree to the influence of career-development theory.

Intellectual traffic between career development psychology and kindred knowledge disciplines has been negligible. With few exceptions, journals and textbooks in child and adolescent behavior ignore occupational socialization processes and virtually none mentions career development theory. A flicker of hope that the climate may be improving is provided by Baltes, Reese, and Lipsitt

(1980) in their extensive review of the literature of lifespan developmental psychology when they declare, "The theme of life-long learning is attracting more and more attention and the role of occupation and work is being increasingly discussed, not only as the outcome of inter- and intragenerational socialization but also as an intrinsic component of the developmental process across the life-span. As Clausen puts it, 'For the average male, no other social role approaches the occupational role in the saliency and pervasiveness of its influence on other aspects of the life course' " (pp. 98–99). In the wake of this pronouncement one is mystified to find literally no treatment of the career development theme or any referencing of career development publications through this lengthy paper. The fact that a substantial review of the career development literature by Super and Hall (1978) had appeared in the same *Annual Review of Psychology* series two years earlier was hardly consoling, since readers might reasonably have expected to find some cross-referencing and updating of the topic in the Baltes, Reese, and Lipsitt paper. The fault may lie as much or more with developmental psychologists as with investigators in the field of vocational behavior. Whatever the explanation, the magnitude of the cross-disciplinary impact of career development theory and research has been minuscule.

Inspection of the primary journals for career development literature leads to the conclusion that productive interest in theory is lagging and that theory making may be temporarily on the shelf. This writer examined all issues of the *Journal of Counseling Psychology* for 1977 (Volume 24). Of ninety-three published papers, a mere eighteen (less than 20 percent) dealt in some respect with vocational psychology. Of these, only three even lightly touched on theory and none treated theory in a seminal manner. Recognizing that the appearance of the newer periodical, *Journal of Vocational Behavior,* has, since the early 1970s, attracted many manuscripts that might earlier have been submitted to the *Journal of Counseling Psychology,* the writer next reviewed the complete contents of Volumes 13 and 15 (three bimonthly issues each) of the *Journal of Vocational Behavior.* Of a grand total of sixty-two published papers, forty-three (69 percent) were judged to have no relevance to career development theory, ten others (16 percent) were judged to be partially or indirectly theory related, and the remaining nine (14.5 percent) were seen as dealing more centrally with theory issues. The middle category included annual "Vocational Behavior and Career Development" literature reviews by Zytowski (1978) and Walsh (1979). The third (directly theory related) category included several validity studies of Crites' Career Maturity Inventory and Holland's Self-Directed Search, and no papers were judged to be new contributions to the substantive content of theory or to the methodology of theory construction or analysis.

We may, then, be at an impasse with theory making. Tomorrow, in looking back, it is possible that we shall be able to interpret this seeming lack of progress as an interlude spent in regrouping, consolidating gains, and clarifying objectives and knowledge-producing strategies.

EPILOGUE: GETTING MOVING AGAIN

This paper has drawn a bleak picture of the impact of theory. It is possible to brighten the scene. Improvement cannot be wrought, however, simply by redoubling the research effort with timeworn and ineffectual practices. George Santayana's admonition is applicable: "Those who cannot remember the past are condemned to repeat it." It is a reasonable assumption that the generation of more powerful and representative conceptual models of career development can make contributions both to the potency of intervention techniques (for example, vocational counseling, career education, CETA programs) and to the refinement of methodology for measuring intervention outcomes. The recommendations that follow, some of which reemphasize positions taken earlier in this paper, are offered as elements in a broad strategy toward fulfilling the latent promise of theory.

1.   Further attempts to create formal theories should be temporarily set aside in favor of developing more modest conceptual maps that set a course for pertinent fact finding and theory building. Blau et al. (1956) argue that "the function of a conceptual scheme of occupational choice and selection is to call attention to different kinds of antecedent factors, the exact relationships between which have to be determined by empirical research before a systematic theory can be developed" (p. 532).

2.   If formal theory making is to be conducted, it should stake out and cultivate delimited themes of career-relevant behavior—for example, development of occupational awareness, the decision-making process, how occupations select people (personnel selection), work-site socialization processes, and job satisfaction. As the theme-bound theories become sufficiently refined through continual hypothesis development and testing, and, concurrently, as we build networks of descriptive and explanatory principles, we can turn our attention to the problem of how the smaller theories can be synthesized into a comprehensive model of occupational behavior. This strategy is also favored by Osipow (1973). As noted earlier, while most current career development theories are, in fact, segmented and theme-bound, they are often mistakenly treated as self-contained global theories.

3.   If there is to be a renewal of effort on theory, and if it is to be generative, a rereading of Crites' (1969) incisive treatment of "The Future of Theory Construction in Vocational Psychology" (pp. 629–635) would be a commendable way to begin.

4.   More career-relevant measures that have meaning for a theory of behavior and that possess acceptable construct validity should be developed. Such instruments must be used in data gathering so that the links between empirical propositions and statements of explanation (employing hypothetical constructs) can be forged (Loevinger, 1957). This is a more modest approach than attempting to erect a large-scale theory.

5.   Research and limited theory on how young people acquire vocational attitudes and vocational self-concepts and move through the career decision process must be fused with research and theory on work adjustment in the organiza-

tional setting. Ultimately, we need to know how and why men and women succeed or fail in the work force.

6. Far more baseline data must be gathered if trustworthy norms of special populations and age- and sex-related career development behaviors are to be established. Such norms are important not only for theory building but also for setting grade-level objectives for curriculum-based career guidance and career education. The National Assessment of Educational Progress (1977) national testing program on career and occupational development is helping to fill the void. A series of monographs reporting the career development needs of youth as revealed by NAEP's Career and Occupational Development assessment has been jointly published by the National Vocational Guidance Association and the Association for Measurement in Education and Guidance (cf. Mitchell, 1978; Westbrook, 1978). Chapter 7 of this volume provides a description of NAEP procedures.

7. The norm-gathering types of research recommended above (points 5 and 6) must be supplemented by experiments that track the effects of preselected stimulus conditions on career-relevant response patterns. Most of the earlier work on career development models was naturalistic; the behaviors typifying the stages of vocational development were described without special effort to identify or manipulate the specific psychosocial variables that produced those behaviors. However, if we can also begin to articulate such antecedent conditions—consequent-behavior relations—we shall contribute to the theory of vocational behavior and to the technology for shaping that behavior. This is the essential rationale of the social-learning approach to the study of career decison-making processes (Krumboltz and Baker, 1973; Krumboltz, Becker-Haven, and Burnett, 1979).

8. Pursuant to the preceding recommendation, to study career development in terms of the controlled observation of environmental conditions and their effects on coping responses is to deal with it as behavioral intervention. It is noteworthy that the summary concept *vocational development* or *career development* originally connoted chiefly the social maturational processes by which an individual's vocational planning, choice, and adjustment emerged in the culture. More recently, the term *development* has been additionally invested with a sense of purposive transitive action, that is, the active facilitation of the individual's vocationally relevant behavior through planned intervention. When the meaning of career development is recast in this manner, its theory and research apparatus must begin to confront the question of outcomes of intervention. This is a direction that investigatory efforts are beginning to take, and indeed must take.

9. If, as proposed, an important research objective in career development has become that of assessing the product—that is, the efficacy of various intervention procedures in counseling and career education—what assessment criteria are to be used? It is now quite common to measure career development gains by score changes on paper-and-pencil vocational-maturity inventories and tests of information about career decision-making and job-seeking principles. Unfortunately nothing in current career development theory establishes these variables as the most dependable indicators of subsequent adult work adjustment. Until evidence is at hand of strong correspondence between short-range and ultimate criteria (that is, employment, job performance, job satisfaction), we cannot be confident that conventional techniques of vocational counseling and guidance are producing the behavior changes that are most critical to work

adjustment. The gathering of such predictive data is not a matter of some urgency to the advancement of both theory and practice. Oliver (1979) offers a balanced discussion of the immediate versus ultimate criterion issues. Her well-documented and tightly reasoned treatment of the measurement of outcomes in career-counseling research could profitably be used as a concise guidebook by many researchers.

10. Guidance programs and counselors face sharp challenges. Congress, state legislatures, local school boards, and research-and-development funding agencies now ask insistent questions about the returns on their monetary investments in career guidance and career education. It is not known how much additional time remains to test our product. Despite the lack of clear direction from theory, and notwithstanding the hazards of using intermediate-range or long-range criteria, the assessment of career development programs may have to incorporate some of the grosser "payoff" measures. It is probably safe to say that public officials and the public at large are not greatly impressed by changes in client verbalizations as a product of counseling or by paper-and-pencil improvements in self-insights and self-esteem ratings. These observers require more pragmatic results. For those students exposed to career education programs, is the school dropout rate lower? Do more of them complete diploma requirements? Do more of them find gainful employment after school completion? It seems clear that those charged with responsibility for testing the outcomes of career development programs will not soon run out of work.

REFERENCES

ADKINS, W. R.   Lifeskills: Structured counseling for the disadvantaged. *Personnel and Guidance Journal*, 1970, *49*, 108–116.

AMERICAN COLLEGE TESTING PROGRAM.   *Career Planning Program, Grades 8–11*. Boston: Houghton Mifflin, 1974.

ASTIN, A. W.   Further validation of the environmental assessment technique, *Journal of Educational Psychology*, 1963, *54*, 217–226.

AUSUBEL, D. P.   *Educational psychology: A cognitive view.* New York: Holt, Rinehart and 1968.

BALTES, P. B., REESE, H. W., and LIPSITT, L. P.   Life-span developmental psychology. In Rosenzweig, M. R., and Porter, L. W. (Eds.) *Annual Review of Psychology*, 1980, *31*, 65–110.

BLAU, P. M., et al.   Occupational choice: A conceptual framework. *Industrial and Labor Relations Review*, 1967, 9, 531–543.

BREWER, J. M.   *History of vocational guidance.* New York: Harper, 1942.

CENTER FOR HUMAN RESOURCE RESEARCH,   *The National Longitudinal Surveys Handbook* (Revised). Columbus: Ohio State University, 1979.

CRITES, J. O.   *Vocational psychology.* New York: McGraw-Hill, 1969.

CRITES, J. O.   *Theory and research handbook for the career maturity inventory.* Monterey, Calif.: CTB/McGraw-Hill, 1973, p. 1.

GINZBERG, E.   *Occupational choice.* New York: Columbia University Press, 1951.

GINZBERG, E.   Toward a theory of occupational choice: A restatement. *Vocational Guidance Quarterly*, 1972, *20*, 169–176.

HAVIGHURST, R. J.   *Human development and education.* New York: Longmans, Green, 1953.

HOLLAND, J. L.   *Making vocational choices: A theory of careers.* Englewood Cliffs, N.J.: Prentice-Hall, 1973.

HOLLAND, J. L., and GOTTFREDSON, G. D.   Using a typology of persons and environments to explain careers: Some extensions and clarifications. In Whiteley, J. M. and Resnikoff, A. (Eds) *Career counseling.* Monterey, Calif.: Brooks/Cole, 1978.

HORST, P.   Educational and vocational counseling from the actuarial point of view. *Personnel and Guidance Journal,* 1956, *35,* 164–170.

HULL, C. L.   *Aptitude testing.* New York: World, 1928.

KRUMBOLTZ, J. D., and BAKER, R. D.   Behavioral counseling for vocational decisions. In H. Borow (Ed.) *Career guidance for a new age.* Boston: Houghton Mifflin, 1973, pp. 235–284.

KRUMBOLTZ, J. D., BECKER-HAVEN, J. F., and BURNETT, K. F.   Counseling psychology. In Rosenzweig, M. R., and Porter, L. W. (Eds.), *Annual Review of Psychology,* 1979, *30,* 555–602.

KRUMBOLTZ, J. D., MITCHELL, A. M., and JONES, G. B.   A social learning theory of career selection. In Whiteley, J. M., and Resnikoff, A. (Eds.), *Career counseling.* Monterey, Calif.: Brooks/Cole, 1978.

LOEVINGER, J.   Objective tests as instruments of psychological theory. *Psychological Reports,* Monograph supplement No. 9, 1957, 636–694.

LOFQUIST, L. H., and DAWIS, R. V.   *Adjustments to work.* New York: Appleton-Century-Crofts, 1969.

MILLER, C. H.   Vocational guidance in the perspective of cultural change. In H. Borow, (Ed.), *Man in a world at work.* Boston: Houghton Mifflin, 1964, pp. 3–23.

MITCHELL, A. M.   *Career development needs of seventeen year olds.* Washington, D.C.: National Vocational Guidance Association, 1978.

OLIVER, L. W.   Outcome measurement in career counseling research. *Journal of Counseling Psychology,* 1979, *26,* 217–226.

OSIPOW, S. H.   *Theories of career development* (2nd Ed.). Englewood Cliffs, N.J.: Prentice-Hall, 1973.

STEPHENS, R. M.   *Social reform and the origins of vocational guidance.* Washington, D.C.: National Vocational Guidance Association, 1970.

SUPER, D. E.   *The dynamics of vocational adjustment.* New York: Harper, 1942.

SUPER, D. E.   A theory of vocational development. *American Psychologist,* 1953, *38,* 185–190.

SUPER, D. E.   *The psychology of careers.* New York: Harper and Row, 1957.

SUPER, D. E., and BACHRACH, P. B.   *Scientific careers and vocational development theory.* New York: Bureau of Publications, Teachers College, Columbia University, 1957.

SUPER, D. E., et al.   *Vocational development: A framework for research.* New York: Bureau of Publications, Teachers College, Columbia University, 1957.

SUPER, D. E., et al.   *Career development: Self-concept theory.* New York: College Entrance Examination Board, 1963.

SUPER, D. E., and HALL, D. T.   Career development: Exploration and planning. In Rosenzweig, M. R., and Porter, L. W. (Eds.). *Annual Review of Psychology,* 1978, *29,* 333–372.

VITELES, M. S.   *Industrial psychology.* New York: Norton, 1932.

VROOM, V. A.   *Work and motivation.* New York: Wiley, 1964.

WALSH, W. B.   Vocational behavior and career development, 1978: A review. *Journal of Vocational Behavior,* 1979, *15,* 120–124.

WARNATH, C. F.   Vocational theories: Direction to nowhere. *Personnel and Guidance Journal,* 1975, *53,* 422–428.

WESTBROOK, B. W.   *Career development needs of adults.* Washington, D.C.: National Vocational Guidance Association, 1978.

ZYTOWSKI, D. G.   Vocational behavior and career development, 1977: A review. *Journal of Vocational Behavior,* 1978, *13,* 141–162.

PART TWO
TECHNICAL REQUIREMENTS

The next series of chapters moves us from a broad perspective to some of the technical requirements and measurement issues faced by career development specialists. Borow's call for the development of measures that possess acceptable construct validity receives attention from three different authors, and the problems inherent in construct definition and validation are treated comprehensively. The appraisal in this section of the limited technical progress in the area provides a sobering reminder of the research and development work yet to be done.

Cole's straightforward treatment of the basic guidelines for establishing the reliability and validity of career development measures contains useful information free of technical jargon. She distinguishes among content, criterion, and construct-validation procedures and uses career decision-making skills as a concrete illustration of the construct-validation problem in career assessment. Her suggestion that commercial demand alone will not support the costs for much needed research and development of improved measures should be noted by budget planners in the state and federal governments.

39

Chapter 4 develops a framework for looking at construct definitions and sources of error in measuring career development variables. Stenner and Rohlf discuss the limitations of classic reliability theory and advocate the concepts of generalizability theory developed by Cronback et al. for the purposes of research design and data analysis. They also provide an illustrative example of generalizability analysis. Borrowing data from one of Bert Westbrook's studies of the Career Maturity Inventory (described in the following chapter), they demonstrate how the person, item, and moment factors, as well as their interactions, can be used to estimate the proportion of variance attributable to each source in generating scores for a particular subscale measurement procedure.

Stenner and Rohlf argue forcefully that generalizability theory provides a model for evaluation studies that requires us to conceptualize better and be more explicit about the constructs we use. They also suggest some relevant special applications for career education measurement in areas such as competency testing, clarifying issues of test bias, and the generalizability of observer ratings and class means. Their concrete examples and specific recommendations for using generalizability theory to improve construct definitions should be helpful to those seeking to understand the requirements of sounder evaluation studies.

Finally, Westbrook, through a series of methodologically sound studies, investigates the validity of a specific career development construct, that of career maturity. Westbrook's discoveries raise serious questions about the validity of the career maturity construct. In particular, his factor analytic studies suggest that the data generated by career maturity measures cannot be differentiated from the scores of basic intelligence, scholastic-aptitude, and academic-achievement measures. All these instruments seem to be tapping a common verbal comprehension factor. Westbrook's chapter suggests that we proceed cautiously in using certain cognitive career development measures for the purposes of differential diagnosis and that we need more performance-based measurement.

Although these chapters, like Borow's in the previous section, cast a critical light on the career development landscape, there is a constructive tone to their message. Before proceeding much further, we must make certain we are clear about what we are measuring and that we have psychometrically sound instruments to do the job. If assessment of career development outcomes is ever to achieve the credibility and importance many of us hope for, improvements in technical precision must be forthcoming.

Establishing reliability
and validity
for measures
of career development

NANCY S. COLE
University of Pittsburgh

The problems of measuring career development outcomes are difficult and important, but they are also basically similar to the issues faced in most other education-related areas. In this short paper, I have made no attempt to duplicate the extensive general guidelines available in the *Standards for Educational and Psychological Tests,* published jointly in 1974 by the American Educational Research Association, the American Psychological Association, and the National Council on Measurement in Education. However, anyone seriously concerned with measures of career development should consult the *Standards* for an exhaustive consideration of the requirement of good measures. In this paper, I have undertaken the more limited task of reviewing some selected validity and reliability issues that seem especially crucial in measuring career development outcomes.

VALIDITY OVERVIEW

The basic question guiding the evaluation of any measuring procedure concerns the extent to which the procedure measures what is intended to be

41

measured and nothing else. Thus, to evaluate the appropriateness of a measurement procedure, one must ask first what the procedure is supposed to measure. Once this goal or use of the procedure is determined, then certain general approaches can be applied to whether in fact the procedure does measure the intended target. This problem is, of course, that of validity. Basically, validity data are evidence about the extent to which it is appropriate to make inferences from the results of the measurement procedure to the phenomenon supposedly being measured.

Validity has traditionally been divided into three general categories (content, criterion-related, and construct) because the phenomena typically measured in education and psychology are of three different types. When that being measured is the extent of accomplishment of some well-specified set of information or skills (called a content domain) and this group of skills is important for its own sake, then the procedures of content validation are applied to determine whether, in fact, a measurement procedure measures the intended skills. When that being measured is some externally measurable criterion, then the procedures of criterion-related validity can be used to determine whether the criterion is adequately approximated by the procedure. When that being measured is some construct that cannot be directly observed, the procedures of construct validation provide ways to judge whether the intended construct is being adequately measured.

It is necessary first to specify clearly the type of phenomenon to be measured to determine the appropriate validation approach. Once the target is determined, we look for evidence supporting or refuting the appropriateness of inferring that a score or outcome of the measurement procedure represents the intended target.

TYPES OF OUTCOMES

Although it is typical of career education programs to be concerned with effects both on traditional areas of school learning as well as on special career-related areas of learning, this discussion will be limited to the special career-related outcome areas, since these areas are the unique province of career education. Two major types of career-related outcome measures seem to be most sought by the field—that is, there are two major phenomena career educators wish to measure. The first type involves measures of the specific information and skills that constitute the domain of instruction about careers. The second type involves measures of attitude or skill constructs that career education programs are designed to foster.

It should be noted here that career education, like all of education, is justified by links to long-range outcomes. At a most basic level, we believe education is important for youngsters because educated adults are more productive members of the society, better citizens, and so on. In this sense, various long-range criteria of adult productivity, citizenship, and the like provide utlimate criteria to which ideally we would relate career education efforts. However, in practice such links are very difficult to establish clearly for any educational effort. Furthermore, such links are not often required by the social and political milieu. Most people will accept the premise that successfully meeting shorter range educational goals will likely have the longer range beneficial effects. Thus, we are usually allowed to focus on much shorter range outcomes in our evaluations, leaving the links to long-range outcomes to broader research studies or assuming by general consensus that the links to the long range will exist. I believe that in career education the immediate social and political demand is for the establishment of links to short-term outcomes. Thus, both of the outcomes addressed here—learning of content domains and attitude or skill constructs—fall into the short-term outcome category.

Measures of an Instructional
Domain about Careers

We seek measures of a career-related instructional domain to answer the question, "Did the students learn the information and skills about which they were instructed?" If the instruction involved information about various careers, then we wish to know if students learned the intended information. If the instruction included preparation of a job application, then we wish to know if students can, in fact, prepare acceptable job applications after the instruction. The instructional objectives provide the domain that should be measured, and for this type of measure, we justify the importance of the measure with the importance of the instructional objectives. Just as we do not feel that we have to justify the need for learning to read and write, so there are many aspects of career education (for example, information about careers and the world of work) that need no long-term justification politically. What we do need to justify is that the career education programs, for which much money is being spent, are accomplishing the agreed upon objectives. For this we need measures of the intended instructional domain.

The approach to validating that a test or any other measurement procedure adequately measures an intended domain is called content validation. Content validation is designed to support or refute one type of test-score interpretation—an interpretation of the test score in terms of knowledge or performance on the entire content domain. Such content-validity evidence does not justify an interpretation in terms of anything external to the content domain. Any inference that learning in the content domain implies longer range outcomes—such as better citizenship or better career choices, for example—is not justified by evidence of content validity. Social convention may allow us to make this longer range link, but evidence of content validity concerns only the inference from the test score to performance on the content domain.

Validating even this limited inference is far more difficult than the surface appearance of the content-validity concept would suggest or than typical content-validation practice would indicate. The major problems concern adequate definition of the domain, consideration of the form and structure of the test questions as they relate to the domain, and reliability of the test as a sample from the domain.

DEFINING A CONTENT DOMAIN

A thorough specification of the intended content domain is required before the process of judging whether the test measures the domain can even begin. Recall that we wish to interpret a test score in terms of what it tells us about a student's performance on a particular content domain. (We are rarely interested only in the student's performance on the particular test questions used among all those that might have been used. We use the particular questions to represent a larger set.) Thus, our desired interpretations are in terms of a content domain. If we cannot fully specify what that domain is, then we have no interpretation to make beyond performance on the small number of specific tasks on the test.

In practice, definitions of content domains take on any of several forms, ranging from the specification of possibly hundreds of detailed behavioral objectives to specification of only a few global content areas. An adequate definition of a content domain is specific enough that any qualified judge can determine whether or not any content element is in the domain. Consider, for example, the two content domain definitions for fourth-grade spelling in Table 3-1.

For fourth-grade spelling, it is possible to determine if any particular word is or is not in the domain described in definition A but not with definition B. However, even A is incomplete because the response form is not specified (for example, the student should write the word in response to its oral presentation). Similarly, for knowledge of occupations, almost anything could fit definition B. Definition A provides considerably more specificity but needs more explication of the type and completeness of description desired from students.

In career education programs, comprehensive lists of instructional objectives have often been compiled, providing a valuable start in content domain definition. Typically, to evaluate a program in a convincing way, it is necessary to describe the objectives of instruction and to measure whether students accomplished those objectives. Thus, the content domain of concern is the domain of the instructional objectives.

As people in many educational areas are finding, it can be very difficult to agree upon an instructional domain. Different schools or programs have different domains, and even within one school or program there may be disagreements about the appropriate domain. This means that one measure is not going to fit perfectly everyone's needs for a content valid measure of each unique program. Sufficient similarity may exist for one measure to fit adequately many programs, or a particular agency, such as the state or federal government, may have one domain to which a large number of schools or programs must conform. However, if local programs are free to set their own

Table 3-1
TWO CONTENT-DEFINITION APPROACHES

FOURTH-GRADE SPELLING

Definition A	*Definition B*
All spelling words at the fourth grade difficulty level according to the word lists of some particular reference.	Fourth-grade spelling words

KNOWLEDGE OF OCCUPATIONS

Definition A	*Definition B*
When given one of the fifty major occupational titles (as cited in some particular reference), the student will describe the type of work, the education level required, and the typical working conditions for that occupation.	The student will know about a wide array of occupations.

---

objectives, then they must carefully define their own domain and follow procedures locally to insure content validity. It is in this latter situation that banks of test items measuring a wide variety of instructional objectives may be useful. Then a particular school could compile its own test to match its own unique combination of instructional objectives.

MATCHING MEASUREMENT
FORM TO DOMAIN

Once the content domain to to be measured is thoroughly defined, the task of content validation is only just begun. The inference from a test score to a domain is supported by content-validity evidence that the test adequately represents the domain both in substantive content and in form. Typically, the test is only a sample of the entire domain and must be judged, as any sample is judged, on its representativeness. The representativeness, or match, of the substantive content of the test to the domain is best judged by experts in the content area, including the potential user. The difficulty lies in the necessity to judge as well the appropriateness of the form of the test to the domain, a necessity rarely addressed in practice but of special concern in career education.

The problem here is that the form of a test task can result in the inclusion of phenomena other than the intended domain being measured. One can see the problem, for example, when the domain concerns arithmetic addition but the test task requires the student to read directions or even read the problems themselves before the addition can be attempted. Such a test form or format would result in a test that measures reading as well as addition. If reading were not an intended part of the content domain, an inference from a score on the test to the domain would not be appropriate—a low test score could indicate a deficiency in reading rather than a lack of knowledge in the addition content domain.

A similar problem exists in the form used to measure many career education instructional outcomes. For example, it is common for reading skill to enter the form of tests designed to measure career-education outcomes though reading has not been the target of instruction in those classes. In addition, it is common for career education instructional objectives to address ways in which a student should actually behave differently after instruction while the paper-and-pencil tests address only *knowledge* of what the instructor said should be done. For instance, in the area of career decision making, a student may respond correctly to a test item that inquires about the content of the *Occupational Outlook Handbook*. The student would thus have demonstrated *knowledge* about an important resource. However, the outcome of greater relevance is whether that student actually uses the *Occupational Outlook Handbook* to answer relevant questions.

Another look at Table 3-1 will further clarify the problem. The fourth-grade spelling domain described under definition A addresses only the content and not the form of response. Does the domain consist of the student's written responses to dictated spelling words? And is this domain the same as multiple-choice questions with four spellings of a word, one correct? And do these two forms differ from multiple-choice questions that offer three correctly spelled different words and one incorrect word to be identified from among the four? If the intended domain is the written response to the dictated word, then the test should have that form. If other forms of tests are to be used, other evidence besides that of content validity will be required to justify the inference from the scores to the intended content domain.

This concern with form is partially related to Mager's (1973) concern that the test task match the verb of the behavioral objective. Suppose the instructional objective is for students to describe characteristics of an occupation when given the name of the occupation, as in definition A. In this case, a multiple-choice question that describes characteristics of some occupation and asks the student to select the correct one from a list of four would be calling for a type of action or behavior from the student that differs from the objective (or domain).

Standard content-validity practice operates as though general judgments of substantive-content similarities between test and domain are sufficient to support the inference from a test score to a domain. Too little attention has been paid to the form of the measurement procedure even though form can both introduce irrelevancies into the task (such as reading or understanding directions for how to answer) and can be addressed to a performance other than the performance to which the instruction is directed. Both these issues of form require more than content judgments to support an inference to the intended domain. These issues are not adequately addressed under content-validation approaches. Instead, they involve construct-validity types of inferences when the form of the test tasks do not directly match the form of response called for in the content domain.

RELIABILITY AND INFERENCES TO A DOMAIN

If a measure is judged to sample in a representative way from a well-defined content domain, one must still consider the question of whether the sample of the domain is sufficiently large to estimate consistently performance on the total domain. This is the question of the reliability of the measurement procedure. Nothing in the content domain definition or analysis of match to the domain ensures the required consistency of the procedure. Yet if we obtained widely varying scores depending on the day or a particular sample of the domain used, we could not have confidence in the scores produced. Thus, in content validation, a thorough reliability check is essential. However, it should be noted that for many uses of measures to evaluate programs it is critical not that there be a high level of reliability of individual student scores, but rather that a sufficiently high reliability be achieved for a group mean. This often means that the amount of testing for single individuals can be reduced or that relatively unreliable measures for individuals may produce adequate reliability for group averages.

Measures of Attitudes, Traits, or Skill Constructs

In a number of instances, career education programs attempt to produce changes in individuals' attitudes or traits. Here the goals are different from the goals to produce learning in a specified instructional domain. Instead, individuals are considered to be developing persons with certain characteristics or traits, and it is thought that career education programs may influence this development. In this case, the phenomenon to be measured is the characteristic or trait of concern—a phenomenon not directly observed but hypothesized and inferred from various types of consistencies in behavior. When such characteristics or constructs are being measured, construct-validation procedures provide the method for judging whether a particular measurement procedure adequately measures the intended construct. That is, construct-validity evidence supports the inference from a score to the intended construct.

The construct-validation process begins with a definition of the intended construct and proceeds with the derivation of observable implications from the defined construct. The process then moves to the collection of data on the measure of the construct to check the consistency of this real-world data with the derived implications. Finally, the process recycles, to alter either the original construct or the measure of it (or both) when the real-world events fail to conform to the expectations derived from the construct. In short, construct validation is similar to proving the correctness of a scientific theory. The task of construct validation is never completed, and in fact the existence of our construct is never proved. The process addresses only the question of whether the constructs and measures of them are useful abstractions for a time.

Some of the most frequently seen constructs of concern in career education are *attitudes toward work, career maturity,* and *career decision-making skill.* Any one of the three would provide an adequate illustration of the difficulties involved in construct validation, but *career decision-making skill* is discussed here, since labeling it a construct may appear at first glance inappropriate.

Following the process described above, we start the construct-validation process by defining what is meant by *career decision-making skill.* Then we ask, If there were such a thing, what would be the real-world implications of the construct? How would people with this skill behave? How would they behave differently from people without the skill?

Decision-making skills of various types have been constructs of great interest in many areas (for example, the physician's decision concerning diagnosis and treatment). However, it is still quite difficult to define the construct. Two general approaches to the definition of decision-making skill have been followed. One concerns the process of decision-making—a person has decision-making skill when he or she can make a decision by pursuing a certain decision-making process. An appropriate decision-making process usually involves such factors as collecting relevant information, weighing possible courses of action, and so on. The second approach is to define decision-making skill by the outcome of the decision making—a person has decision-making skill when he or she can make a good decision (or the right or best decision). However, as Chapter 9 points out, it is often difficult to identify a correct or best decision relating to a person's career. Usually we are concerned with both appropriate processes and outcomes in defining career decision-making skill, since the processes could be the focus of instruction presumably designed to produce the best career-decision outcome.

From these definitions the next step is to derive observable implications. If we had a measurement procedure purporting to measure career decision-making, how would we expect such a measure to relate to observable conditions in the world? If there is such a thing as career decision-making skill, what types of observable behaviors would people varying on such a skill produce? A very preliminary and partial answer will serve to illustrate the process. (It would take someone with expertise in career decision-making to provide the full definitions required and to derive the most useful and telling implications.) People high in career decision-making skill should differ from people low in it in the following ways:

1. They would use more of the good decision-making processes.
2. They would know more about good decision-making processes. (Note that we would want to distinguish clearly knowledge of processes from actual use of the processes of good decision making.)
3. They would make better hypothetical career decisions.
4. They would make better decisions in noncareer areas. (Here the extent to which career decision making can usefully be differentiated from other types of decision-making skill would be examined. Presumably even if some differentiation could be shown, some relationship would still exist.)

5. They would do better academically. (In this area some degree of relationship would likely be expected. However, if we think decision-making skill is something different from intelligence, for example, the extent to which the two can be differentiated would also have to be investigated.)
6. They would have had instruction in career decision making. (If the skill does not improve with instruction, then this affects our notion of what the skill is.)

Starting from a list such as this, the construct-validation process involves numerous studies to determine the extent to which people with high scores on the career decision-making skill measure are different from those with low scores in the expected ways. This process means doing small intensive studies of the career decision-making processes people use to validate the measure in relation to implication 1, even though it might not be feasible to observe and measure such processes directly on a large scale. Also, if the measure relates too highly to academic performance or intelligence test scores, then it cannot be distinguished clearly enough from those constructs to give it a different name (implication 5). (See chapter 5 for a detailed illustration of this problem with the construct of career maturity.) And studies would have to be done before and after career decision-making instruction to see if changes in behavior as a result of instruction can be identified. If the measure did not show change after instruction as indicated in implication 6, we would either have to reject the measure as inadequate or alter our ideas about the nature of the skill as attainable through instruction.

If the results of many such intensive studies of the measure show the measure to provide results consistent with the theoretical expectations for it, then we tentatively conclude that the measure has construct validity—that we can make reasonable inferences from the measure to the career decision-making skill construct. However, as noted, the construct-validation process never ends. We continue to learn more and more about the type of appropriate inference to be made from the measure as data of all sorts are collected on it.

SUMMARY AND RESEARCH SUGGESTIONS

There are two major types of validation processes (content and construct) on which we need to concentrate for assessing career development. These two validation processes, though generally well understood theoretically, are quite complex and difficult to apply in practice. Because an adequate theoretical guide for validating measures is in place, the need is to support better practical implementation of validation procedures, especially in the areas identified here as underdeveloped.

Actually, validation issues in career education are not essentially different from those raised in other educational areas. However, the cost and time required to implement good validation procedures is immense for proper evaluation of career education programs. Traditionally, the cost of research on measurement procedures has been borne by the sales of the procedures. This has worked reasonably well for high-volume, high-income measures. However, low-volume or new measures have almost always yielded extremely weak validation evidence.

In many areas of education, the federal government has demanded evaluation. Often, measures existed for at least some of the intended outcomes of the new federal programs, and typically these existing measures (for example, standardized achievement tests in compensatory education programs) were accepted as the primary evaluation tool. Career education is both fortunate and unfortunate in the general shortage of existing instruments. The fortunate part is that the field is not forced to live with instruments that are conveniently available but may be only marginally related to intended outcomes. The unfortunate part is that it must pay the high price of building good instruments.

Efforts are being made to define objectives of career education programs more effectively. As these definitions of objectives improve, domain-based instruments can be built. The new instruments will need study, and as they are studied we will learn more about the process of instruction in the objectives.

Both theoretical development and measurement efforts would profit from investments to develop and refine measures of the theoretical constructs. As data on the measures are collected, we will be able to refine both the measures and the theories about the constructs. Study devoted to the measures should have payoffs beyond the measures themselves to a better understanding of the theoretical constructs. The level of commercial demand for career education measures may not be sufficient to support the needed research and development on career development measures. If not, other forms of support will be required to achieve the development and refinement of the measures so essential to good evaluation and the development of career education programs.

REFERENCES

AMERICAN PSYCHOLOGICAL ASSOCIATION. *Standards for educational and psychological tests.* Washington, D.C.: American Psychological Association, 1974.

MAGER, R. F. *Measuring instructional intent.* Belmont, Calif.: Lear Siegler/Fearon, 1973.

4

Construct definition methodology and generalization theory applied to career education measurement

A. JACKSON STENNER and RICHARD J. ROHLF

NTS Research Corporation

The field of career education measurement is in disarray. Evidence mounts that today's career education instruments are verbal-ability measures in disguise (see chapter 5 in this volume). A plethora of trait names such as career maturity, career development, career planning, career awareness, and career decision making have, in the last decade, appeared as labels to scales composed of multiple-choice items. Many of these scales appear to be measuring similar underlying traits, and certainly the labels have a similar sound or "jingle" to them. Other scale names are attached to clusters of items that appear to measure different traits and at first glance appear deserving of their unique trait names—for example, occupational information, resources for exploration, work conditions, and personal economics. The items of these scales look different and the labels correspondingly are dissimilar or have a different "jangle."

As instrument developers and users, we commit the "jingle fallacy" (Green, 1974) when we give the same or nearly the same name to clearly distinct underlying traits. Similarly, we commit the "jangle fallacy" when different labels are assigned to essentially the same underlying trait. When a trait label such as *career maturity* is assigned to a set of items that in fact measures verbal ability, we have committed the jangle fallacy. When we find evidence that two similarly named scales are only moderately correlated, there exists the possibility of the jingle fallacy.

Whether or not a given scale is a measure of verbal ability as opposed to career maturity is, of course, a question of validity—that is, Is the scale actually a measure of "what it is intended to measure"? This chapter asserts that the current state of affairs in career-education measurement exists because of the lack of carefully defined and operationalized career-education constructs. Herein we suggest a theory and methodology that researchers and practioners will, we hope, find useful in their continuing efforts to develop and refine measurement in the field of career education.

CONSTRUCT DEFINITION

Constructs are the means by which science orders observations. We take it on faith that the universe of our observations can be ordered and subsequently understood by means of a comparatively small number of constructs or inferred organizing influences. Observations are aggregated and constructs created through the mental processes of abstraction and induction. When we observe a group of children and describe some of the children as more aggressive than others, we employ a construct. We create the construct *aggression* by observing that certain behaviors tend to vary together and this pattern of covariation among observations we come to designate as aggression. In describing the differences in behavior among children, we might conclude that one child is much more aggressive than the other children. We arrive at this conclusion informally by summing up the frequency of observed aggressive acts and we use the total score as an index of each child's level of aggression. These total scores are then compared and we arrive at decisions about each child.

This process of weighting individual observations, aggregating the observations into a total score, and then checking the quality of the construct score by determining how well the total score can predict the original observations happens so fast and so frequently and works so well in our everyday lives, that there is seldom need to reflect critically on the process itself. The search for pattern or regularity among observations is, it seems, just as central to our daily lives as it is to scientific activity. Perhaps because the process of observation, abstraction, and construct formation is so fundamental to daily functioning, it is taken for granted in behavioral-science research. Often, observations in the form of questionnaire items and test questions are aggregated without adequate examination of the assumptions and implications inherent in the summation and averaging procedures. The simple fact that observations are combined and a total score computed means that we entertain a hypothesis that the observations are in some way related to one another. If the observations are uncorrelated, then combining them into a total score is a meaningless undertaking, since the total or construct score will carry no information about the original observations and consequently will be of no value in explaining anything else. If, however, the observations are correlated, then the construct score has meaning. Precisely what meaning depends upon the perceived nature of the organizing influences responsible for the correlations among observations.

A construct, then, is a theory that expresses the way its inventor "construes" a set of interrelated observations. Construct labels (for example, career maturity, occupational information, career decision making) serve as shorthand expressions for hypotheses regarding the nature of the predominant organizing influences responsible for correlations among observations.

What constitutes an observation? In career education measurement, the most common "observation" would be a person's response to a test or rating item. Such observations provide information about a person's placement on a scale and serve as indicants of the extent to which the subject possesses the attribute or trait being measured. A set of such indicants (items) constitutes an instrument. The underlying structure or organizing influence operating on these observations is often determined by some combination of statistical structural analysis—for example, factor analysis—and a logical analysis of the item content. Corroboration of the underlying structure is then frequently sought by confirmation via hypothesis testing and correlations with other instruments measuring conceptually similar and dissimilar constructs.

All observations, whether made in service of the behavioral or physical sciences, are prone to error. Error is given more attention in behavioral sciences measurement, probably because it exists in such abundance. Because of its abundance, the process of construct definition must incorporate a theory of error. Various approaches to estimating the reliability of a measurement procedure rest on different assumptions about error and how it affects the observations we make.

Classical reliability theory is based on Spearman's model of an *observed score* (for example, observation). Basically, an observed score is a function of two components, a true score and an error score. Within this framework, models of reliability have been formulated to assess the relative importance of each component. Campbell (1976) gives an excellent review of the historical development of reliability theory. All traditional measures of reliability (alpha, equivalent forms, retest) describe the agreement among repeated measurements of the same individuals. Although these reliability measures differ in their definition of error, they all assume *a single, undifferentiated* source of error. Coefficient alpha attributes error to inconsistency in the extent to which individual items measure an attribute. Measures of stability, such as test-retest or equivalent-forms reliability coefficients, attribute error to changes in testing conditions, mood of examinee, and so on.

In recent times, authors such as Tryon (1957), Cronbach et al. (1963), Cronbach et al. (1972), Nunnally (1967), and Lord and Novick (1968) have departed from the classic concept of true versus error scores and have instead incorporated what has come to be known as the *domain-sampling theory of reliability.* The notion of a true score was replaced by a *domain* or *universe score,* which is an individual's score if all observations in a domain or universe could be averaged. Measurement error in this framework is the extent to which a sample value differs from the population value.

This change in focus from a true score to a universe score resulted in increased importance being placed on defining the "universe" from which a particular sample of items has been drawn and to which we want to generalize. Initially, the concept of universe was restricted to a universe of content—for example, sampling of reading comprehension items from a universe of possible reading comprehension items. However, the work of Cronbach et al. (1972) has broadened this original conceptualization. His work, referred to as *generalizability theory,* speaks to sampling of "conditions of measurement" that include additional sources of variation to that of just variation among samples of items, or components of content. This broadened conceptualization can be viewed as a change from a focus on the reliability of an instrument to a focus on the reliability of a *measurement procedure.*

For example, suppose the career maturity of a group of students is rated on a number of items by a number of different teachers on several different occasions. The traditional view of a content domain would focus on the items as a sample from the universe of all such similar items. However, Cronbach's generalizability theory forces us (1) to acknowledge that there are probably systematic differences in item scores across occasions that do not reflect true change in level of career maturity, and (2) to recognize that there are systematic differences among students reflected in observed scores that are not necessarily due to difference in career maturity—for example, socioeconomic status. Thus, from this perspective we are not only concerned with a universe of possible career maturity items, but, in addition, we need to think in terms of a universe of possible teachers, and a universe of possible occasions. Actually, Cronbach and his colleagues do not talk in terms of different universes, rather, they would consider each of the above a "facet" in the universe of measurement conditions. The more facets one chooses to include in defining a construct, the broader becomes the universe of generalization. Cronbach also refers to facets as either *random* or *fixed.* A fixed facet would be one that would not vary; that is, it would be a constant in the universe. For example, if raters were considered to be a fixed facet in a measurement procedure, the investigator would be planning to use the same rater(s) whenever a measurement was taken. Given this condition, there would be no systematic differences in observed scores due to idiosyncratic differences in rating behavior among raters. However, if raters were considered to be a random facet, the investigator would be broadening the construct definition of career maturity such that a person's universe score would be an average score across the universe of career-maturity items judged across all possible raters. In the fixed-facet case, the universe score would be an average score across the universe of items as judged by a particular rater or set of raters.

As discussed above, the process of construct definition begins with the recognition that observed scores (observations) are determined by some set of underlying organizing influences. In addition to "wanted" influences causing variation among scores, we must also recognize that there are "unwanted" (error) influences exercising potentially biasing or misleading effects on observed scores. Generalizability theory enables us to specify these sources of variance in observed scores in terms of characteristics of the object of measurement, characteristics of the indicants (items), characteristics of the context of measurement, and the interactions both within and across those categories.

In addition to a conceptual model, generalizability theory, using analysis-of-variance procedures, provides the techniques by which we can specify the sources of variance (both wanted and unwanted) in observed scores and estimate the magnitude of their effects. The procedure also yields a generalizability coefficient(s) that can be interpreted in a manner similar to traditional reliability coefficients—for example, in estimating the standard error of measurement. However, before these analysis-of-variance procedures can be applied, it is necessary to design a study in which sources of variance are systematically varied.

Generalizability theory makes a distinction between G and D studies. A G study is a study in which data is collected in order to examine a wide range of sources of variance affecting a measurement procedure, whereas a D study (for *Decision*) selects either the G-study design or some modification of that design for use in estimating the generalizability coefficient that can be expected in some subsequent application of the measurement procedure. A D study does not involve the gathering of data, but rather uses the variance estimates from the sources designed into the G study to estimate what the generalizability coefficient would be under alternative construct definitions and sampling specifications. For example, suppose that the authors of a career maturity scale employ a $p{:}c \times i \times occ$ (persons nested within class crossed with items crossed with occasion) G-study design. That is, the career maturity scale is administered to several classes on at least two occasions. Under this design, the broadest permissible construct definition generalizes over items and occasions with either person or class as the object of measurement. Suppose that an investigator had limited time available for student testing and wanted to know what the effect would be of reducing by 50 percent the number of items on the scale. This scenario could be set up and a generalizability coefficient estimated given specification of the object of measurement and construct definition (which facets are considered fixed and which random). This application of generalizability theory is analogous to power analysis (Cohen, 1977), in which different sampling scenarios are evaluated to determine the probability of detecting an effect. In D studies, different measurement scenarios (alternative construct definitions coupled with alternative sampling frequencies) are evaluated to determine the precision with which objects of measurement can be differentiated.

AN ILLUSTRATION OF
GENERALIZABILITY THEORY

Before proceeding with an example, it may prove useful to reflect on the meaning of a generalizability coefficient as well as its general form. A generalizability coefficient is simply the ratio of true-score variance (or universe-score variance) to the sum of true-score variance and error variance:

$$\hat{\Sigma}_\rho^2 = \frac{\text{true-score variance}}{\text{true-score variance} + \text{error variance}} = \frac{\tau}{\tau + \delta}$$

The components that enter true-score variance and error variance change as the construct definition changes, but the basic expression for a generalizability coefficient remains the same. Following are several descriptive comments about the generalizability coefficient that may help you to gain an intuitive grasp of what this ratio means:

1. One task of measurement is to differentiate among objects (for example, classrooms or children) on some scale while simultaneously generalizing over selected facets. The higher the generalizability coefficient, the better is the differentiation or separation among objects.

2. Children or classrooms differ on a scale for many reasons (we usually refer to these reasons as sources). Some of these reasons are important to us and represent what we want to measure, and others are of no interest and represent noise. Differences among students that arise due to reasons we are interested in we call *true-score differences,* whereas differences due to reasons we are not interested in we call *error differences.* A generalizability coefficient is simply the ratio of average squared differences between objects that arise from wanted sources divided by the average squared differences between objects arising from wanted and unwanted sources.

3. Observed-score variance is the sum of true-score variance and error variance. Thus, the generalizability coefficient represents the proportion of observed-score variance that is due to "wanted" sources of variance. If the generalizability coefficient is high, then a high proportion of the variance in observed scores is due to wanted sources of variation, whereas if the coefficient is low, it means that only a small proportion of differences among objects is due to wanted sources of variation.

4. We can conceive of the generalizability coefficient as a heuristic that describes the confidence with which we can reject the null hypothesis that the true scores of all objects are equal. Statisticians would use an F ratio for this purpose and, in fact, for the simple persons x items ($p \times i$) design:

$$\hat{\Sigma}_\rho^2 = \frac{F-1}{F} \quad \text{or} \quad F = \frac{1}{1 - \Sigma_\rho^2}$$

5. The generalizability coefficient is the squared correlation between observed scores and true scores. The true score is the average score we would obtain if all

observations across the random facets of the universe of generalization could be exhaustively sampled. Errors of measurement (unwanted reasons that objects have different scores) contribute to ordering people differently on observed scores (which are samples) than they would be ordered if their scores could be averaged over all facets of interest (for example, items or days during a two-week period). The generalizability coefficient provides an indication of how differently people are likely to be ordered if exhaustive sampling of all relevant observations was possible.

In summary, the generalizability coefficient provides an estimate of the precision of measurement given a construct definition. It is meaningless to refer to a reliability or generalizability coefficient without reference to the governing construct definition. What construct definition is most appropriate in a given situation is a substantive question that often cannot be answered by measurement specialists. What definition to employ is a complex question that takes us back to what we want our construct to mean. Ascribing meaning to constructs and increasing our understanding of variance arising from applications of our measurement procedures is what the process of construct definition is all about.

Table 4-1 provides estimated G-study variance components for a $p \times i \times m$ design, and Table 4-2 displays different D-study designs or measurement scenarios. The data used in this illustration were graciously provided by Dr. Bert Westbrook and represent a subsample of the ninth-grade data used in his chapter of this volume. The sample consists of sixty students responding to the fifty attitude items of the Career Maturity Inventory (CMI).

Examination of Table 4-1 reveals that a large proportion (60 percent) of the variance of this instrument is unexplained by facets of the measurement procedure. The second and third largest components of variance are the item (i)

TABLE 4-1
ILLUSTRATIVE EXAMPLE OF GENERALIZABILITY
ANALYSES FOR THE ATTITUDE SUBSCALE OF THE CMI

SOURCE	NOTATION	SS	df	MS	ESTIMATED VARIANCE COMPONENT	ESTIMATED PROPORTION OF UNIVERSE VARIANCE ATTRIBUTABLE TO EACH SOURCE
Person	P	68.87	59	1.167	.00889	04
Item	i	270.41	49	5.519	.04328	18
Moment	m	1.20	1	1.204	.00030	00
Person × Item	$p \times i$	661.62	2891	.229	.04111	17
Person × Moment	$p \times m$	11.55	59	.196	.00098	00
Item × Moment	$i \times m$	11.87	49	.242	.00159	01
Person × Item × Moment	$p \times i \times m_e$	423.88	2891	.147	.14662	60

TABLE 4-2
ILLUSTRATIVE SCENARIO TABLE

SCENARIO NUMBER	CONSTRUCT DEFINITION		SAMPLING SPECIFICATIONS	SOURCES OF VARIANCE							GENERALIZABILITY COEFFICIENT
	Random Facets	Fixed Facets		p	i	m	$p \times i$	$p \times m$	$m \times i$	$p \times i \times m_e$	
1	Items	Moments	$N_i = 50$ $N_m = 1$	τ	—	—	δ	τ	—	δ	.72
2	Moments	Items	$N_m = 1$ $N_i = 50$	τ	—	—	τ	δ	—	δ	.78
3	Items Moments		$N_i = 50$ $N_m = 1$	τ	—	—	δ	δ	—	δ	.72
4	Items Moments		$N_i = 50$ $N_m = 2$	τ	—	—	δ	δ	—	δ	.81
5	Items Moments		$N_i = 100$ $N_m = 3$	τ	—	—	δ	δ	—	δ	.92

and person × item ($p \times i$) interaction, respectively. The person (p) component explains 4 percent of the universe variance. The moment (m), person × moment ($p \times m$) interaction and item by moment ($i \times m$) interaction explain very small proportions of the variance.

A major advantage of generalizability theory is that the theory specifies which sources of variance are to be ignored, which contribute to true score (τ), and which contribute to error (δ) in estimating the generalizability of a measurement procedure under a particular construct definition. Whether stated or not, there are two essential aspects of a measurement procedure that must be made explicit before any reliability or generalizability coefficients can be interpreted. These are (1) the construct definition—that is, which facets are to be considered random and which fixed—and (2) the sampling frequencies for each facet included in the construct definition.

Table 4-2 presents construct definitions and sampling specifications for five scenarios. Scenario 1 displays the generalizability coefficient under the classical reliability formulation in which moments (that is, short-term occasions) are fixed ($N_m = 1$) and items are random. The generalizability coefficient ($\Sigma\rho^2 = .72$) under this scenario accurately describes the precision of measurement only if our interest centers on how well students can be differentiated on a single occasion. This coefficient corresponds to the traditional coefficient alpha (or $KR - 20$).

In Scenario 2, moments are random and items are fixed. This construct definition corresponds to the traditional stability, or retest, coefficient. In other words, within the framework of generalizability theory, the traditional retest coefficient may be computed under a generalizability design of the form $p \times i \times m$ where items constitute a fixed facet and moments constitute a random facet. Note that in this case the retest coefficient is higher than the internal consistency coefficient because the $p \times m$ variance component accounts for virtually no variance whereas the $p \times i$ interaction (which contributes to the true score when items are fixed) accounts for 17 percent of the universe variance.

Scenarios 3, 4, and 5 all employ the broadest permissible construct definition (items and moments random) but the sampling frequencies for items and/or moments differ. In Scenario 3 we estimate what the generalizability coefficient would be if fifty items were administered on one occasion (that is, moment). Note that the generalizability coefficient under this construct is coincidentally the same as that observed under Scenario 1. As a rule, when the construct definition is broadened and the sampling specifications are unchanged, the generalizability coefficient goes down. Similarly, when the construct definition is narrowed and consequently the universe of generalization is narrowed, the generalizability coefficient is increased. The reasoning for this expectation is straightforward; if the universe under examination is quite broad, then a larger number of observations must be sampled to attain a specified level of precision, whereas a narrower universe permits a smaller number of observations to attain the same precision. Under Scenario 4, the item sample remains at $N_i = 50$ but the number of testing sessions is increased, $N_m = 2$, resulting in an improvement in the generalizability coefficient ($\Sigma_\rho^2 = .81$). Finally, under Scenario 5 sampling frequencies are increased for both items ($N_i = 100$) and moments ($N_m = 3$), resulting in a substantial increase in precision of measurement.

Classical reliability theory, as practiced in the field of career education measurement, is unnecessarily restrictive. Disciples of classical theory compute a number of equivalence coefficients by correlating student performance on split halves of an instrument or by computing coefficient alpha (KR − 20) for an instrument administered on a single occasion. Similarly, stability or retest coefficients are computed by correlating student performance on one occasion with performance, say, two weeks later. Finally, interrater reliability coefficients are computed by correlating the ratings of two or more raters of the same behavior. Each of these forms of reliability coefficient reflects a single undifferentiated source of error and, more importantly, derives from different construct definitions. Coefficient alpha accurately reflects an instrument's reliability under the highly restricted construct definition that treats items as the *only* random facet and, consequently, the $p \times i$ interaction (confounded with the residual) as the only source of error. The stability coefficient properly reflects an instrument's reliability under a construct definition that treats occasions as the only random source of variance and the persons × occasion interaction as the only source of error.

It is important to recognize that traditional forms of reliability permit error variance to be confounded with true-score variance because they do not differentiate among the many possible sources of error. For example, the test-retest reliability coefficient will not "break out" a $p \times i$ interaction, and thus that variance will be a "hidden" component of the true-score variance. Likewise, the $p \times occ$ interaction will be a hidden component of the true-score variance when the coefficient alpha is calculated. The result could be an artificially inflated estimate of true-score variance, which, in turn, would result in an inflated reliability coefficient. The attractiveness of generalizability theory is that it permits simultaneous consideration of items, occasions, and other facets as random sources of error.

Generalizability theory provides a framework that enables us to better conceptualize the constructs we use. Unfortunately, many investigators do not invest sufficient time in construct-definition activities. Time and again, researchers move ahead to answer substantive research questions without carefully defining the constructs that figure in their theories or program evaluations. The most common mistake found in the behavioral sciences is that investigators will state a conceptually broad construct definition but will use a reliability estimate based on a much narrower definition, thus yielding a coefficient that exaggerates the precision with which the construct can be measured. Elsewhere we have argued that career education will go the way of many previous fads unless, as a field, it can stake out a set of well-defined constructs and related instrumentation (Stenner, Strang, Baker, 1978). So far, efforts in this regard have been disappointing.

SOME SPECIAL APPLICATIONS

Many seemingly diverse issues in measurement can be accommodated within generalizability theory. Cronbach (1972) states,

> What appears today to be most important in G Theory is not what the book gave greater space to. In 1972 G Theory appeared as an elaborate technical apparatus. Today the machinery looms less large than the questions the theory enables us to pose. G Theory has a protean quality. The procedures and even the issues take a new form in every context. G Theory enables you to ask your questions better; what is most significant for you cannot be supplied from the outside [p. 199].

In the discussion to follow we attempt to illustrate the range of applications for which generalizability theory, coupled with construct-definition methodology, can be useful.

Toward a Theory of the Indicant
A historical convention for which we can find no rational explanation has contributed to the avoidance of a potentially fruitful type of construct-validation study. The convention is to report person scores as number of items (or indicants) correct and item scores as proportion of respondents answering an item correctly. Thus, person scores and item scores are expressed in different metrics, leading some investigators to assume that there is a fundamental difference in the way people and items can be analyzed. For example, construct-validity studies often emphasize relationships between theoretically relevant variables and the construct under study and use the person as the unit of analysis. On the other hand, little work has been done in explaining variance in item scores. Some authors, including ourselves, contend that many career-development scales containing items of the multiple-choice variety in fact measure verbal ability and not career maturity (see Westbrook's chapter in this volume). One approach to investigating this contention that, on the surface, seems more direct than focusing on person-score correlations, would involve predicting item scores using a set of item readability and syntax measures as well as theoretically derived ratings of the extent of career maturity called for by each item. If the readability and syntax measures explain a large proportion of the variance in item scores and the theory-based ratings explain little of the variance, then it is likely that the so-called career development ideas are really verbal-reasoning items in disguise. If a construct is really well defined, then it should be possible to explain the behavior of indicants of that construct—that is, explain variance in item or indicant scores. Unfortunately, this is a test that few constructs

in the behavioral sciences, let alone career education, have passed. (A discussion and illustration of this methodology has been described by Stenner and Smith, in press.)

Generalizability of Ratings

Many outcomes in career education do not readily lend themselves to paper-and-pencil testing. For example, outcomes such as employability skills, personal work habits, and job-interview behavior are better measured by trained observers in either real or simulated settings. Generalizability theory provides a framework for estimating the dependability of these ratings.

Suppose a career education program sets about to improve the job-interview behavior of a group of students. Five employers from the local community are called upon to interview each student and complete a rating scale. One highly informative design for examining the generalizability of these ratings would be $p \times i \times r$ (persons crossed with items crossed with raters). Thus, each student would be rated by each employer on all items. Under this design, the broadest permissible construct definition generalizes over items and raters.

Separate estimates of alpha or interrater agreement would overestimate the precision with which the construct as defined can be measured. The generalizability coefficient more accurately reflects measurement precision and provides information on how the precision can be increased to an acceptable level. One excellent illustration of this type of analysis is provided by Gilmore, Kane, and Naccarato (1978). Note that this design does not include the "occasion" facet. If a sizable $p \times occ$ interaction exists, our estimate of measurement precision may be inflated if we have defined our construct to be stable over time.

Competency Testing

The objectives of some career education programs state that all students will attain a particular mastery level in reading and mathematics. In assessing this objective, instrumentation is needed that has a special kind of reliability. Discussion above focused on developing instruments that would maximally differentiate among objects (for example, students). In competency or mastery testing, the objective is to differentiate among two groups of students, those who have attained the minimal performance level and those who have not. Generalizability theory provides a framework for studying the dependability of mastery or competency decisions. The most thorough treatment of this application of generalizability theory is provided by Brennan and Kane (1977).

Generalizability of Class Means

Some career-education evaluations employ class or school rather than student as the unit of analysis (Stenner, Strang, and Baker, [1978]; Kane and Brennan [1977]; Kane, Gilmore, and Crooks [1976]). Haney (1974) and Kane and Brennan (1977) have suggested that generalizability theory provides a conceptually and practically appealing approach to estimating the reliability of class means. The simplest design from which we can estimate the generalizability of class means is $p{:}c \times i$ (persons nested within class crossed with items). Note that this is the familiar persons $\times$ items design (from which coefficient alpha is computed) with the addition that knowledge is available on class membership. Under this design we can estimate the reliability of persons nested within classes and class means. In a more complex design, such as $p{:}c{:}s \times i$, the object of measurement might be persons (p), classes (c), or schools (s). In general, this type of split-plot design can prove particularly useful in an evaluation in which multiple units of analysis (for example, students, classes, and schools) are employed (Hayman, Rayder, Stenner, and Madey, 1979). As a rule, generalizability coefficients should be computed for each unit of analysis employed in a research or evaluation study.

In passing, we should note that applications of generalizability theory in which class or school is the object of measurement have focused exclusively on the mean or first moment of the distribution. Lohnes (1972), in an excellent but largely ignored paper, demonstrated that using the variance of a class or school distribution as an independent variable might also be useful in predicting outcomes. In such studies, interest is centered on differentiating classrooms not in terms of their means but rather in terms of their variances while generalizing over occasions or some other random facet.

Issues of Test Bias

Much attention and controversy have surrounded the issues of race and sex bias in testing. Although there are many types of bias, perhaps the most pernicious is that which gives members of particular racial, ethnic, or sex groups unfair advantage in responding to certain kinds of items. It is somewhat ironic that although career education has as one of its goals the eradication of sex-role stereotyping (Hoyt, 1975) we were unable to find any studies of sex bias in career education measurement.

Some forms of item bias can be effectively studied within the framework of generalizability theory. For example, a simple $p{:}s \times i$ (persons nested within sex group crossed with items) will provide information on possible sex bias. In this design the component of variance related to sex bias is the $s \times i$ (sex by item) interaction. If this component of variance is large, then items have a different meaning (that is, they measure something different) for males and females. Examination of the items contributing most heavily to the interaction can sometimes lead to explanations for the source of the bias (for example, terminology unfamiliar to males or females). Students can also be nested within race groups to evaluate racial bias or nested within reading-level groups to evaluate the extent to which item meaning is conditional on student reading level.

Although the literature on bias has focused almost exclusively on racial, ethnic, and sex characteristics, the notion of bias is a generic concept. Any characteristic of the object of measurement that interacts with a random facet represents bias. For social and other reasons, item scores that are conditional on race and sex (that interact with race and sex) have received the bulk of attention. From theoretical as well as practical perspectives, other types of bias pose equally troublesome problems. For example, items that take on radically different meanings depending upon the examinee's reading level are just as invalid as indicators of career maturity as items that are conditional on the sex or race of the examinee.

REFERENCES

BRENNAN, R. L., and KANE, M. T. An index of dependability for mastery tests, *Journal of Educational Measurement*, 1977, *14*, 3, 277–289.

CAMPBELL, J. P. *Psychometric theory.* In M. D. Dunnette (Ed.), *Handbook of industrial and organizational psychology.* Chicago: Rand McNally, 1976.

COHEN, J. *Statistical power analysis for the behavioral sciences* (Rev. Ed.). New York: Academic Press, 1977.

CRITES, J. *Career maturity inventory.* Monterey, Calif.: CTB/McGraw-Hill, 1973.

CRONBACH, L. J., GLESER, G. C., NANDA, H., and RAJARATNAM, N. *The dependability of behavioral measurements: Multifacet studies of generalizability.* New York: Wiley, 1972.

CRONBACH, L. J., RAJARATNAM, N., and GLESER, G. *Theory of Generalizability: A liberalization of reliability theory.* British *Journal of Statistical Psychology,* 1963, *16* (part 2), 137–163.

GILMORE, G. M., KANE, M. T., and NACCARATO, R. W. *The generalizability of student ratings of construction: Estimation of the teacher and course components. Journal of Educational Measurement,* 1978, *15*, 1–13.

GREEN, D. R. (Ed.). *The aptitude-achievement distinction.* Monterey, Calif. CTB/McGraw-Hill, 1974.

HANEY, W. *The dependability of group mean scores.* Unpublished special qualifying paper, Harvard Graduate School of Education, October 1974.

HAYMAN, J., RAYDER, N., STENNER, A. J., and MADEY, D. L. *On aggregation, generalization, and utility, in educational evaluation. Educational Evaluation and Policy Analysis,* July–August, 1979, *1* (4), pp. 31–39.

HOYT, K. B. *An introduction to career education: A policy paper of the U.S. Office of Education.* Washington, D.C.: U.S. Department of Health, Education, and Welfare, 1975.

KANE, M. T., and BRENNAN, R. L. *The generalizability of class means. The Review of Educational Research,* 1977, *47* (1), 267–292.

KANE, M. T., GILMORE, G. M., and CROOKS, T. J. *Student evaluations of teaching: The generalizability of class means. Journal of Educational Measurement,* 1976, *13*, 171–183.

LOHNES, P. *Statistical descriptors of school classes. American Educational Research Journal,* 1972, *9*, 547–556.

LORD, F. M., and NOVICK, M. R. *Statistical theories of mental test scores.* Reading, Mass.: Addison–Wesley, 1968.

NUNNALLY, J. C. *Psychometric theory.* New York: McGraw-Hill, 1967.

STENNER, A. J., and SMITH, M.   *Testing construct theories.* In press.

STENNER, A. J., STRANG, E. W., and BAKER, R. F.   *Technical assistance in evaluating career education projects: Final report.* Durham, N.C.: NTS Research Corporation, 1978.

TRYON, R. C.   Reliability and behavior domain validity: Reformulation and historical critique. *Psychological Bulletin,* 1957, *54,* 229–249.

5

Construct validation of career maturity measures

BERT W. WESTBROOK
North Carolina State University

For several years, I have been interested in the testing issues in career development. About ten years ago, I began looking at the literature in this area and discovered that such people as Donald Super and John Crites had been emphasizing the need for measures of what they called vocational maturity. Since no standardized measures existed at that time, it appeared to be an opportunity to develop a test that could be used in the evaluation of career-development programs. So we launched into a project before we had time to think about all the problems involved and in spite of occasional heckling to the effect that "fools rush in where angels fear to tread." When Donald Super reviewed my proposal to construct and validate vocational maturity measures in two years, he advised me that "research always takes longer."

Our PERT network prevailed, however, and in 1970 we put together a

Appreciation is expressed to Brenda Rogers, who reviewed this paper and provided many helpful suggestions.

Some of the data reported in this chapter have already appeared in Westbrook, B. W., Cutts, C. C., Simonson, S. S., and Arcia, M., The validity of the Crites model of career maturity, *Journal of Vocational Behavior*, 1980, *16*, 249–281.

test we initially called the Vocational Maturity Battery, Tests 1−6 (Revised Form) (Westbrook, 1970). Later we changed the name (not the test) to the Cognitive Vocational Maturity Test. In January, 1972, we submitted a report to the *Journal of Vocational Behavior,* where it was published in July 1973 (Westbrook and Parry-Hill, 1973a). The test and all the technical data were published in a technical report (Westbrook and Parry-Hill, 1973b), but the report is more readily available from the *JSAS Catalog of Selected Documents in Psychology* (Westbrook and Parry-Hill, 1975). Some of the strengths and weaknesses of the Cognitive Vocational Maturity Test can be found in other places (Westbrook and Mastie, 1973; Westbrook and Mastie, 1974; and Super, 1974).

Some of our problems, experiences, and suggestions have appeared in various publications (Westbrook and Cunningham, 1970; Westbrook and Mastie, 1972; Westbrook and Parry-Hill, 1975; Westbrook, 1971; Westbrook, 1974).

Vocational maturity has experienced a name change. It is now called career maturity. Basically, however, the problems in measuring it have not changed. A number of problems are associated with the construct validity of career maturity. We have carried out studies that provide some support for the construct of career maturity (Westbrook, 1976a, 1976b, 1976c, 1976d). More recently, we have collected data that raise serious questions about the assumptions we have made about career maturity (Westbrook, Cutts, Madison, and Arcia, 1980).

WHAT RESEARCH SAYS
ABOUT CAREER MATURITY

What does research say about career maturity and its measurement? The remainder of this paper is devoted to a discussion of a number of generalizations based partly on our own research and partly on a review of the literature. These generalizations appear in italics at the start of each subsection.

Consensus in the Field
There is very little consensus as to the number of career-maturity variables that can be reliably measured, the best organization of them, or their most appropriate names.

Table 5-1 represents the current state of the art, offering the variable lists of the investigators who have developed measures of career development. All the investigators give somewhat different names to their scales. The number of scales ranges from one for the ETS Guidance Inquiry to ten for the Assessment of Career Development. No two instrument titles or scales have identical names, although the word *career* appears in several of the titles and scales. One investigator classifies the items in separate categories, another puts some of the

TABLE 5-1
CAREER MATURITY SCALE NAMES

Vocational Development Inventory Attitude Scale (Crites, 1965)
Cognitive Vocational Maturity Test (Westbrook, 1970)
       Fields of Work
       Job Selection
       Work Conditions
       Education Required
       Attributes Required
       Duties
Career Development Inventory (Super et al., 1971)
       Planning Orientation
       Resources for Exploration
       Information and Decision-Making
Assessment of Career Development (American College Testing Program, 1972)
       Occupational Characteristics
       Occupational Preparation Requirements
       Career Planning Knowledge
       Career Planning Involvement
       Exploratory Occupational Experiences—Social, Health, and Personal Services
       Exploratory Occupational Experiences—Business, Sales, and Management
       Exploratory Occupational Experiences—Business Operations
       Exploratory Occupational Experiences—Technologies and Trades
       Exploratory Occupational Experiences—Natural, Social, and Medical Sciences
       Exploratory Occupational Experiences—Creative and Applied Arts
       Exploratory Occupational Experiences—Summary
Career Maturity Inventory (Crites, 1973)
       Career Choice Attitudes
       Career Choice Competencies
              Self-Appraisal
              Occupational Information
              Goal Selection
              Planning
              Problem Solving
New Mexico Career Education Test Series (Healy and Klein, 1973)
       Career Planning
       Knowledge of Occupations
       Job Application Procedures
       Career Development
       Career Oriented Activities
       Attitude Toward Work
Career Awareness Inventory (Fadale, 1974)
       Identity
       Training
       Models
       Functions
       Prestige
       Clusters
       Characteristics
Career Decision Scale (Osipow, 1976)

TABLE 5-1 (continued)

Career Skills Assessment Program (College Entrance Examination Board, 1977, 1978)
        Self-Evaluation and Development Skills
        Career Awareness Skills
        Career Decision-Making Skills
        Employment-Seeking Skills
        Work Effectiveness Skills
        Personal Economics Skills
Career Maturity Inventory (Crites, 1978)
        Career Choice Attitudes, Screening Form
        Career Choice Attitudes, Counseling Form
                Involvement
                Orientation
                Decisiveness
                Independence
                Compromise
        Career Choice Competencies
                Self-Appraisal
                Occupational Information
                Goal Selection
                Planning
                Problem-Solving
Career Development Inventory (Super et al., 1979)
        Career Planning
        Career Exploration
        Career Decision-Making
        World-of-Work Information
        Knowledge of Preferred Occupation

---

items together, and still another redivides groups of items differently. Each names the variables in his or her own way. Until scale names can be linked conclusively to a definite theory, choice must be made on other grounds.

Scale names are a source of confusion. Career development theory needs a set of constructs on which many investigators agree and which all can interpret similarly. Furthermore, for each such construct there should be several indicators derived from various sorts of data. We are far from that state at present.

Given the present Babel of scale names, the only useful way to discuss career maturity or career development variables is to refer to the measure used—for example, "the Crites Planning score," "the Super Planning Orientation score," "the New Mexico Career Planning score," and so on.

The Coverage of Behavior
Career maturity tests differ substantially in their coverage of cognitive, psychomotor, and affective behavior.

If we accept the existing measuring instruments as operational definitions of the performance domain of career development, then it is apparent that there is not much agreement on what constitutes career development. A content analysis of six career development tests (Westbrook, 1974) revealed that they differ in several respects, and substantially in their coverage of cognitive, psychomotor, and affective behavior. The tests also differ in terms of the range of behaviors covered within each of the three domains and vary enormously in their coverage of specific behaviors.

Some tests cover an extremely wide range of behaviors. An example is the Assessment of Career Development, which covers behaviors in the cognitive, psychomotor, and affective domains. The content outline in Table 5-2 lists a total of seventy-one career development behaviors on the Assessment of Career Development, which probably includes a greater variety of behaviors than any available instrument.

TABLE 5-2
ACD CONTENT OUTLINE

I. OCCUPATIONAL AWARENESS

    A. Occupational Knowledge
        1. Occupational characteristics
           a. Duties
               (1) Identify occupational titles of given job descriptions (Unit 1—Items 1–3, 25, 32–34, 37, 39–40)
               (2) Identify job descriptions for given occupational titles (Unit 1—Items 44–49)
               (3) Identify type of work (things or machines, people, ideas or theories, data or records) for given occupations (Unit 1—Items 50–58)
           b. Psychosocial aspects
               (4) Identify occupations with irregular working schedule (Unit 1—Items 6, 10, 16)
               (5) Identify jobs involving physical danger (Unit 1—Item 7)
               (6) Identify jobs requiring worker to be on feet while working (Unit 1—Item 9)
               (7) Identify jobs involving mental and emotional stress (Unit 1—Item 13)
               (8) Identify jobs that would satisfy given values (Unit 1—Items 20–24)
               (9) Identify occupations involving working with groups of people (Unit 1—Item 4)
               (10) Distinguish between indoor and outdoor jobs (Unit 1—Item 27)
               (11) Identify workers who are employed by given organizations (Unit 1—Item 65)
           c. Worker attributes
               (12) Identify occupations requiring given abilities (Unit 1—Items 5, 8, 14)
               (13) Identify workers having similar interests (Unit 1—Item 18)
               (14) Identify occupations associated with given interest types (Unit 1—Item 17)
               (15) Identify occupations associated with given personality characteristics (Unit 1—Items 11, 26)
               (16) Identify occupations associated with given types of work experience (Unit 1—Item 28)
               (17) Identify appropriate jobs for given individuals whose attributes are described (Unit 1—Items 66–72)
        2. Occupational preparation requirements
           a. School course requirements

TABLE 5-2 (continued)

       (18) Identify names of school courses that provide training for given occupations (Unit 1—Item 64)

       (19) Identify names of occupations for which given school courses would be most helpful (Unit 1—Items 30, 36, 43)

   b. Educational level requirements

       (20) Identify titles of occupations requiring least amount of education (Unit 1—Item 12)

       (21) Identify titles of occupations requiring most amount of education (Unit 1—Item 19)

       (22) Identify education levels required of given occupations (Unit 1—Items 38, 59–63)

       (23) Identify titles of occupations requiring given education level (Unit 1—Items 29, 31, 35, 42)

       (24) Identify titles of occupations requiring an apprenticeship (Unit 1—Items 15, 41)

B. Exploratory Occupational Experiences

       (25) The learner reports degree of involvement (none, once or twice, or several times) in experiences and worker activities typical of jobs in the Business Operations Cluster (Unit 6—Items 5, 11, 17, 23, 29, 35, 41, 47, 53, 59, 65, 71, 77, 83, 89)

       (26) The learner reports degree of involvement in experiences and worker activities typical of jobs in the Industrial Technologies and Trades Cluster (Unit 6—Items 6, 12, 18, 24, 30, 36, 42, 48, 54, 60, 66, 72, 78, 84, 90)

       (27) The learner reports degree of involvement in experiences and worker activities typical of jobs in the Science and Medicine Cluster (Unit 6—Items, 1, 7, 13, 19, 25, 31, 37, 43, 49, 55, 61, 67, 73, 79, 85)

       (28) The learner reports degree of involvement in experiences and worker activities typical of jobs in the Creative and Applied Arts Cluster (Unit 6—Items 2, 8, 14, 20, 26, 32, 38, 44, 50, 56, 62, 68, 74, 80, 86)

       (29) The learner reports degree of involvement in experiences and worker activities typical of jobs in the Personal, Social, and Health Services Cluster (Unit 6—Items 3, 9, 15, 21, 27, 33, 39, 45, 51, 57, 63, 69, 75, 81, 87)

       (30) The learner reports degree of involvement in experiences and worker activities typical of jobs in the Sales and Promotion Cluster (Unit 6—Items 4, 10, 16, 22, 28, 34, 40, 46, 52, 58, 64, 70, 76, 82, 88)

II. SELF-AWARENESS

A. Preferred Job Characteristics

   1. Job values

      a. Most important job value

        (31) The learner identifies the job value which he or she feels would be most important on the job (Unit 2—Item 1)

      b. Second most important job value

        (32) The learner identifies the second most important job value (Unit 2—Item 2)

      c. Least important job value

        (33) The learner identifies the least important job value (Unit 2—Item 3)

   2. Working condition preferences

      a. Indoor versus outdoor work

        (34) The learner indicates a preference for indoor or outdoor work (Unit 2—Item 4)

      b. Working with people versus working alone

TABLE 5-2 (continued)

---

      (35) The learner indicates a preference for working with people or working alone (Unit 2—Item 5)

  c. Working at variety of tasks versus same task

      (36) The learner indicates a preference for working at a variety of tasks or the same task (Unit 2—Item 6)

  d. Work with hands versus work at desk

      (37) The learner indicates a preference for working with hands doing physical labor or working at a desk with little physical activity (Unit 2—Item 7)

B. Career Plans

  1. Educational plans

      (38) The learner indicates the greatest amount of education he or she plans to complete (Unit 3—Item 1)

  2. Occupational preferences

      (39) The learner writes the name of the job that he or she is thinking about most (Part A) and identifies the Job Family in which his or her first job choice best fits (Part B) (Unit 3—Item 2)

      (40) The learner writes the name of his or her second job choice (Part A) and identifies the Job Family in which his or her second job choice best fits (Part B) (Unit 3—Item 3)

  3. Certainty of occupational preferences

      (41) The learner indicates the degree of certainty that his or her first job choice will be the same in one year (Unit 3—Item 4)

C. Perceived Need for Help with Career Planning

      (42) The learner reports that he or she would or would not like help in improving study skills (Unit 4—Item 46)

      (43) The learner reports that he or she would or would not like help in improving reading skills (Unit 4—Item 47)

      (44) The learner reports that he or she would or would not like help in improving math skills (Unit 4—Item 48)

      (45) The learner reports that he or she would or would not like help in choosing courses (Unit 4—Item 49)

      (46) The learner reports that he or she would or would not like help in discussing personal concerns (Unit 4—Item 50)

      (47) The learner reports that he or she would or would not like help in discussing a health problem (Unit 4—Item 51)

      (48) The learner reports that he or she would or would not like help in making career plans (Unit 4—Item 52)

      (49) The learner reports that he or she would or would not like help in obtaining money to continue education after high school (Unit 4—Item 53)

      (50) The learner reports that he or she would or would not like help in finding after-school or summer work (Unit 4—Item 54)

III. CAREER PLANNING AND DECISION MAKING

A. Career Planning Knowledge

  1. Knowledge of basic career development principles

    a. Continuous nature of career development and decision making

      (51) The learner will be able to distinguish between accurate and inaccurate statements describing the nature of career development (Unit 5—Items 17, 18, 22)

TABLE 5-2 (continued)

---

      b. Impact of work on one's life
         (52) The learner will be able to distinguish between accurate and inaccurate statements describing the impact of work on one's life (Unit 5—Items 2, 6, 19)
      c. Multipotentiality of people for occupations
         (53) The learner will be able to distinguish between accurate and inaccurate statements describing the concept of multipotentiality of people for occupations (Unit 5—Items 4, 7, 21)
   2. Knowledge of reality factors
      a. Post-high-school education and training
         (54) The learner will be able to distinguish between accurate and inaccurate statements about post-high-school education and training (Unit 5—Items 9, 10, 11, 13, 30)
      b. Labor market functioning and trends
         (55) The learner will be able to distinguish between accurate and inaccurate statements about labor market functioning and trends (Unit 5—Items 12, 14, 15, 34, 35)
   3. Knowledge of the career planning process
      a. When to start
         (56) The learner will be able to distinguish between accurate and inaccurate statements dealing with the time that an individual should begin career planning (Unit 5—Items 3, 5, 20)
      b. How to proceed
         (57) The learner will be able to identify valid statements describing sources of information about occupations (Unit 5—Items 8, 29)
         (58) The learner will be able to identify statements that describe valid career planning/exploration principles (Unit 5—Items 1, 16, 28, 31–33)
         (59) The learner will be able to distinguish **among** statements describing one's interests, abilities, and values (Unit 5—**Items** 23–27)
         (60) Given a description of a school or **career** problem that an individual is having, the learner will be able to identify **the** most appropriate solution to the given problem (Unit 5—Items 36–40)
B. Career Planning Involvement
   1. Seeking information
      a. Reading, viewing, and consulting references
         (61) The learner reports the extent to which he or she has engaged in career planning activities dealing with reading, viewing, and consulting references (Unit 4—Items 1, 4, 5, 11)
      b. Talking and discussing
         (62) The learner reports the extent to which he or she has engaged in career planning activities that involve talking about and discussing career plans with others (Unit 4—Items 2–3, 6–10)
   2. Doing and experiencing
      a. Observing workers and work setting
         (63) The learner reports the extent to which he or she has engaged in career planning activities that involve observing workers and work settings (Unit 4—Items 12, 13)
      b. Engaging in self/career exploratory activities
         (64) The learner reports the extent to which he or she has engaged in exploratory career planning activities that involve taking courses that provide information about jobs (Unit 4—Items 17, 18)

TABLE 5-2 (continued)

---

        (65) The learner reports the extent to which he or she has engaged in exploratory career planning activities that involve summer or part-time work experience in a job related to an occupation under consideration (Unit 4—Item 19)

        (66) The learner reports the extent to which he or she has engaged in exploratory career planning activities of an informal nature such as hobbies and clubs (Unit 4—Items 14–16)

  c. Practicing employment-seeking skills

        (67) The learner reports the extent to which he or she has engaged in activities that might increase his or her employment-seeking skills (Unit 4—Items 20–22)

3. Focusing on information and experience resources

        (68) The learner reports the extent to which he or she has engaged in activities that might be of help in determining whether or not his or her preferred occupations are suitable ones (Unit 4—Items 26–32)

4. Making career plans

  a. Planning activities

        (69) The learner reports whether or not he or she has made certain plans that will facilitate the implementation of his or her own career goals (Unit 4—Items 23–25)

  b. Self-evaluation of career planning

        (70) The learner is asked to give his or her own opinion of the suitability of the job choice named (Unit 4—Items 33—38)

IV. REACTIONS TO CAREER GUIDANCE EXPERIENCES

        (71) The learner is asked to give his or her opinion of how much school has helped in career planning (Unit 4—Items 39–45)

The Coverage of Instructional Objectives

Some instructional objectives in the cognitive domain are assessed by nearly all career development tests.

An analysis of six career development tests, using criteria suggested by Baker and Schutz (1972), revealed that a total of fifty-four instructional objectives can be assessed by existing tests. Table 5-3 presents the list of the fifty-four instructional objectives, the test names, and the number of each test item that can be used to assess a specific instructional objective. The six career development tests were analyzed to determine which test items could be used to assess specific instructional objectives in the cognitive domain only. Each item on each test was assigned to a specific instructional objective. This analysis allows us to look more precisely at the kinds of behaviors assessed by career development tests.

Table 5-4 shows the five instructional objectives that are assessed by at least four career development tests. The five objectives can be described as follows: the ability to make appropriate vocational choices, the ability to identify valid sources of occupational information, knowledge of educational requirements of jobs, knowledge of job duties, and the ability to identify the most

TABLE 5-3
ITEM NUMBERS OF TEST ITEMS ON CAREER DEVELOPMENT TESTS THAT CAN BE USED TO
ASSESS SPECIFIC INSTRUCTIONAL OBJECTIVES IN THE COGNITIVE DOMAIN

INSTRUCTIONAL OBJECTIVES	CAREER DEVELOPMENT TESTS					
	Career Develop- ment Inventory	Career Maturity Inven- tory	Assessment of Career Develop- ment	New Mexico Career Education Test Series	Cognitive Vocational Maturity Test	ETS Guid- ance Inquiry
INDIVIDUAL ATTRIBUTE APPRAISAL						
1. Given a list of statements describing abilities and interests, the learner will be able to identify any statement that describes an individual's abilities.			Unit 5, Items 25, 27			Items 27, 31, 32
2. Given a list of statements describing abilities, interests, and values, the learner will be able to identify any statement that describes an individual's interests.			Unit 5, Item 23			Item 33
3. Given a list of statements describing abilities, interests, and values, the learner will be able to identify any statement that describes an individual's values.			Unit 5, Item 24			Items 5, 28, 30, 34
4. Given a description of the characteristics of an individual and a list of conclusions, the learner will be able to identify the conclusion that represents the most accurate appraisal of the individual.	Item 86	Competence Test Items 1–20				Items 4, 7, 25

(continued)

TABLE 5-3 (continued)

INSTRUCTIONAL OBJECTIVES

	Career Development Inventory	Career Maturity Inventory	Assessment of Career Development	New Mexico Career Education Test Series	Cognitive Vocational Maturity Test	ETS Guidance Inquiry
GENERAL OCCUPATIONAL INFORMATION						
5. The learner will be able to distinguish between accurate and inaccurate statements describing job-market characteristics.	Items 65, 66		Unit 5, Items 6, 10, 14, 15, 17, 18, 22, 34, 35			Item 18
6. Given a description of a type of information needed about an occupation, the learner will be able to identify valid sources from which the information can be obtained.	Items 34–47, 62, 63		Unit 5, Items 29, 31, 8	Career Planning Test, Items 1, 3, 5, 7, 9, 11, 13, 15, 17, 19		Item 17
ATTRIBUTE REQUIREMENTS						
7. Given a description of a special ability and a list of jobs, the learner will be able to identify occupations that require given types of abilities.			Unit 1, Items 8, 14		Items 78, 79, 80, 83, 84, 86, 89, 90, 91, 44, 45	
8. Given the name of a specific type of interest, the learner will be able to identify, from a list of occupational titles, the name of the occupation that would enable an individual to satisfy the given interest.			Unit 1, Item 17		Items 77, 81, 82, 94	

CAREER DEVELOPMENT TESTS

9. Given a list of occupational titles, the learner will be able to identify the occupational titles of workers having similar interests			Item 16
10. Given the name of a specific occupation, the learner will be able to identify, from a list of names of different types of values, the value that is likely to be important for the given occupation.	Item 83	Unit 1, Item 18	
11. Given a description of a value that is important to an individual, the learner will be able to identify an occupation that would provide the individual with an opportunity to satisfy the given value.		Unit 1, Items 20–24	
12. Given a description of a type of work experience that an individual has had and a list of occupational titles, the learner will be able to identify and name the occupation for which the experience would be most helpful.		Unit 1, Item 28	Items 76, 87, 88, 92, 95
13. Given a description of a type of personality and a list of occupations, the learner will be able to identify the occupation that would be most suitable for an individual with the given personality.		Unit 1, Items 11, 26	

EDUCATION AND TRAINING REQUIREMENTS

14. Given a list of occupational titles, the learner will be able to identify the title of the occupation requiring the *least* amount of education.		Unit 1, Item 12	Items 56, 57, 63, 65, 68, 70, 74, 75

(continued)

TABLE 5-3 (continued)

INSTRUCTIONAL OBJECTIVES

CAREER DEVELOPMENT TESTS

	Career Development Inventory	Career Maturity Inventory	Assessment of Career Development	New Mexico Career Education Test Series	Cognitive Vocational Maturity Test	ETS Guidance Inquiry
15. Given a list of occupational titles, the learner will be able to identify the title of the occupation requiring the most education.			Unit 1, Item 19		Items 58, 64, 66, 69	
16. The learner will be able to identify the educational level required for entry into a specific occupation, given the name of a specific occupation and a list of different levels of education.	Items 67–74		Unit 1, Items 38, 59–63		Item 67	Items 9–15
17. Given a description of a particular level of education and a list of occupational titles, the learner will be able to identify the name of the occupation that matches the educational-level description.			Unit 1, Items 29, 31, 35, 42		Items 72, 71, 62, 61, 60, 59	
18. The learner will be able to identify any occupation requiring an apprenticeship, given a list of occupations.			Unit 1, Items 15, 41		Item 73	
19. The learner will be able to arrange occupations from highest to lowest in amount of education and training required, given a list of occupations.				Knowledge of Occupations Test, Items 16, 17		
20. The learner will be able to classify occupations into different fields of work, given the name of the field of work and a list of occupations.					Items 1–20	

JOB DUTIES

		Competence Test Items 21–40	Unit 1, Items	Knowledge Test	Items
21.	Given an occupational title and a list of job descriptions, the learner will be able to identify the correct job description for the given title.	Competence Test Items 21–40	Unit 1, Items 44–49		Items 96, 97, 103, 104, 108–110, 112–117, 120
22.	Given a brief description of a job performed by an individual and a list of occupational titles, the learner will be able to identify the correct occupational title for the given job description with 80 percent accuracy.		Unit 1, Items 1–4, 25, 32–34, 37, 39–40	Knowledge of Occupations Test Items 1, 3, 5, 7, 9, 11, 13	Items 98–102, 105–107, 111, 118–119

WORK CONDITIONS

			Unit 1, Items		Items
23.	The learner will be able to identify occupations that require working irregular hours, given a list of occupations, some of which require working regular hours and some of which require working irregular hours.		Unit 1, Items 6, 10, 16		Items 52, 93
24.	The learner will be able to identify jobs that involve physical danger, given a list of jobs, some of which involve physical danger, and some of which do not involve physical danger.		Unit 1, Item 7		Items 41, 85
25.	The learner will be able to distinguish between those jobs which involve a great deal of standing and those jobs which involve a great deal of sitting, given a list of standing and sitting jobs.		Unit 1, Item 9		Item 37

(continued)

TABLE 5-3 (continued)

INSTRUCTIONAL OBJECTIVES			CAREER DEVELOPMENT TESTS			
	Career Development Inventory	Career Maturity Inventory	Assessment of Career Development	New Mexico Career Education Test Series	Cognitive Vocational Maturity Test	ETS Guidance Inquiry
26. The learner will be able to distinguish between the occupational titles of persons who spend most of their time outdoors and the occupational titles of persons who spend most of their time indoors, given a list of outdoor and indoor jobs.			Unit 1, Item 27		Items 38, 40	
27. Given the name of an occupation, the learner will be able to classify the occupation into one of the following categories: (1) an occupation involving work mainly with things or machines. (2) an occupation involving work mainly with people, (3) an occupation involving work mainly with data.			Unit 1, Items 50–58		Item 39	
28. Given a list of occupational titles, the learner will be able to identify occupations that involve mental and emotional stress.			Unit 1, Item 13			
29. Given a list of occupational titles, the learner will be able to identify occupations that allow the worker to perform his or her job at home.					Item 42	

30. Given a list of occupational titles, the learner will be able to identify the occupational titles of workers who have the highest income.		Knowledge of Occupations Test, Items 14, 15	Items 43, 47, 49, 50, 51, 53, 54, 55
31. Given a list of occupational titles, the learner will be able to identify the occupation that requires the greatest amount of walking.			Item 46
32. Given a list of occupational titles, the learner will be able to identify any job that requires the worker to be away from home for extended periods of time.			Item 48
33. The learner will be able to rank occupations in order from highest to lowest in terms of the amount of supervision received.		Knowledge of Occupations Test, Items 18, 19	
34. The learner will be able to identify the type of organization in which an occupation would most likely be found, given the name of an occupation and a list of names of types of organizations.	Unit 1, Item 65		
35. Given a list of occupational titles, the learner will be able to identify any occupation that requires the use of tools.			Item 36
36. Given the name of an occupation and a list of names of tools (or equipment) employed in different occupations, the learner will be able to identify the name of the tool or equipment used in the given occupation.	Items 75–79		

(continued)

TABLE 5-3 (continued)

INSTRUCTIONAL OBJECTIVES

	CAREER DEVELOPMENT TESTS					
	Career Development Inventory	Career Maturity Inventory	Assessment of Career Development	New Mexico Career Education Test Series	Cognitive Vocational Maturity Test	ETS Guidance Inquiry
JOB SELECTION						
37. Given a list of statements, the learner will be able to identify any statement that is an accurate description of a job-selection principle.	Items 80, 81, 82, 84, 91	Attitude Scale, Items 1, 2, 5, 7, 8, 11, 12, 17, 20, 21, 22, 24, 25, 26, 30, 31, 32, 36, 37, 39, 42, 44, 45, 46	Unit 5, Items 1, 2, 3, 4, 5, 7, 20, 21, 16, 28, 32, 33			
38. Given a description of the characteristics and background of an individual, the learner will be able to identify, from a list of jobs, the job that would be most appropriate for the individual.	Items 85, 87	Competence Test Items 41–60	Unit 1, Items 66–72	Knowledge of Occupations Test Items 2, 4, 6, 8, 10, 12	Items 21–35	
SCHOOL COURSES						
39. The learner will be able to identify statements describing rules to follow in selecting school courses, given a list of statements.						Items 6, 20

40. Given a description of the abilities of an individual, the learner will be able to identify the most appropriate school course for the individual to enroll in.		Item 3
41. Given the name of a school course and a list of occupations, the learner will be able to identify the name of the occupation for which the given school course would be most helpful.	Unit 1, Items 5, 30, 36, 43	Item 22
42. Given the name of an occupation and a list of school courses, the learner will be able to identify the name of the school course that would provide the best preparation for the given occupations.	Unit 1, Item 64	
SCHOOL CURRICULA		
43. The learner will be able to identify the characteristics of different curricula, given a list of characteristics and the names of different curricula.		Items 1, 19, 21, 23, 24
44. Given a brief description of the characteristics of an individual and a list of types of curricula, the learner will be able to identify the most appropriate curriculum for the individual.		Item 8
CAREER PLANNING		
45. Given an occupational title and a list of steps that a person could complete to prepare for and enter the given occupation, the learner will be able to identify the correct sequence of steps required to enter the given occupation.	Competence Test, Items 61–80	Knowledge of Occupations Test, Items 20, 21, 22, 23, 24, 25

(continued)

TABLE 5-3 (continued)

INSTRUCTIONAL OBJECTIVES

	Career Development Inventory	Career Maturity Inventory	CAREER DEVELOPMENT TESTS Assessment of Career Development	New Mexico Career Education Test Series	Cognitive Vocational Maturity Test	ETS Guidance Inquiry
SCHOOL AND CAREER PROBLEM SOLVING						
46. Given a description of a problem that a person is having in school or in choosing an occupation, the learner will be able to identify, from a list of solutions, the best solution to the given problem.	Items 88, 89, 90	Competence Test, Items 81–100	Unit 5, Items 36–40	Career Planning Test, Items 2, 4, 6, 8, 10, 12, 14, 16, 18, 20		
EMPLOYMENT-SEEKING SKILLS						
47. The learner will be able to identify statements describing desirable practices to follow in making arrangements for, preparing for, and participating in a job interview.				Job Application Procedures Test, Items 2, 3, 6, 7, 14, 16, 18, 19		
48. Given a description of an individual's qualifications, the learner will be able to identify the most appropriate career decision for the individual.				Job Application Procedures Test, Items 8, 10, 11, 15, 20		
49. The learner will be able to identify statements describing desirable practices to follow in filling out job-application forms and resumés.				Job Application Procedures Test, Items 1, 5, 13, 17		

85

50. The learner will be able to identify appropriate sources for locating jobs, given a list of appropriate and inappropriate sources.

Job Application Procedures Test, Items 4, 9, 12

GENERALLY USEFUL ON-THE-JOB SKILLS

51. Given a description of a problem that an individual is having in carrying out a job, the learner will be able to identify the factor that accounts for the existence of the problem or the learner will be able to identify the most appropriate action to take in order to solve the problem.

Career Development Test, Items 2, 4, 5, 7, 8, 11, 13, 14, 17, 20, 22, 23, 25

52. The learner will be able to identify the most appropriate action an individual should take in order to become advanced in an occupation, given a list of alternative actions that a person should take.

Career Development Test, Items 6, 9

53. The learner will be able to identify factors that may result in inefficiency, demotion, or loss of jobs.

Career Development Test, Items 1, 3, 15, 16, 19, 21

54. The learner will be able to identify factors that contribute to job success and advancement on the job.

Career Development Test, Items 10, 12, 18, 24

TABLE 5-4
FIVE INSTRUCTIONAL OBJECTIVES ASSESSED BY AT LEAST FOUR CAREER DEVELOPMENT MEASURES

INSTRUCTIONAL OBJECTIVES	CAREER DEVELOPMENT TESTS					
	Career Development Inventory	Career Maturity Inventory	Assessment of Career Development	New Mexico Career Education Test Series	Cognitive Vocational Maturity Test	ETS Guidance Inquiry
38. Given a description of the characteristics and background of an individual, the learner will be able to identify, from a list of jobs, the job that would be most appropriate for the individual.	Items 85, 87	Competence Test, Items 41–60	Unit 1, Items 66–72	Knowledge of Occupations Test, Items 2, 4, 6, 8, 10, 12	Items 21–35	
6. Given a description of a type of information needed about an occupation, the learner will be able to identify valid sources from which the information can be obtained.	Items 34–47, 62, 63		Unit 5, Items 29, 31, 8	Career Planning Test, Items 1, 3, 5, 7, 9, 11, 13, 15, 17, 19		Item 17
16. The learner will be able to identify the educational level required for entry into a specific occupation, given the name of a specific occupation and a list of different levels of education.	Items 67–74		Unit 1, Items 38, 59–63		Item 67	Items 9–15
22. Given a brief description of a job performed by an individual and a list of occupational titles, the learner will be able to identify the correct occupational title for the given job description with 80 percent accuracy.		Competence Test, Items 21–40	Unit 1, Items 1–4, 25, 32–34, 37, 39–40	Knowledge of Occupations Test, Items 1, 3, 5, 7, 9, 11, 13	Items 98–102, 105–107, 111, 118–119	

	Items 88, 89, 90	Competence Test, Items 81–100	Unit 5, Items 36–40	Career Planning Test, Items 2, 4, 6, 8, 10, 12, 14, 16, 18, 20
46. Given a description of a problem that a person is having in school or in choosing an occupation, the learner will be able to identify, from a list of solutions, the best solution to the given problem.				

appropriate solution to a problem that a student is having in school or in choosing a career.

The Coverage of
Particular Objectives

Career development tests vary enormously in their coverage of a particular objective.

Some tests include only one item to measure a particular objective, while other tests provide separate subtests of twenty or more items to assess the same objective.

Table 5-5 shows, for example, that the Career Development Inventory includes only two items to measure objective 38, the ability to make an appropriate job choice, while the Career Maturity Inventory provides a separate subtest of twenty items to assess the same objective.

The Emphasis on
Occupational Information

Career development tests vary in their emphasis on occupational information.

Some tests appear to be overloaded with occupational-information items, while other tests are composed of items in a variety of areas. Apparently, some test authors believe that career development involves having a great deal of knowledge about the characteristics and requirements of occupations. Table 5-6 shows the results of an earlier analysis (Westbrook, 1974) revealing that the Cognitive Vocational Maturity Test is more heavily loaded with occupational-information items (87 percent) than the Assessment of Career Development (23 percent).

Do the authors of tests that stress occupational information really believe that it is critical to occupational adjustment, or is occupational information merely an area that lends itself more readily to the preparation of objective items?

The Behavior Measured

Although several scales from different tests have similar names, the items do not look as if they are measuring the same behavior.

Crites' "Planning" items require the learner to identify the correct sequence of steps needed to enter a given occupation. Super's "Planning Orientation" items require the respondent to report how much thinking, planning and/or talking he or she has done about career decisions with an adult who knows something about the respondent. One of the ACT's "Career Planning Knowledge" items requires the learner to identify the statement that most accurately identifies what the labor force will be like ten years from now. And one of Healy and Klein's "Career Planning" items requires the learner to select the

TABLE 5-5
THE NUMBER OF TEST ITEMS ON CAREER DEVELOPMENT MEASURES THAT CAN BE USED TO ASSESS SPECIFIC INSTRUCTIONAL OBJECTIVES IN THE COGNITIVE DOMAIN

INSTRUCTIONAL OBJECTIVES	CAREER DEVELOPMENT TESTS					
	Career Development Inventory	Career Maturity Inventory	Assessment of Career Development	New Mexico Career Education Test Series	Cognitive Vocational Maturity Test	ETS Guidance Inquiry
38. Given a description of the characteristics and background of an individual, the learner will be able to identify, from a list of jobs, the job that would be most appropriate for the individual.	2	20	7	6	15	0
6. Given a description of a type of information needed about an occupation, the learner will be able to identify valid sources from which the information can be obtained.	14	0	3	10	0	1
16. The learner will be able to identify the educational level required for entry into a specific occupation, given the name of a specific occupation and a list of different levels of education.	8	0	6	0	1	7
22. Given a brief description of a job performed by an individual and a list of occupational titles, the learner will be able to identify the correct occupational title for the given job description with 80 percent accuracy.	0	20	11	7	11	0

(continued)

TABLE 5-5 (continued)

INSTRUCTIONAL OBJECTIVES

CAREER DEVELOPMENT TESTS

INSTRUCTIONAL OBJECTIVES	Career Development Inventory	Career Maturity Inventory	Assessment of Career Development	New Mexico Career Education Test Series	Cognitive Vocational Maturity Test	ETS Guidance Inquiry
46. Given a description of a problem that a person is having in school or in choosing an occupation, the learner will be able to identify, from a list of solutions, the best solution to the given problem.	3	20	5	10	0	0

TABLE 5-6
**PERCENT OF ITEMS MEASURING OCCUPATIONAL
INFORMATION ON TWO CAREER DEVELOPMENT TESTS**

NAME OF TEST	PERCENT OF ITEMS MEASURING OCCUPATIONAL INFORMATION
Cognitive Vocational Maturity Test	87
Assessment of Career Development	23

Note: An occupational-information item is defined as an item that includes an occupational title in its item content.

statement that best describes what a person should do in order to make up his or her mind about becoming a librarian.

Whether these four items are measuring the same or different behaviors is certainly a debatable question. However, they appear to assess different instructional objectives. We might ask ourselves whether these items represent the most appropriate concept of planning and, if not, what an acceptable substitute would be.

Overgeneralization

We have a tendency to overgeneralize regarding the domain sampled by career development tests.

A multiple-choice question may measure the ability to recognize accurate conclusions about hypothetical people whose characteristics have been described, as illustrated by the two items in Table 5-7. But can it be assumed that such a test also measures the ability to appraise accurately one's own career-relevant capabilities? According to Martin Katz (1978), we cannot make such an assumption. The items "cannot serve as work samples of CDM [career decision making] because they do not engage each person in CDM in his or her own identity" (Katz, 1978, p. 223). Katz recommends that we measure career decision making by assessing whether students know what information they need, whether they can get the information they want, and whether they can use the information.

Correlation between Variables

There is no evidence that variables called career maturity have more in common with each other than they have in common with noncareer-maturity variables.

The Crites model (1965, 1973a, 1978a) of career maturity provides a useful conceptual framework for testing substantive hypotheses regarding the

TABLE 5-7
**SELF-APPRAISAL ITEMS FROM THE COMPETENCE
TEST OF THE CAREER MATURITY INVENTORY**

19. Wayne likes to do things rather than study about them. His interest in school is not very strong, but he spends a great deal of time on his hobby – photography. He has developed into a good photographer over the years and has just sold some of his pictures. He realizes the competition in photography as a field is tough, but he thinks he has the talent.
    What do you think?
    A. Before he decides anything, he should ask his friends what they think.
    B. With the start he has, there's no doubt that he has the talent in photography to be outstanding.
    C. It is unlikely that he has enough talent in photography to be successful in such a highly competitive field.
    D. He has enough developed talent to continue in photography until he can decide if he should stay in the field.
    E. Don't know.
20. Cynthia has tried to become interested in several different things, but she has not stayed with any of them for very long. She will start an activity, such as flower arranging or dancing, but then quit in a short time. It is hard for her to figure out what she likes to do.
    What do you think?
    F. She may just be going through a time of trying different things; an interest will develop in one of them later on.
    G. It's almost impossible for her to know for sure what her interests are.
    H. She could be interested in anything she wants; she should go ahead and get into something.
    I. Her parents know her best; she should ask them what her interests are.
    J. Don't know.

Source: *Career Maturity Inventory* devised by John O. Crites. Reprinted by permission of the publisher, CTB/McGraw-Hill, Del Monte Research Park, Monterey, Calif. 93940. Copyright © 1973, 1978 by McGraw-Hill, Inc. All rights reserved. Printed in the United States of America.

construct of career maturity. Crites (1965, 1973a, 1978b) has proposed the hierarchical model, shown in Figure 5-1, that is organized according to four dimensions: Consistency of Career Choices, Realism of Career Choices, Career Choice Competencies, and Career Choice Attitudes. Each dimension is composed of various specific variables which are fairly highly correlated with each other. Consistency of Career Choices is subdivided into Time, Field, and Level. Realism of Career Choice is subdivided into Abilities, Interests, and Personality. The dimension of Career Choice Competencies consists of Problem Solving, Planning, Occupational Information, Self-Appraisal, and Goal Selection. The dimension of Career Choice Attitudes includes Involvement, Orientation, Independence, Preference, and Conception (Crites, 1973a).

Career maturity variables in the Crites model should have more in common with each other than they have with variables that are not included in the model. Therefore, scores on measures of variables in the model should

FIGURE 5-1
A MODEL OF CAREER MATURITY IN ADOLESCENCE

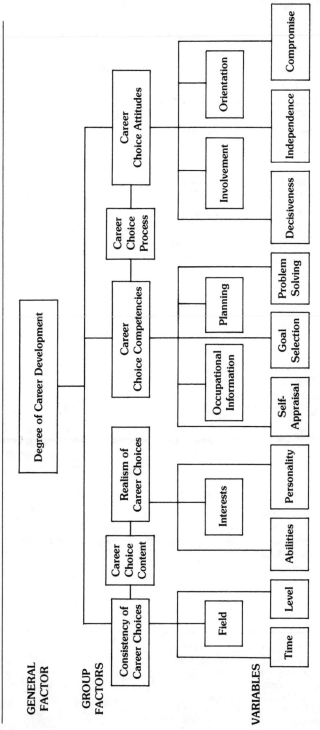

Source: *Career Maturity Inventory* devised by John O. Crites. Reprinted by permission of the publisher, CTB/McGraw-Hill, Del Monte Research Park, Monterey, Calif. 93940. Copyright © 1973, 1978 by McGraw-Hill, Inc. All rights reserved. Printed in the United States of America.

correlate more highly with each other than they correlate with scores on measures of noncareer-maturity variables such as intelligence and school achievement. In previous investigations of the relationship among career maturity
measures, a total of thirty reported correlations ranged from .41 to .67, with a
median of .57 (American College Testing Program, 1974; Crites, 1973a; Forrest
and Thompson, 1974; Gasper and Omvig, 1976; Hansen and Ansell, 1973;
Westbrook and Parry-Hill, 1973; Westbrook, 1976a, 1976c, 1976d). However,
contrary to theoretical expectation, previous studies have reported higher correlations, on the average (mdn. $r = .67$), between career maturity measures and
measures of intelligence and school achievement (Clemmons, 1973; Crosby,
1975; Dillard, 1976; Lawrence and Brown, 1976; LoCascio et al., 1976;
Maynard and Hansen, 1970; Mowsesian and Holley, 1977; Westbrook and
Parry-Hill, 1973). Generalizations should not be drawn from these studies, however, because none of the investigators followed the Campbell-Fiske procedure
of administering two career maturity measures and a measure of intelligence or
achievement to a common sample of students (Campbell and Fiske, 1959;
Campbell, 1960; Thorndike and Hagen, 1977).

    Table 5-8 shows the results of some research we did at North Carolina
State University. The table shows that the Attitude Scale of the Career Maturity

TABLE 5-8
**CORRELATIONS OF CAREER MATURITY MEASURES
WITH OTHER CAREER MATURITY MEASURES AND
WITH MENTAL ABILITY MEASURES**

INVESTIGATORS	CAREER MATURITY MEASURES VERSUS OTHER CAREER MATURITY MEASURES		CAREER MATURITY MEASURES VERSUS MENTAL ABILITY MEASURES	
	Measures[a]	r	Measures[a]	r
Westbrook, Cutts, Madison, Arcia (1980)	AS-CT Subtests	.48[b]	AS-OLMAT	.56
Westbrook, Cutts, Madison, Arcia (1980)	CT Total—AS	.59	CT Total—OLMAT	.73
Westbrook, Cutts, Madison, Arcia (1980)	AS-CT Subtests	.34[b]	AS-SAT Math	.46
Westbrook, Cutts, Madison, Arcia (1980)	AS-CT Total	.47	AS-SAT Verbal	.49
Westbrook, Cutts, Madison, Arcia (1980)			CT Total—SAT V	.54
Westbrook, Cutts, Madison, Arcia (1980)			CT Total—SATM	.50
Westbrook (1976a)	CVMT-AS	.57		
Westbrook (1973)			CVMT-CTMM	.70
Median		.47		.54

[a]AS = Attitude Scale of the Career Maturity Inventory
CT = Competence Test of the Career Maturity Inventory
OLMAT = Otis-Lennon Mental Ability Test
SAT = Scholastic Aptitude Test
CVMT = Cognitive Vocational Maturity Test
CTMM = California Test of Mental Maturity
[b]Median of five correlations

Inventory correlates more highly with the Otis-Lennon Mental Ability Test than it does with the part scores of the CMI Competence Test. The Competence Test correlates more highly with the Otis-Lennon Mental Ability Test than with the Attitude Scale. The Attitude Scale correlates more highly with the math portion of the Scholastic Aptitude Test than with the part scores of the Competence Test. The Attitude Scale correlates more highly with the verbal test of the Scholastic Aptitude Test than with the total score on the Competence Test. The total score on the Competence Test correlates more highly with the SAT verbal than it does with the Attitude Scale. Finally, the Cognitive Vocational Maturity Test correlates more highly with the California Test of Mental Maturity than it does with the Attitude Scale of the Career Maturity Inventory. This research indicates that career maturity variables do not have more in common with each other than they have in common with mental ability and mental maturity.

Similar Test Scores
Many career development tests yield several scores that are not distinguishable from each other statistically.

What is the rationale and the justification for dividing career development knowledge into so many differently named parts? Our research results indicate that the part scores are so highly intercorrelated that, for the most part, they are probably measuring the same thing. For example the Cognitive Vocational Maturity Test provides separate scores for six cognitive areas of career maturity, but the intercorrelation of the part scores range from the .60s to the .80s (Westbrook and Parry-Hill, 1973a, 1973b, 1975). As Table 5-9 shows, the Career Maturity Inventory provides six scores that are intercorrelated from the .50s to the .70s among ninth graders (Westbrook and Cutts, 1978). Taking account of the unreliability, are they really measuring anything different? For example, Table 5-9 shows that, on the Career Maturity Inventory, a test entitled Occupational Information shows a correlation of .72 with a test named Goal Selection (Westbrook, Cutts, Madison, and Arcia, 1980). When the correlation is corrected for attenuation, the correlation of .97 suggests that both appear to measure so nearly the same behavior that there would be few cases indeed in which we could feel with confidence that a person has done better on one of these tests than on the other.

Career Maturity as a
Multidimensional Construct
There is no evidence that career maturity is a multidimensional construct.

The Crites model of career maturity is hypothesized to be multidimensional. According to Crites (1965, 1973a, 1974a, 1974b, 1978a), the model is hierarchical and consists of sixteen variables organized under four dimensions. If measures were available for each of the variables in the model, a factor pattern derived from the matrix of intercorrelations should consist of a general factor and

TABLE 5-9
MEANS, STANDARD DEVIATIONS, AND
INTERCORRELATIONS[a, b] OF THE CAREER MATURITY
INVENTORY ($N = 193$)

MEASURES	M	SD	SA	OI	GS	PL	PS	CTT	AS
Self-Appraisal	9.25	4.03	(.76)[c]	.63	.62	.62	.53		.55
Occupational Information	10.44	4.25	.83	(.76)	.72	.58	.56		.59
Goal Selection	10.25	4.41	.83	.97	(.73)	.58	.51		.53
Planning	9.96	3.65	.80	.74	.76	(.80)	.55		.54
Problem Solving	7.67	3.30	.76	.80	.75	.77	(.64)		.56
Competence Test Total	47.57	16.16						(.90)[c]	.67
Attitude Scale	30.20	6.20	.71	.77	.70	.68	.79	.80	(.78)

Source: From B.W. Westbrook and C.C. Cutts, "Career Maturity of Ninth Grade Pupils: Real or Imaginary?" (Unpublished manuscript, 1978).

Note: Career Maturity Inventory administered May, 1976.
[a]Values below the diagonal are corrected for attenuation.
[b]Values in parentheses are KR 20's.
[c]Estimated

four group factors (Westbrook, 1971). A review of the literature revealed only two factorial investigations (Prediger, 1979; Wilton, 1979) of variables in the Crites model, and neither of these studies demonstrates the multidimensionality of the Crites model.

Table 5-10 shows that a factor analysis of career maturity measures and noncareer-maturity measures yields only one factor. The results of the factor analysis suggest that only one factor can be considered meaningful in terms of the patterns of loadings and according to Kaiser's (1960) "eigenvalue-one" criterion (Westbrook, Cutts, Madison, and Arcia; 1980). All the tests have high loadings on the one factor. We can find no support for more than one major dimension running through career maturity measures, and therefore no evidence that any career maturity measure is providing more than one piece of information. The results cast doubt on the use of test patterns on career maturity measures for diagnosis.

The results of our factor analytic studies (Westbrook, Cutts, Madison, and Arcia, 1980) indicate that career maturity measures, mental ability measures, and school achievement measures have high loadings on the one factor that has been identified. All these measures seem to require the ability to understand written language and may be described as a verbal comprehension factor. I have not been able to discover any evidence that any career maturity instrument provides measures of more than one major dimension. Nor have I been able to uncover any evidence that career maturity measures can be differentiated from measures of intelligence, scholastic aptitude, reading, and language.

TABLE 5-10
FACTOR LOADINGS AND PROPORTIONS OF
COMMON-FACTOR, SPECIFIC, AND ERROR VARIANCE
IN THE CAREER MATURITY AND NONCAREER
MATURITY MEASURES FOR NINTH GRADERS (*N* = 312)

				PROPORTIONS	
MEASURES[a]	Factor I	Specific S	Error E	Communality h^2	Reliability KR-20
Career maturity measures					
CMICT Self-appraisal	.79	.13	.24	.63	.76
CMICT Occupational Information	.82	.08	.24	.68	.76
CMICT Goal Selection	.78	.11	.27	.62	.73
CMICT Planning	.80	.16	.20	.64	.80
CMICT Problem Solving	.77	.05	.36	.59	.64
CMI Attitude Scale	.68	.32	.22	.46	.78
Noncareer maturity measures					
OLMAT Deviation IQ	.85	.22	.05	.73	.95
MAT Reading grade equivalent	.89	.18	.04	.78	.96
MAT Language grade equivalent	.85	.23	.04	.73	.96
Eigenvalue	5.84				

Source: B. W. Westbrook, C. C. Cutts, S. S. Madison, and M. A. Arcia, "The Validity of the Crites Model of Career Maturity," *Journal of Vocational Behavior*, 1980, *16*, 249–281. Copyright © 1980 by Academic Press, Inc. Reprinted by permission.

[a]Abbreviations: CMICT, Career Maturity Inventory Competence Test; CMI, Career Maturity Inventory; OLMAT, Otis-Lennon Mental Ability Test; MAT, Metropolitan Achievement Test.

Strengthening the Research Base

We need a stronger research base before we use these instruments for differential diagnosis in career counseling.

To illustrate this point, the Career Maturity Inventory is recommended as "an assessment device which might be useful to the practicing counselor" (Crites, 1973b, p. 34). The instrument could be used for differential diagnosis if evidence could be marshalled to support the contention that it "yields scores for six major aspects of vocational maturity" (Super, 1974, p. 164). According to the author, an individual could have "relatively high scores on the Self-Appraisal and Occupational Information subtests but a low score on Goal Selection" (Crites, 1973b, p. 37). The author suggests that these results, plotted on a profile, might mean that "an individual (or group) has sufficient information about himself (or itself) and the world of work but cannot synthesize [Super, 1957] it into a realistic career choice" (Crites, 1973b, p. 37).

To investigate this question, we administered the instrument in question to samples of ninth graders and adults (Westbrook, Cutts, Madison, and Arcia, 1980). The results indicate that the reliability of the difference scores ($r = .29$) is much lower than the reliability of the two tests taken separately ($r = .73, .73$) because the two tests are fairly highly correlated with each other ($r = .65$). It becomes a problem when the counselor wishes to use test patterns on the profile for diagnosis. The judgment that the client's self-appraisal ability lags behind his or her occupational information is a judgment that must be made a good deal more tentatively than a judgment about the client's self-appraisal score or occupational-information score taken separately. Many differences will be found to be quite small relative to their standard deviation, and consequently quite undependable.

Age Differentiation
Age differentiation may be a necessary condition for establishing construct validity but it should not be considered a sufficient condition.

One criterion that has been used in the validation of some career maturity and career development tests is age differentiation. Such tests as the Career Maturity Inventory, the Assessment of Career Development, and the Cognitive Vocational Maturity Tests have been checked against chronological age or grade to determine whether the scores show a progressive increase with advancing age or grade. Since career development skills are expected to increase with age and grade, it is argued that test scores should likewise show such an increase, if the test is valid. Table 5-11 shows the evidence presented by Crites (1973b) to support his contention that the Attitude Scale is measuring a developmental variable. It should be noted, however, that age and/or grade differentiation may be a necessary but not a sufficient condition for validity. Thus, if the test scores fail to improve with age, such a finding might indicate that the test is not a valid measure of the behaviors it was designed to sample. On the other hand, to prove

TABLE 5-11
MEAN SCORES ON THE ATTITUDE SCALE ($N = 50$)

Grade	N	Mean	SD
6	116	28.12	5.51
7	2077	29.21	5.55
8	3747	32.84	5.49
9	3770	34.29	5.09
10	1690	35.31	5.28
11	2203	36.02	5.24
12	2258	37.23	5.19
13	533	38.97	4.52

Source: The data in this table are from J. O. Crites, *Administration and Use Manual of the Career Maturity Inventory* (Monterey, Calif.: CTB/McGraw-Hill, 1979), p. 39.

that a test measures something that increases with age or grade does not define the area covered by the test very precisely. A measure of height or weight would also show regular age and grade increments, although it could hardly be designated as a career development test.

Career Maturity and Sex

There is some evidence that there is a relationship between career maturity and sex.

Tables 5-12 and 5-13 show that females score higher than males and that, for the most part, the differences are statistically significant. Although the scores are significantly different, it is yet to be determined whether these results should be attributed to real differences between males and females or to the test.

Career Maturity and Ethnic Background

There is some evidence that there is a relationship between career maturity and ethnic background.

Tables 5-14 and 5-15 show that whites score significantly higher than blacks on all the measures. Whether these results are due to real differences

TABLE 5-12
MEANS, STANDARD DEVIATIONS, AND t TESTS ON THE CAREER MATURITY INVENTORY, SCHOLASTIC APTITUDE TEST, AND THE CAREER DECISION SCALE FOR MALES AND FEMALES

	MALES[a]		FEMALES[b]		
SCALE	*M*	*SD*	*M*	*SD*	*t*
Career Maturity Inventory					
Competence Test					
Self-appraisal	13.78	3.34	15.66	2.25	3.84**
Occupational Information	17.09	2.53	17.91	2.14	2.30*
Goal Selection	13.76	3.32	14.57	2.75	1.74
Planning	13.27	4.35	15.86	2.44	4.17**
Problem Solving	9.84	3.83	12.53	2.54	4.83**
Total score	67.93	12.70	76.52	8.20	4.66**
Attitude Scale	36.15	5.12	38.74	4.14	3.69**
SAT Verbal	345.82	69.91	378.94	82.95	2.63**
SAT Math	343.64	78.47	372.57	84.91	2.20*
Career Decision Scale	33.53	8.61	30.43	7.11	2.59*

Source: B. W. Westbrook, C. C. Cutts, S. S. Madison, and M. A. Arcia, "The Validity of the Crites Model of Career Maturity," *Journal of Vocational Behavior*, 1980, *16*, 249–281. Copyright ©1980 by Academic Press, Inc. Reprinted by permission.

Note: All students in this sample were enrolled in a technical college in central North Carolina.
[a]*n* = 55.   *p < .05.
[b]*n* = 145.   **p < .01.

TABLE 5-13
MEANS, STANDARD DEVIATIONS, AND t TESTS FOR MALES AND FEMALES ON THE CAREER MATURITY INVENTORY, OTIS-LENNON MENTAL ABILITY TEST, AND METROPOLITAN READING AND LANGUAGE TESTS

TEST		MALES			FEMALES		
	n	M^a	SD	n	M^a	SD	t
Career Maturity Inventory							
Competence Test							
Self-appraisal	177	8.69	3.77	135	10.61	4.12	4.28**
Occupational Information	177	10.24	3.81	135	11.40	3.87	2.65**
Goal Selection	177	8.73	3.71	135	10.01	3.46	3.12**
Planning	177	8.66	4.16	135	10.26	4.07	3.41**
Problem Solving	177	6.68	2.99	135	7.76	3.47	2.95**
Total score	177	42.84	14.49	135	49.94	15.81	4.12**
Attitude Scale	177	28.50	5.57	135	29.57	6.21	1.60
Otis-Lennon Mental Ability Test	155	89.62	12.58	125	89.55	13.57	.04
Metropolitan Reading Test	143	6.47	2.33	110	6.84	2.25	1.28
Metropolitan Language Test	143	6.87	2.33	108	7.61	2.27	2.52*

Source: B. W. Westbrook, C. C. Cutts, S. S. Madison, and M. A. Arcia, "The Validity of the Crites Model of Career Maturity," *Journal of Vocational Behavior*, 1980, 16, 249–281. Copyright © 1980 by Academic Press, Inc. Reprinted by permission.

Note: Students in this sample were enrolled in grade 9.

^{a} Raw scores are reported for the Career Maturity Inventory; grade equivalents are reported for the Reading and Language tests; and Deviation IQs are reported for the Otis-Lennon Mental Ability Test.

*$p < .05$.
**$p < .01$.

TABLE 5-14
**MEANS, STANDARD DEVIATIONS, AND *t* TESTS FOR
BLACKS AND WHITES ON CAREER MATURITY AND
NONCAREER MATURITY TESTS**

SCALE		BLACKS			WHITES		
	n	*M[a]*	*SD*	*n*	*M[a]*	*SD*	*t*
Career Maturity Inventory							
Competence Test							
Self-appraisal	191	8.50	3.53	120	11.13	4.27	5.64*
Occupational Information	191	9.62	3.45	120	12.49	3.86	6.83*
Goal Selection	191	8.29	3.39	120	10.88	3.53	6.45*
Planning	191	8.55	3.87	120	10.61	4.40	4.33*
Problem Solving	191	6.27	2.83	120	8.59	3.34	6.31*
Total score	191	41.15	13.16	120	53.48	15.94	7.09*
Attitude Scale	191	27.51	5.87	120	31.27	5.12	5.76*
Otis-Lennon Mental Ability Test	175	84.96	10.47	104	97.27	13.27	8.08*
Metropolitan Reading Test	158	5.94	2.04	94	7.79	2.27	6.66*
Metropolitan Language Test	156	6.65	2.10	94	8.10	2.43	5.00*

[a] Raw scores are reported for the Career Maturity Inventory; grade equivalents are reported for the Reading and Language Tests; and Deviation IQs are reported for the Otis-Lennon Mental Ability Test.
$+ p < .01$.

TABLE 5-15
**MEANS, STANDARD DEVIATIONS, AND *t* TESTS ON
THE CAREER MATURITY INVENTORY, SCHOLASTIC
APTITUDE TEST, AND CAREER DECISION SCALE FOR
WHITES AND BLACKS**

SCALE	WHITES[a]		BLACKS[b]		
	M	*SD*	*M*	*SD*	*t*
Career Maturity Inventory					
Competence Test					
Self-appraisal	15.50	2.35	13.89	3.47	2.93**
Occupational Information	18.05	1.96	13.89	2.81	3.64**
Goal Selection	14.65	2.74	13.29	3.35	2.79**
Planning	15.59	2.81	13.64	4.25	2.89**
Problem Solving	12.08	2.79	10.78	4.14	1.99*
Total score	75.88	8.56	68.24	13.51	3.59*
Attitude Scale	38.59	4.03	36.09	5.71	2.75**
SAT Verbal	378.36	76.90	340.44	87.59	2.82**
SAT Math	374.03	81.24	332.18	86.14	3.00**
Career Decision Scale	30.28	6.61	34.73	9.82	2.86**

[a]$n = 155$.   *$p < .05$.
[b]$n = 45$.   **$p < .01$.

Source for Tables 5-14 and 5-15: B. W. Westbrook, C. C. Cutts, S. S. Madison, and M. A. Arcia, "The Validity of the Crites Model of Career Maturity," *Journal of Vocational Behavior*, 1980, *16*, 249–281. Copyright ©1980 by Academic Press, Inc. Reprinted by permission.

in the career maturity of blacks and whites or to the tests has not yet been determined.

Reliability

The reliability of some career maturity measures has not been firmly established.

Table 5-16 shows the internal consistency reliability coefficients reported for many career maturity measures. Table 5-17 shows the stability coefficients for several career maturity measures. Many of these coefficients would be considered borderline at best for an instrument that is recommended for individual diagnosis.

Reading Ability

Career maturity attitude variables have less in common with reading ability than do career maturity competency variables.

TABLE 5-16
**INTERNAL CONSISTENCY RELIABILITY COEFFICIENTS
FOR GROUP MEASURES OF CAREER MATURITY**

		r	
Investigator	*Test Title*	*Range*	*Median*
College Board (1978)	Career Skills Assessment Program	.85–.93	.91
Westbrook and Parry-Hill (1973)	Cognitive Vocational Maturity Test	.67–.91	.84
Prediger (1979)	Career Decision Scale		.84
Crites (1973, 1978)	CMI Competence Test, 5 Subtests	.58–.90	.83
American College Testing Program (1974)	Assessment of Career Development	.61–.93	.80
Prediger (1979)	Career Development Inventory	.78–.90	.79
Westbrook, Cutts, Madison, and Arcia (1980)	CMI Attitude Scale, Form A-1		.78
Westbrook, Cutts, Madison, and Arcia (1980)	CMI Competence Test, 5 Subtests	.65–.80	.76
Mowsesian and Holley (1977)	CMI Attitude Scale, Form A-1	.70–.81	.75
Crites (1978a)	CMI Attitude Scale, Form A-2	.73–.75	.74
Crites (1973, 1978)	CMI Attitude Scale, Form A-1	.65–.84	.72
Hanna and Neely (1978a)	CMI Attitude Scale, Form A-1	.70–.71	.71
Neely (1981)	CMI Competence Test, 5 Subtests	.51–.80	.70
Prediger (1979)	Assessment of Career Decision Making	.32–.73	.69
Crites (1978a)	CMI Attitude Scale, Counseling Form	.50–.72	.67
Moore and McLean (1977)	CMI Attitude Scale, Form A-1	.58–.64	.61
Median			.75

TABLE 5-17
**STABILITY COEFFICIENTS OF CAREER
MATURITY MEASURES**

Investigator	Measure	Grade	N	Test-Retest Interval	r Range	Median
Osipow, Carney, and Barak (1976)	Career Decision Scale	13+	56	2 weeks		.90
Osipow, Carney, and Barak (1976)	Career Decision Scale	13+	59	2 weeks		.82
Forrest and Thompson (1974)	Career Development Inventory Scales, Form I	10	82	2–4 weeks	.71–.85	.82
Mowsesian and Holley (1977)	CMI Attitude Scale, Form A-1	8	155	3 months		.78
American College Testing Program (1976)	Assessment of Career Development	11	340	9 weeks	.44–.87	.76
American College Testing Program (1974)	Assessment of Career Development	9	445	9 weeks	.56–.86	.71
Crites (1937a)	CMI Attitude Scale, Form A-1	6–12	1648	12 months		.71
Forrest and Thompson (1974)	Career Development Inventory Scales, Form I	10	1000	6 months	.63–.71	.67
Westbrook, Cutts, Madison, and Arcia (1980)	CMI Attitude Scale, Form A-1	9	193	5 months		.67
Mowsesian and Holley (1977)	CMI Competence Test Subtests	8	155	3 months	.58–.66	.64
Moore and McLean (1977)	CMI Attitude Scale, Form A-1	14–15	202	4 months		.60
Westbrook, Cutts, Madison, and Arcia (1980)	CMI Competence Test Subtests	9	193	5 months	.47–.65	.55
Median						.71

The Metropolitan Reading Test correlates more highly with the CMI Competence Test ($r = .77$) than it does with the CMI Attitude Scale ($r = .54$). We can use such statistics to interpret the criticism that career maturity measures are indistinguishable from achievement or ability tests. For the set of data in the ninth-grade study we get the breakdown in Figure 5-2; other samples give the same general impression (Mowsesian and Holley, 1977; Clemmons, 1973; Westbrook and Parry-Hill, 1973; Lawrence and Brown, 1976; LoCascio, Nesselroth, and Thomas, 1976; Crosby, 1975). For the data collected in the ninth-grade study, we estimate that 59 percent of the CMI Competence Test duplicates information in the reading test, and 19 percent is new information.

The Attitude Scale overlaps much less with reading ($r = .54$), indicating

FIGURE 5-2
OVERLAP OF CAREER MATURITY INVENTORY
SCORES WITH A CONCURRENT MEASURE OF
READING ABILITY

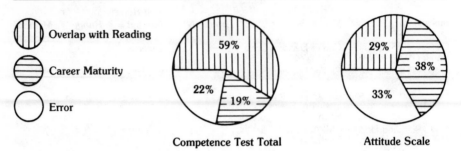

Source: B. W. Westbrook, C. C. Cutts, S. S. Madison, and M. A. Arcia, "The Validity of the Crites Model of Career Maturity," *Journal of Vocational Behavior*, 1980, *16*, 249–281. Copyright © 1980 by Academic Press, Inc. Reprinted by permission.

that 29 percent (.54 squared) of the CMI Attitude Scale duplicates information in the reading test. Since the reliability of the attitude scale is .67, 33 percent would be error and 38 percent is new information. Hence, although the CMI Attitude Scale has a larger error component than the CMI Competence Test, the CMI Attitude Scale provides almost 20 percent more new information, primarily because it demands less in reading ability. Whether or not the additional new information is a significant career maturity factor remains to be determined.

Reading Loads
Career maturity measures can be ranked according to their "reading load."

As Table 5-18 shows, the first five scales correlate most highly with the reading test and can be described as cognitive measures of career maturity. For the most part, these measures assess the learners' knowledge of occupational information and career decision-making skills.

The scales that are least highly correlated with the reading test seem to have different characteristics: they do not attempt to measure what the learner knows; they tend to be self-report measures in which the learner reports how he or she feels, what the learner thinks he or she can do, or what the learner is actually doing to facilitate his or her career maturity.

Some very promising measures of career maturity appear to be those that are (1) highly reliable and (2) uncorrelated with reading. The following scales have reliabilities of at least .84 and correlate less than .10 with the ITED Reading Test: Career Development Inventory Planning, Career Decision Scale, and Assessment of Career Development Involvement.

TABLE 5-18
RANKING OF CAREER MATURITY/CAREER
DECISION-MAKING MEASURES IN TERMS OF THEIR
CORRELATION WITH THE ITED READING TEST
(*N* = 230 HIGH SCHOOL JUNIORS)

SCALES	CORRELATION WITH ITED READING
1. CSAP Career Decision-Making Skills (.91)[a]	.60
2. ACD Career Planning Knowledge (.68)	.56
3. CDI Career Decision Making (.78)	.53
4. CDI World of Work Information (.79)	.51
5. CMI Goal Selection	.46
6. CMI Attitude Scale (.76)	.37
7. ACDM I STYLE (.60)	−.29
8. ACDM D STYLE (.69)	−.24
9. ACDM CR TASK (.52)	.18
10. ACDM R STYLE (.72)	.15
11. ACDM CH TASK (.71)	−.11
12. ACD CERTAINTY	−.10
13. CDI PLANNING (.90)	.08
14. CDS Career Indecision (.84)	.07
15. ACDM CL TASK (.32)	−.07
16. ACD INVOLVEMENT (.90)	.02
17. ACDM EX TASK (.73)	.00

Note: Data are from Prediger (1979).

[a]Internal consistency estimates are in parentheses.

The Validity of the Career Maturity Inventory

The Career Maturity Inventory may be the most widely used measure of career maturity, but its validity has been seriously questioned.

In his review, Katz (1978) expresses "reservations" (p. 1563) about the attitude scale because (1) most of the items are keyed false, (2) "agreement between judges and keys hardly seems to represent content validity in the generally accepted sense" (p. 1562), and (3) the nonsignificant correlations between the attitude scale and Super's Indices of Vocational Maturity (IVM) "speaks poorly for content validity since the IVM was derived from virtually the same definition of 'career maturity' as the CMI" (p. 1563).

Zytowski (1978) identified several problems with the CMI Attitude Scale: (1) only five validity studies are cited in the manual and all of them were conducted prior to 1968; (2) the author did not "clarify where the CMI is more successfully or validly applied and where it is not" (p. 1566); (3) mean differences across states are greater than mean differences across grades; (4) evidence is not reported to support the statement that "those in the lowest quarter . . . can be considered as possibly delayed or impaired in their career development . . . and can be invited to participate in some facilitating experience" (Crites, 1973b, p. 32); and (5) gain scores are "unimpressive in terms of the total possible score or standard error of measurement" (p. 1566). With respect to the last point, Crites (1973b) has criticized Smith and Herr's (1972) evidence on sex differences because "the N's for the statistical test were quite large" and the differences between means were "quite small," for example, only 1.09 raw score points in grade 10 (Crites, 1973b, p. 6). However, the "norms" for the Attitude Scale (Crites, 1973b, p. 39) show small raw-score differences across grade level: 1.09 between grades six and seven; 1.02 between grades nine and ten; and only 0.71 between grades ten and eleven. If these are insignificant, then the developmental nature of the Attitude Scale may be in question. The revised manual (Crites, 1978b) shows even smaller differences between grades: 0.46 between grades six and seven; 0.70 between grades eight and nine; 0.74 between grades nine and ten; and 0.69 between grades eleven and twelve.

Katz (1978) criticizes the competence test because (1) the test-taker can choose the keyed responses without reading the stems, (2) "the items may be good measures of test-taking savvy, but miss the major components of the competency they purport to measure" (p. 1564), and (3) "the 8th grade means for four of the five competence tests are higher than the 9th grade means in the standardization sample" (p. 1565). Katz (1978) does not recommend the Career Maturity Inventory for use "as a criterion of competencies involved in career decision-making or career development, for diagnostic measurement, or for any other purpose" (p. 1565).

Zytowski (1978) expresses concern about the following: (1) on the Competence Test, the twelfth graders answer correctly only about four more items than do the sixth graders; (2) several in-progress studies and periodic supplements were promised but never delivered; (3) the claims of the Career Maturity Inventory are "substantially overdrawn" (p. 1567); and (4) the Career Maturity Inventory "appears to need a great deal more study, resulting perhaps in some revision, before it can receive better than this qualified endorsement for its extensive claimed uses" (p. 1567).

The Career Maturity Inventory
as a Criterion Measure

The Career Maturity Inventory has been used widely as a criterion measure for career education programs, but Bonnet's analysis (1978) revealed that only a small fraction of the programs reported statistically significant results.

When the Attitude Scale was used as a criterion measure, only two out of thirty-four studies yielded significant results. Similarly low success rates were obtained with the Competence Test subtests: goal selection, three out of twenty-five; problem solving, two out of eighteen; self-appraisal, two out of nineteen; occupational information, two out of twenty; and planning, two out of twenty-five. Whether or not the low success rate is due to the inadequacy of the test or the programs remains to be determined.

SUMMARY

Westbrook et al. (1980) have posed several questions for which we do not have sufficient answers:

> How can career maturity variables be distinguished from noncareer maturity variables? What should be the magnitude of the relationship between career maturity and intelligence, scholastic aptitude, and school achievement? Should career maturity be viewed as an independent variable or as a dependent variable, as aptitude or achievement? Is career maturity multidimensional or unidimensional? Can career maturity be established as a meaningful construct on its own, separate from other existing constructs? If career maturity is a meaningful construct, shouldn't it be possible for students of high intelligence to be career immature and students with low intelligence to be career mature? Should students be required to take routinely a battery of several "different" career maturity tests, when the studies by Prediger (1979) and Wilton (1979) suggest that the measures of Career Choice Attitudes and Career Choice Competencies are providing substantially the same information [p. 277]?

In addition, Westbrook et al. (1980) have briefly described several studies that might help answer some of those questions:

1. Administer separate measures of all sixteen variables in the Crites (1978a) model and intercorrelate and factor analyze the scores to determine whether the model is multidimensional.
2. Use the multitrait-multimethod matrix design (Campbell and Fiske, 1959) to investigate the construct validity of career maturity measures.
3. Administer career maturity measures/indicators to students at different ability levels to determine which items and indicators are highly correlated with each other but uncorrelated with mental ability.
4. Construct and try out new measures of career maturity that are less demanding in reading, verbal, and language skills; that have fewer occupational-information items than existing measures; and that include variables such as career indecision, career salience, and realism of career choice.
5. Investigate procedures for increasing the reliability of existing career maturity measures, such as increasing the length of the Attitude Scale or combining the scores on the subtests of the Competence Test.
6. Administer career maturity measures to students and ask the students' teachers to provide independent rating of each pupil's career maturity level.
7. Studies of the relationship between career maturity and career adjustment are greatly needed.
8. Also needed are further studies to determine the relationship between career maturity and the appropriateness of vocational choices (Westbrook, 1976b), particularly simulated occupational choice (Katz, Norris, and Pears, 1978).

9. Perhaps an updated content analysis (Westbrook, 1974) or a comparative test review (Westbrook and Mastie, 1973) would be helpful if it included more recent measures, such as the College Board's Career Skills Assessment Program (1978).

10. A recent nationwide assessment (Westbrook, 1978) indicates the need for studies of adult career maturity.

11. Although suggestions for further research are easier to recommend than to carry out (Westbrook and Cunningham, 1970), there is a possibility that accumulated studies will increase our understanding of the construct of career maturity (Westbrook and Mastie, 1972).

The following paragraph summarizes Westbrook et al.'s (1980) outlook on the construct of career maturity:

A major goal of future investigations should be to collect more evidence on the construct validity of career maturity measures. If over the course of numerous investigations career maturity measures produce theoretically parsimonious findings that fit the construct name *career maturity* applied to them, then investigators will be encouraged to continue using them in research, and to use the name *career maturity* to refer to the instruments. On the other hand, if the evidence is dismal in this regard, it will discourage scientists from investing in additional research with the instruments, and we will wonder if the instruments really fit the trait name that has been employed to describe them [p. 278].

REFERENCES

AMERICAN COLLEGE TESTING PROGRAM. *Handbook for the assessment of career development.* Boston: Houghton Mifflin, 1974.

BOKER, R. L., and SCHUTZ, R. E. (Eds.). *Instructional product development.* New York: Van Nostrand Reinhold, 1971.

BONNET, DEBORAH G. *A synthesis of results and programmatic recommendations emerging from career education evaluation in 1975–76.* Washington, D.C.: U.S. Government Printing Office, 1978.

CAMPBELL, D. T., and FISKE, D. W. Convergent and discriminant validation by the multitrait-multimethod matrix. *Psychological Bulletin,* 1959, *56,* 81–105.

CAMPBELL, D. T. Recommendations for APA test standards regarding construct, trait, and discriminant validity. *American Psychologist,* 1960, *15,* 546–553.

CLEMMONS, J. S. Attributes associated with career awareness among North Carolina sixth graders. Unpublished manuscript, Division of Research, State Department of Public Instruction, Raleigh, North Carolina, 1973.

COLLEGE ENTRANCE EXAMINATION BOARD. *About the achievement tests, 1974–75.* New York: College Entrance Examination Board, 1974.

COLLEGE ENTRANCE EXAMINATION BOARD. *Career skills assessment program.* New York: College Entrance Examination Board, 1978.

CRITES, J. O. Measurement of vocational maturity in adolescence: I. Attitude Test of the Vocational Development Inventory. *Psychological Monographs,* 1965, *79,* (2, Whole No. 595).

CRITES, J. O.   Career Maturity. *Measurement in education*, 1972, *4* (2), 1–8.

CRITES, J. O.   *Theory and research handbook for the Career Maturity Inventory.* Monterey, Calif.: CTB/McGraw-Hill, 1973. (a)

CRITES, J. O.   *Administration and use manual for the Career Maturity Inventory.* Monterey, Calif.: CTB/McGraw-Hill, 1973. (b)

CRITES, J. O.   *Career Maturity Inventory Attitude Scale, Form A-1.* Monterey, Calif.: CTB/McGraw-Hill, 1973. (c)

CRITES, J. O.   *Career Maturity Inventory Competence Test, Research Edition.* Monterey, Calif.: CTB/McGraw-Hill, 1973. (d)

CRITES, J. O.   Career development processes: A model of career maturity. In E. L. Herr (Ed.), *Vocational guidance and human development.* Boston: Houghton Mifflin. 1974. (a)

CRITES, J. O.   The Career Maturity Inventory. In D. E. Super (Ed.), *Measuring vocational maturity for counseling and evaluation.* Washington, D.C.: National Vocational Guidance Association, 1974. (b)

CRITES, J. O.   *Theory and research handbook for the Career Maturity Inventory* (2nd ed.). Monterey, Calif.: CTB/McGraw-Hill, 1978. (a)

CRITES, J. O.   *Administration and use manual for the Career Maturity Inventory* (2nd ed.). Monterey, Calif.: CTB/McGraw-Hill, 1978. (b)

CRITES, J. O.   *Career Maturity Inventory Attitude Scale, Screening Form A-2.* Monterey, Calif.: CTB/McGraw-Hill, 1978. (c)

CRITES, J. O.   *Career Maturity Inventory Attitude Scale, Counseling Form B-1.* Monterey, Calif.: CTB/McGraw-Hill, 1978. (d)

CRITES, J. O.   *Career Maturity Inventory Competence Test.* Monterey, Calif.: CTB/McGraw-Hill, 1978. (e)

CROSBY, R.   The relationship of mental maturity to vocational group of trade and industrial juniors. *Journal of Industrial Education*, 1975, *13*, 40–47.

DILLARD, J.   Relationship between career maturity and self-concepts of suburban and urban middle and urban lower-class preadolescent black males. *Journal of Vocational Behavior*, 1976, *9*, 311–320.

FORREST, D. J., and THOMPSON, A. S.   The Career Development Inventory. In D. E. Super (Ed.), *Measuring vocational maturity for counseling and evaluation.* Washington, D.C.: National Vocational Guidance Association, 1974.

FRUCHTER, B.   *Introduction to factor analysis.* New York: Van Nostrand, 1954.

GABLE, R. K., THOMPSON, D. L., and GLANSTEIN, P. J.   Perception of personal control and conformity and vocational choice as correlates of vocational development. *Journal of Vocational Behavior*, 1976, *8*, 259–267.

GASPER, T. H., and OMVIG, C. P.   The relationship between career maturity and occupational plans of high school juniors. *Journal of Vocational Behavior*, 1976, *9*, 367–375.

GUILFORD, J. P., and FRUCHTER, B.   *Fundamental statistics in psychology and education* (6th ed.). New York: McGraw-Hill, 1978.

HANNA, G. S., and NEELY, M. A.   Reliability of the CMI Attitude Scale. *Measurement and Evaluation in Guidance*, 1978, *11*, 114–116.

HANSEN, J. C.   Review of Career Maturity Inventory by J. Crites. *Journal of Counseling Psychology*, 1974, *21*, 168–172.

HANSEN, J. C., and ANSEL, E. M.   Assessment of vocational maturity. *Journal of Vocational Behavior*, 1973, *3*, 89–94.

HARCOURT, BRACE, JOVANOVICH. *Metropolitan Achievement Test.* New York: Harcourt Brace Jovanovich, 1970.

HARMON, L. W. The counselor as consumer of research. In L. Goldman (Ed.), *Research methods for counselors.* New York: Wiley, 1978.

HEALY, C. C., and KLEIN, S. P. *Manual for the New Mexico Career Education Test Series.* Hollywood, Calif.: Monitor Publishing, 1973.

HERR, E. L., and ENDERLEIN, T. E. Vocational maturity: The effects of school, grade, curriculum and sex. *Journal of Vocational Behavior,* 1976, *8,* 227–238.

HOTELLING, H. The selection of variates for use in prediction, with some comments on the general problem of nuisance parameters. *Annals of Mathematical Statistics,* 1940, *11,* 271–283.

KAISER, H. F. The varimax criterion for analytic rotation in factor analysis. *Psychometrika,* 1958, *23,* 197–200.

KATZ, M. R. Review of the Career Maturity Inventory by J. O. Crites. In O. K. Buros (Ed.), *The eighth mental measurements yearbook.* New Jersey: Gryphon, 1978, 1562–1565.

KATZ, M. R., NORRIS, L., and PEARS, L. Simulated occupational choice: A diagnostic measure of competencies in career decision-making. *Measurement and Evaluation in Guidance.* 1978, *10,* 222–232.

LAWRENCE, W., and BROWN, D. An investigation of intelligence, self-concept, socioeconomic status, race, and sex as predictors of career maturity. *Journal of Vocational Behavior,* 1976, *9,* 43–52.

LoCASCIO, R., NESSELROTH, J., and THOMAS, M. The Career Development Inventory: Use and findings with inner city dropouts. *Journal of Vocational Behavior,* 1976, *8,* 285–292.

MAYNARD, P. O., and HANSEN, J. C. Vocational maturity among inner city youths. *Journal of Counseling Psychology,* 1970, *17,* 400–404.

MOORE, T. L., and McLEAN, J. E. A validation study of the Career Maturity Inventory Attitude Scale. *Measurement and Evaluation in Guidance,* 1977, *10,* 113–116.

MORACCO, J. C. Vocational maturity of Arab and American high school students. *Journal of Vocational Behavior,* 1976, *8,* 367–373.

MOWSESIAN, R., and HOLLEY, S. I. Reliability and validity of the CMI by sex, ethnicity and time. Paper presented at the Annual Meeting of the American Educational Research Association, New York, April, 1977.

OMVIG, C. P., and THOMAS, E. G. Relationship between career education, sex, and career maturity of sixth and eighth grade pupils. *Journal of Vocational Behavior,* 1977, *11,* 322–331.

OSIPOW, S. H., CARNEY, C. G., and BARAK, A. A scale of educational-vocational undecidedness: A typological approach. *Journal of Vocational Behavior,* 1976, *9,* 233–243.

OSIPOW, S. H., CARNEY, C. C., WINER, J., YANICA, B., and KOSCHIER, M. *The Career Decision Scale* (3rd Rev. ed.). Columbus, Ohio: Marathon Consulting and Press, 1976.

OTIS, A. O., and LENNON, R. T. *Otis-Lennon Mental Ability Test.* New York: Harcourt Brace Jovanovich, 1969. (a)

OTIS, A. O., and LENNON, R. T. *Technical handbook for the Otis-Lennon Mental Ability Test.* New York: Harcourt Brace Jovanovich, 1969. (b)

PREDIGER, DALE. Career decision-making measures in the context of Harren's model. Paper presented at the meeting of the American Personnel and Guidance Association, Las Vegas, April, 1979.

SMITH, E. D., and HERR, E. L. Sex differences in the maturation of vocational attitudes among adolescents. *Vocational Guidance Quarterly,* 1972, *20,* 177–182.

SMITH, E. J.   Reference group perspectives and the vocational maturity of lower socioeconomic black youth. *Journal of Vocational Behavior,* 1976, *8,* 321 – 336.

SORENSON, G.   Review of the Career Maturity Inventory. *Measurement and Evaluation in Guidance,* 1974, *7,* 54 – 57.

SUPER, D. E.   Retrospect, circumspect, and prospect. In D. E. Super (Ed.), *Measuring vocational maturity for counseling and evaluation.* Washington, D.C.: National Vocational Guidance Association, 1974.

THORNDIKE, R. L., and HAGEN, E.   *Measurement and evaluation in psychology and education* (3rd ed.). New York: Wiley, 1977.

TITLEY, R. W., TITLEY, B., and WOLFF, W. W.   The major changers: Continuity or discontinuity in the career decision process? *Journal of Vocational Behavior,* 1976, *8,* 105 – 111.

TRYON, W. A.   The test-trait fallacy. *American Psychologist,* 1979, *34,* 402–406.

WESTBROOK, B. W. (Ed.).   Vocational Maturity Battery, Tests 1 – 6, Revised Form. Unpublished test, Department of Psychology, North Carolina State University, Raleigh, North Carolina, 1970.

WESTBROOK, B. W.   *Toward the validation of the construct of vocational maturity* (Center Technical Paper No. 6). Raleigh; North Carolina State University, Center for Occupational Education, 1971.

WESTBROOK, B. W.   Content analysis of six career development tests. *Measurement and Evaluation in Guidance,* 1974, *7* (3), 172 – 180.

WESTBROOK, B. W.   Criterion-related and construct validity of the Career Maturity Inventory Competence Test with ninth-grade pupils. *Journal of Vocational Behavior,* 1976, *9,* 377 – 383. (a)

WESTBROOK, B. W.   Interrelationship of career choice competencies and career choice attitudes of ninth-grade pupils: Testing hypotheses derived from Crites' model of career maturity. *Journal of Vocational Behavior,* 1976, *8,* 1 – 12. (b)

WESTBROOK, B. W.   The relationship between career choice attitudes and career choice competencies of ninth-grade pupils. *Journal of Vocational Behavior,* 1976, *9,* 119 – 125. (c)

WESTBROOK, B. W.   The relationship between vocational maturity and appropriateness of vocational choices of ninth-grade pupils. *Measurement and Evaluation in Guidance,* 1976, *9,* 75 – 80. (d)

WESTBROOK, B. W.   *Career development needs of adults.* Washington, D.C.: National Vocational Guidance Association and Association for Measurement and Evaluation in Guidance, 1978.

WESTBROOK, B. W.   Career maturity: The concepts, the instruments, and the research. In S. H. Osipow and W. B. Wolsh (Eds.), *Handbook of vocational psychology.* New Jersey: Lawrence Erlbaum Associates, in press.

WESTBROOK, B. W., and CUNNINGHAM, J. W.   The development and application of vocational maturity measures. *Vocational Guidance Quarterly,* 1970, *18* (3), 171 – 175.

WESTBROOK, B. W., and CUTTS, C. C.   Career maturity of ninth grade pupils: Real or imaginary? Unpublished manuscript, 1978.

WESTBROOK, B. W., CUTTS, C. C., MADISON, S. S., and ARCIA, M.   The validity of the Crites model of career maturity. *Journal of Vocational Behavior,* 1980. *16,* 249 – 281.

WESTBROOK, B. W., and MASTIE, M. M.   On pathfinding: Some suggestions for increasing our understanding of the construct of vocational maturity. *Journal of Industrial Teacher Education,* 1972, Spring, *9,* 39 – 46.

WESTBROOK, B. W., and MASTIE, M. M.   Three measures of vocational maturity: A beginning to know about. *Measurement and Evaluation in Guidance,* 1973, *6,* 6 – 16.

WESTBROOK, B. W., and MASTIE, M. M.   The Cognitive Vocational Maturity Test. In D. E. Super (Ed.), *Measuring vocational maturity for counseling and evaluation.* Washington: National Vocational Guidance Association, 1974.

WESTBROOK, B. W., and PARRY-HILL, J. W.   The measurement of cognitive vocational maturity. *Journal of Vocational Behavior,* 1973, *3,* 239–252. (a)

WESTBROOK, B. W., and PARRY-HILL, J. W.   *The construction and validation of a measure of vocational maturity* (Center Technical Paper No. 16). Raleigh; North Carolina State University, Center for Occupational Education, 1973. (b)

WESTBROOK, B. W., and PARRY-HILL, J. W.   The construction and validation of a measure of vocational maturity. *JSAS Catalog of Selected Documents in Psychology,* 1975, *5,* 256 (Ms. No. 968).

WILTON, T. L.   Sex differences in career development: Social desirability as a cultural role mediator in analyzing locus of control and career maturity of middle school students. Paper presented at the meeting of the Eastern Educational Research Association, Kiawah Island, South Carolina, February 22, 1979.

ZYTOWSKI, D. G.   Review of the Career Maturity Inventory by J. O. Crites. In O. K. Buros (ed.), *The eighth mental measurements yearbook.* New Jersey: Gryphon, 1978, 1565–1567.

PART THREE

ALTERNATIVE ASSESSMENT PROCEDURES

Having identified some of the important technical requirements in career development measurement and having seen how difficult it is to define constructs that can be measured without contamination, we turn now to some specific ways to measure career development outcomes. The big problem in career education measurement is to insure that we are measuring what we want to measure and only what we want to measure. Cole emphasized this fundamental problem in her discussion of content validity in chapter 3, and in chapter 6 Shoemaker provides a specific set of procedures to implement that idea. Shoemaker's basic notion is that we must begin with a clearly articulated "skills framework," which is essentially a well-organized set of instructional objectives. Next, a large pool of test questions (an item domain) can be constructed to measure each of the components in the skills framework. Finally, instruments of various lengths and difficulty levels for various subpopulations can be constructed from the desired item domains. Shoemaker provides examples of skills frameworks from four sources, including one of the most advanced attempts to measure career development outcomes, the Career and

Occupational Development test devised by the National Assessment of Educational Progress (NAEP).

Hulsart and Burton in chapter 7 describe the specific issues that needed to be resolved to measure career and occupational development in the NAEP program. NAEP attempts to assess the skill level of the general population at various age levels by randomly sampling representative subgroups. To construct what Shoemaker calls a skills framework, NAEP draws upon the talents, not just of measurement experts, but of a wide array of lay people and occupational specialists. This "task force" then defines the skills framework. Of course, a different group of people appointed to the task force might well define a different set of desired objectives. Hulsart and Burton point out how the desired objectives have evolved over recent years. They address several important issues in measuring outcomes: How can one distinguish the skills that are to be measured in a career program from skills that are developed in all the other subject matter areas such as English, mathematics, and social studies? Should the test measure skills required for performing specific occupations, or should it measure more general skills that would be useful across many occupations? How can one measure skills that involve sequential steps over a long period of time? How can one measure attitudes and emotional responses without invading the privacy of individuals? How can one measure what people can do as opposed to what they say they can do? How can the results of the measurement process be interpreted and communicated to interested persons? The NAEP effort has probably been the most sophisticated attempt to assess career development outcomes, and this experience can provide an enlightened basis for further attempts to improve the measurement process.

The NAEP testing exercises require students to answer using paper and pencil. The examinees can reveal the extent of their knowledge, their ability to solve verbal problems, and their own estimates of skills that they might be able to exercise in the real world. However, the exercises give subjects no opportunity to show what they can really do. Finch in chapter 8 examines the possibilities of performance testing, suggesting that people need some opportunity to demonstrate their skills, not merely write about them. Finch discusses a number of important questions. Are the added costs of performance testing worth the potential benefits? How can the validity of a performance test be checked? What unusual problems affect the reliability of performance tests compared to paper-and-pencil tests? Finch points out that successful performance almost inevitably requires a combination of skills and knowledge and therefore that it may not be possible to develop separate tests for individually specified skills, as Shoemaker advocated in chapter 6. The acid test for career education ultimately involves performance testing. If students merely learn to mark test-answer sheets differently and fail to perform more successfully in real life, then the career education movement has been for nothing. If we could be sure that paper-and-pencil tests, which are more easily administered and less expensive, correlated highly with actual performance, we might be more confident in using such tests as intermediate criteria of success. At the moment we do not have that assurance. Finch's chapter argues forcefully for the inclusion of some performance measures, at least as ways of validating paper-and-pencil tests.

If we cannot afford to measure actual performance in real life, perhaps we can measure actual performance in a simulated life situation. In chapter 9, Krumboltz, Hamel, and Scherba describe an attempt to simulate the process of career decision making. The two-hour simulation was developed as a criterion measure in an effort to determine whether people could be trained to make better career decisions. What *is* a better decision? Is a good decision determined by the process that one goes through to make it regardless of the outcome? Or is it judged by the outcome regardless of the process? Or must both process and product be considered? Since their experiment was designed to identify the process that would produce a good outcome, the investigators first had to develop a way to measure good outcomes. Eventually they defined a good outcome as one that yields consequences consistent with the values of the decider. In short, good deciders get what they want. The problem then became one of designing an instrument that would measure whether each decider got what he or she wanted. The outcome that was best for one person was not necessarily best for another. Chapter 9 describes how the simulation was constructed, the rationale underlying it, the method for determining the values of the subjects, and the rationale for using fictitious occupations and fictitious occupational information. Some preliminary data are reported on the most popular values and the performance of community college students on the criterion measures of goodness of choice. Validity and reliability studies await future researchers. Simulation exercises might represent a first approximation to the more realistic performance testing advocated by Finch.

Evaluating career education programs using item domains

JUDITH SAULS SHOEMAKER

National Institute of Education

In the flurry to develop career education programs and appropriate grade-level activities, the development of adequate test instruments for evaluating the effectiveness of such programs has generally been neglected. The reasons for this neglect are easy to understand. Expected student outcomes and definitions of basic terms such as *career, work,* and *decision making* are still being formulated (Super, 1976). Stated objectives tend to be broad and general in nature, encompass many diverse cognitive and affective skills, and are usually stated as long-term, end-of-schooling objectives. All these factors make development of adequate test instruments difficult at best. Additionally, tests developed locally for use in career education programs rely primarily on face validity and assess easy-to-measure skills and attitudes, such as knowledge of specific occupations. Standardized tests may cover more complex areas but often present a mismatch, with instruction requiring the user to select one subtest

This article was written by the author in her private capacity. No official support or endorsement by NIE, U.S. Department of Education, is intended or should be inferred.

from one battery and another subtest from another battery. National norms, when provided, may not be appropriate for local programs.

One procedure by which "adequate" assessment instruments may be developed for evaluating career education programs has as its core the construction of an *item domain* (not an item pool). As an overview, the item domain associated with a given career education program constitutes an operational definition of that program and is structured by a framework that organizes, usually in a hierarchy, the knowledge, skills and attitudes taught. This framework, called a *conceptual framework,* provides the critical link between the instructional program and appropriate assessment instruments. As such, the resulting item domain is particularly appropriate both for instruction and for evaluating program effectiveness. In the following discussion, the relationship is described between an item domain and an instructional program, a procedure is outlined for constructing item domains for career education programs, and examples are given of how such item domains may be used to evaluate programs.

RELATIONSHIPS BETWEEN ITEM DOMAINS AND EDUCATIONAL PROGRAMS

This discussion of the ideal relationship between an educational program and its associated item domain, illustrated in Figure 6-1, is based on the work of Shoemaker (1975, 1976) and Shoemaker and Shoemaker (1978b). Briefly, the purpose of every educational program is to teach a certain set of skills or to change students' behavior on these skills. Every educational program can be described or defined as the domain of skills it seeks to teach. This domain of skills often exists in the form of written program goals and objectives; in practice, the domain of skills consists of those skills actually taught by the program whether or not these skills are articulated.

The skills within the domain of skills are ordered by an organizing principle that helps to identify the sequence of instruction (hence, the branching structure in Figure 6-1). The resulting structure may be a learning hierarchy based on difficulty or complexity of skills, or it may parallel a developmental process. For example, the skills to be taught by a career education program might be structured developmentally by following the steps in a career-choice model: career awareness, career exploration, career preparation, and career access. When the domain of skills is structured using the organizing principle, the result is the skills framework. This framework is the key to the construction of the item domain, since it forms the structure for the item domain as well as for program evaluation. Examples of organizing principles associated with career development programs are given in step 2 under "Constructing an Item Domain," on page 121.

FIGURE 6-1.
**INTERRELATIONSHIPS AMONG EDUCATIONAL
PROGRAM, ITEM UNIVERSE, AND ITEM DOMAIN**

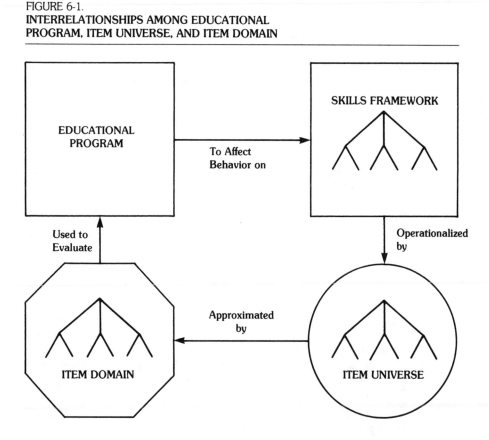

Associated with each skill there exists a set of all possible items that could be used to measure proficiency on that skill. Collectively, across all skills to be taught, these sets of all possible items constitute the item universe associated with that program. The item universe, if it could be constructed, would be an extremely large number of items. In practice, we deal with only a subset of these items. This subset is called an *item domain* and contains a manageable number of items extracted by experts from the large item universe. In short; an item domain is a "workable item universe" (Shoemaker, 1975) although it, too, may contain a large number of items.

The structure of the item domain parallels the structure of the item universe and, hence, the structure of the program's skills framework. Thus, performance on the item domain is equivalent to performance on the item universe. When an item domain is used to evaluate the effectiveness of an educational program, the results will correspond exactly to the structure of skills taught by the program and will be directly interpretable in terms of the program. It is this correspondence between an item domain and the educational program that differentiates an item domain from an item pool. Typically, the latter consists of an unstructured collection of items written for other purposes and may or may not cover the program's domain of skills.

Since the item domain corresponds exactly to the skills taught by the educational program, it can be used to judge the adequacy of alternative assessment approaches. As a result the evaluator will find that most standardized tests will not be appropriate for judging the effectiveness of educational programs.

CHARACTERISTICS OF AN ITEM DOMAIN

An item domain associated with an educational program will, in most cases, be a large collection of items with the following characteristics:

1. Items within the domain will define operationally each skill associated with the educational program.
2. Items within the domain will span comprehensively the relevant range of participant behaviors associated with each skill.
3. An explicitly stated skills framework is associated with the item domain that (a) defines the interrelationships among skills and (b) provides a framework within which results are to be interpreted.
4. The skills framework associated with the item domain defines an integrated and meaningful body of knowledge, skills, or attitudes.

BUILDING TEST INSTRUMENTS USING ITEM DOMAINS

Item domains may be used to construct the evaluation instruments associated with a given program. Items carefully selected from the item domain, collectively maintaining its structure, can be used to develop domain-, criterion-, or objectives-referenced tests. Technically, a test built from an item domain that relates directly to the domain of skills taught by an educational program is called a domain-referenced test. Criterion-referenced tests were originally defined in exactly the same way: "A criterion-referenced test is used to ascertain an individual's status with respect to a well-defined behavior domain" (Popham, 1975). As Hambleton, Swaminathan, Algina, and Coulson (1978) have stated in a review of the topic, "domain-referenced testing" is a more descriptive term for what is currently called criterion-referenced testing. In practice, criterion-referenced testing is primarily associated with a performance standard (or criterion), the identification of mastery/nonmastery states, and minimum proficiency levels.

An objectives-referenced test is composed of items designed to measure a set of objectives, which may or may not completely span a conceptual framework. Hambleton et al. (1978) described the differences between criterion-referenced and objectives-referenced tests in this manner:

> The primary distinction between criterion-referenced tests and objectives-referenced tests is as follows: In a criterion-referenced test, the items are a representative set of items from a clearly defined domain of behaviors measuring an objective, whereas with an objectives-referenced test, no domain of behaviors is specified, and items are not considered to be representative of any behavior domain [p. 3].

Accordingly, items developed by NAEP for their career and occupational development instruments (see chapter 7) are objectives-referenced and, indeed, the publication presenting all released items in career and occupational development is organized by objectives (National Assessment of Educational Progress, 1977b). These objectives tend to be a laundry list of desired terminal outcomes and are not necessarily a comprehensive set or hierarchy of skills.

CONSTRUCTING AN ITEM DOMAIN

The following steps briefly describe how to construct an item domain associated with a given career education program.

Step 1: Selecting Task Force Members and Providing Background Information

The task force will supply the necessary expert judgment to successfully identify the skills framework and build the item domain. Five to seven people should be selected for their experience with career education programs and their knowledge of the career development process. Additional members might include counselors and community representatives. Before the first meeting, this panel of experts should be informed of the scope of its tasks and be provided with any materials that might be relevant.

Step 2: Developing a Skills Framework

The development of a skills framework for a given career education program will be the most difficult step in constructing an item domain. Due to the newness of career education as an educational program, few frameworks exist from which to build. However, statements of objectives do exist and various theories have been developed that attempt to describe the career development process, as Borow has summarized in chapter 2. But there does not currently exist an integrated, theory-based description of the skills, knowledge and attitudes of career development. The construction of such a framework will be a major effort for the task force.

An investigator might consider several alternatives when developing a skills framework. It is not true that one and only one organizational principle is appropriate for a given educational program. The individual skills may be considered "building blocks" to be assembled and reassembled in accordance with many different organizing principles. Thus, two programs seeking to teach the same set of skills may be structured and sequenced quite differently while their item domains nevertheless contained the same items, each structured to parallel the associated skills framework. Four examples of organizing frameworks that would be associated with a given career education program are provided by Bailey (1977), Wise, Charner, and Randour (1976), National Assessment of Educational Progress (1977a), and Westbrook (1974). Each is described briefly here.

A recent analysis of elementary and secondary career education curriculum materials conducted by Bailey (1977) produced a domain of career development behaviors defined by grade levels. The organizing principle used was career development stages, each associated with a range of grades: awareness stage (grades $K-3$), accommodation stage (grades $4-6$), orientation stage (grades $7-8$), and exploration and preparation stage (grades $9-12$). Bailey's analysis is given in Table 6-1.

Frameworks for career education programs might also stem from hypothesized relationships among components defining career development. For example, in an article presenting a skills framework for career awareness, Wise, Charner, and Randour (1976) identified two sets of skills related to career awareness: (1) self-assessment skills, specifically "the skills involved in assessing one's stock of knowledge, values, preferences, and self-concepts in relation to some type of work or work setting," and (2) decision-making skills used to "identify and assess career opportunities." Also identified were subskills in each area. Finally, sample questions for student assessment were provided. A description of their framework is given in Figure 6-2.

Another example of a skills framework for Career Education is the Cycle II objectives for Career and Occupational Development developed by NAEP (1977a). Their framework, describing desired behaviors for four age levels (9 years, 13 years, 17 years, and adult), is given in Table 6-2.

An alternative approach to developing a skills framework for career education was suggested by Westbrook (1974) in a study designed initially, not to develop a skills framework, but to classify items of six current career development tests to determine what they were measuring. In his analysis of a total of 609 test items, he found that they could be described by 54 different descriptive behavioral statements. These 54 behaviors were used subsequently to develop an "outline of career development behaviors" that describes skills in the cognitive, psychomotor, and affective domains. These behaviors are reported by Westbrook in chapter 5, Table 5-3. Such a framework might be useful in constructing a skills framework for a given career education program; however, it is restricted to behaviors actually measured by the six tests.

TABLE 6-1

**GOAL STATEMENTS FOR THE CAREER EDUCATION
MODEL DEFINED BY BAILEY (1977)**

AWARENESS STAGE: GRADES K – 3

A1. Becomes aware of self characteristics
A2. Becomes aware of different types of work roles
A3. Shows awareness of responsibility for own behavior
A4. Knows how to organize information for learning and action
A5. Learns cooperative social behavior
A6. Shows interest in learning about work

ACCOMMODATION STAGE: GRADES 4 – 6

B1. Develops greater self knowledge
B2. Develops concepts about the world of work
B3. Displays increased responsibility for own behavior
B4. Learns how to gather information and make decisions
B5. Shows awareness of the nature of group membership
B6. Accepts differences in work attitudes and values

ORIENTATION STAGE: GRADES 7 & 8

C1. Clarifies occupational self-concept
C2. Surveys the structure and interrelatedness of the American economic system
C3. Recognizes responsibility for own career planning
C4. Practices information-seeking and decision-making methods
C5. Participates in simulated, group work activities
C6. Appreciates the role of work in meeting social and individual needs

EXPLORATION AND PREPARATION STAGE: GRADES 9 – 12

D1. Crystallizes and implements occupational self-concept
D2. Executes plans to qualify for post-secondary career objectives
D3. Displays commitment to implementation of a career plan
D4. Demonstrates competency in decision-making skills and strategies
D5. Demonstrates effective interpersonal skills in relation to work
D6. Demonstrates effective work habits and attitudes

Step 3: Selecting and Defining the Skills to Be Assessed

After constructing the skills framework, the task force should list and define briefly each skill to be assessed by the item domain. In practice, this seemingly pedestrian assignment is extremely difficult and is complicated by decisions on the level and scope of skills to be assessed. Questions such as the following are typically encountered: Should only "terminal" skills be assessed? How many "prerequisite" skills should be assessed? Should we measure only those skills specifically taught by the program? The level of skills to be assessed must come from the task force and will depend on the amount of detail needed

FIGURE 6-2
A FRAMEWORK FOR CAREER AWARENESS DEVELOPED
BY WISE, CHARNER, AND RANDOUR (1976).

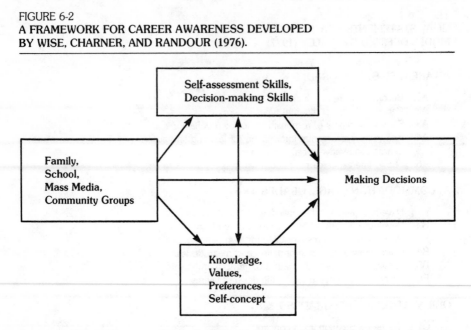

Source: R. Wise, I. Charner, and M. L. Randour, "A Conceptual Framework for Career Awareness in Career Decision-Making," *The Counseling Psychologist,* 1976, *6,* 47 – 53.

in the evaluation of the program and the nature of the selected organizing principle or frameworks, Usually, the task force will identify a minimum number of prerequisite skills per major skill essential for a sound program evaluation. The scope of the items should relate directly to the skills framework, which may encompass skills not directly taught by the program. As noted earlier, the framework and its corresponding item domain should span comprehensively a given body of knowledge, skills or attitudes. In this sense, the skills identified by the task force might be called "program free," in that the skills will not be specifically tailored or restricted to that which the program purports to address.

The National Assessment of Educational Progress calls this step the "construction of item samples." Beginning with the stated objectives and sub-objectives, content experts identify specific behaviors that indicate proficiency on the associated subobjective. Sample test items, or item forms, are produced for the specific behaviors and submitted subsequently to item writers.

Step 4: Selecting and/or Constructing
Items for Each Skill

At this point, the task force should select and/or construct items for each skill. Two general approaches to this task are possible. First, without considering any specific items, the group can define initially the skill categories and then

TABLE 6-2
**OUTLINE OF CYCLE II CAREER AND OCCUPATIONAL
DEVELOPMENT OBJECTIVES**

I.   **KNOWLEDGE, ABILITIES AND ATTITUDES RELEVANT TO CAREER
     DECISIONS**

  A. *Awareness and knowledge of individual characteristics*

    1.   Abilities
       a.   Know one's own abilities
       b.   Understand one's own abilities relative to those of others
       c.   Recognize the multiple causes and effects of abilities
    2.   Interests
       a.   Know one's own interests
       b.   Understand one's own interests relative to those of other individuals
       c.   Recognize the multiple causes and effects of interests
    3.   Values
       a.   Know one's own values
       b.   Understand one's own values relative to those of other individuals.
       c.   Recognize the multiple causes and effects of values

  B. *Knowledge of career and occupational characteristics*

    1.   Major duties
       a.   Know the major duties of specific occupations
    2.   Entry requirements
       a.   Know the entry requirements of different occupations
    3.   Work conditions
       a.   Know differences in work conditions among different occupations
       b.   Understand that differences in work conditions influence the lifestyle of
            workers and their families
       c.   Recognize that work conditions may conflict with individual interests and
            values
    4.   Benefits and employment practices
       a.   Know employment benefits—including social security, medical, vacation
            and retirement benefits—related to occupations
       b.   Know legal requirements protecting persons seeking employment
       c.   Recognize factors that encourage or discourage formation of labor and
            management organizations
       d.   Compare and evaluate specific occupations in terms of employee benefits
    5.   Social and technological change
       a.   Recognize that social and technological changes can modify entry
            requirements and job responsibilities, necessitating adjustments in career
            planning and preparation
       b.   Understand that technological, economic, political and social changes result
            in decreases in the availability of some kinds of occupations and increases in
            others
       c.   Accept the effects of social and technological changes on the availability and
            desirability of specific careers and occupations
    6.   Occupational classifications
       a.   Know that many occupations possessing similar characteristics can be
            grouped into occupational families or clusters

                                                                          (continued)

Note: Used by the National Assessment of Educational Progress (1977a, pp. 3 – 7).

TABLE 6-2 (continued)

---

    b. Recognize occupational classifications such as public/private, profit/nonprofit, and union/nonunion

    c. Understand the differences in duties, responsibilities and entry requirements between different occupations within an occupational cluster or family

C. *Making and implementing career and occupational decisions*

  1. Individual characteristics and occupational requirements
    a. Recognize that abilities, interests and values affect career choice
    b. Identify occupational characteristics that are congruent with one's own abilities, interests and values
    c. Recognize that many limitations can be overcome and do not necessarily prevent success in desired careers

  2. Career decision making
    a. Know that career decision making is a narrowing process
    b. Know that career decision making is an ongoing process
    c. Know that career choices may occur at different ages
    d. Know that career choice is an individual decision
    e. Know that external factors can affect career choice
    f. Use decision-making skills in initiating career choice
    g. Recognize the importance of timing in career decision making

  3. Career preparation
    a. Recognize the importance of adequate planning for entry into a career
    b. Understand that persons with broad education in a family or group of occupations tend to qualify for a number of specific occupations, thereby increasing opportunities for meaningful employment
    c. Demonstrate the ability to prepare a plan for entry into a possible occupation or career

  4. Career modification or change
    a. Recognize that people can modify and change careers
    b. Recognize relevant factors bearing on possible career changes
    c. Recognize advantages and disadvantages of making career modification or change
    d. Recognize when it is advantageous to change or modify existing careers and occupations

  5. Sources of additional knowledge
    a. Know sources and methods for obtaining additional knowledge for career development
    b. Participate in activities leading to more informed and realistic perception of career development
    c. Evaluate sources of information to determine their usefulness in gaining additional knowledge relating to career development

II. KNOWLEDGE, ABILITIES AND ATTITUDES NECESSARY FOR SUCCESS IN A CAREER OR OCCUPATION

  A. *Skills generally useful in careers*

    1. Numerical skills
      a. Know the applications of numerical skills in various careers
      b. Know how to perform basic numerical calculations

TABLE 6-2 (continued)

---

    c. Know metric measurements and how to perform simple calculations using metric measurements

    d. Read numerical values from graphs, charts and tables and understand their use

    e. Interpret statistical data from charts, tables and graphs

    f. Understand and calculate percentages, ratios and proportions

    g. Compare numerical values to determine extremes, central characteristics and trends

    h. Convert measurements into equivalent quantities on a different scale

    i. Estimate relative magnitude in numerical terms

    j. Perform calculations for jobs common to specific age levels

    k. Use graphs, charts and tables in making graphic representations of numerical quantities

2. Communication skills

    a. Recognize communication skills needed to become successful in careers

    b. Listen to and understand spoken and visual instructions, directions and information

    c. Read and follow written instructions, directions and information

    d. Read and understand pictorial, graphic and symbolic information

    e. Give directions, explain, describe and demonstrate clearly

    f. Give organized and informative oral presentations

    g. Write organized, legible and articulate reports and summaries

    h. Prepare concise letters, messages, want ads and telegrams

3. Manual/perceptual skills

    a. Identify and use common tools, fasteners and equipment to perform simple household or job tasks

    b. Read and understand gauges, scales and other common measurement instruments

    c. Construct, fabricate and assemble, using appropriate tools, equipment and materials

    d. Repair and maintain items common in households and occupations

    e. Plan and develop visual presentations

    f. Distinguish between adequate and inadequate construction and repairs

4. Information-Processing, problem-solving and decision-making skills

    a. Know specific procedures and principles used in information processing, problem solving and decision making

    b. Analyze information and define problems

    c. Collect and organize data

    d. Identify possible solutions and alternatives

    e. Make decisions or choose alternatives in terms of relevant criteria

    f. Implement plans

    g. Based on feedback, evaluate and modify plans

    h. Learn and apply procedures and principles that are basic to further learning

    i. Devise plans, new ideas and better ways of doing things

5. Interpersonal skills

    a. Know the importance of interpersonal skills

    b. Work and interact effectively with peers, teachers and supervisors

    c. Demonstrate effective leadership

6. Employment-Seeking skills

    a. Know where to find information regarding job openings

(continued)

TABLE 6-2 (continued)

      b. Use appropriate procedures in applying for a job or position

    7. Career-Improvement skills

      a. Know that most careers require the continuous attainment of new knowledge and abilities

      b. Know methods of gaining knowledge and abilities necessary to improve existing career and occupational skills

      c. Engage in activities that improve skills within a planned career

B. Personal characteristics related to career success

    1. Responsibility and initiative

      a. Know that accepting responsibility and practicing initiative can contribute to job success

      b. Demonstrate the ability to plan for completion of an assigned or accepted responsibility

      c. Use initiative when appropriate in performing an assigned or accepted responsibility

      d. Demonstrate resourcefulness and efficiency in accomplishing an assigned or accepted responsibility

      e. Know that good grooming, appropriate dress and health care contribute to job success

      f. Accept responsibility for one's own behavior

    2. Adaptability to variable conditions

      a. Know factors that can cause changes in working conditions

      b. Adjust to varied work conditions

    3. Attitudes and values

      a. Know the bases of various attitudes towards work

      b. Identify and analyze one's own attitudes towards work

      c. Recognize and evaluate the personal and societal consequences of one's own attitudes towards work

      d. Encourage and assist others to develop and use abilities to achieve maximum competence

      e. Recognize the contributions and abuses of various organizations and individuals to the well-being of society

      f. Recognize and appreciate effort, accomplishment and excellence in the completion of an accepted or assigned responsibility

      g. Value constructive work in terms of meeting societal goals

    4. Personal fulfillment

      a. Know that people need to experience personal satisfaction and that one's own career can be a source of such satisfaction

      b. Establish personal goals that contribute to self-fulfillment

      c. Accept the diversity of career goals and lifestyles of others

      d. Seek personal fulfillment through achievement in school, career and personal life

construct appropriate items for each category. The definitions of each skill might be item forms or item specifications and would be dependent on the definitions provided in step 3. This is the approach commonly used by the NAEP.

The second approach is more common and begins with a collection of a pool of items related to the program's skills that are appropriate for the grade level of the students. These items are then sorted and assigned to the skill areas identified in step 3. For each skill area, the items might be sorted by ability level: simple, intermediate, and complex. When using previously written items, the task force must be alert to *compound items,* that is, items that measure more than one skill. Such items, when they are reviewed, seem to be appropriate for more than one skill area. (Do not be tempted to "kill two birds with one stone.") Interpretations of correct results on such items are difficult, since correct performance could be attributed to proficiency in more than one skill. Such items should be revised until performance on the item is directly related to proficiency in one skill.

After items have been assigned to skills and the task force is satisfied that each item does indeed measure the associated skill, the task force will need to construct appropriate items for any skill areas left unmeasured. Unfortunately but expectedly, these areas will be the higher level and more complex skill areas such as "career decision-making" and "attitudes toward work."

Two questions arise in the selection of items: (1) What form should the items take? and (2) How many items should be used to measure a given skill? The item format (for example, multiple choice, true/false, free response) should be the one that permits the skill to be assessed in the simplest, most direct manner possible, allowing for age-level appropriateness and available item-scoring resources. The number of items per skill has been addressed by Millman (1973) but, in general, no mystical number exists for measuring proficiency on each and every skill. The number of items per skill depends on the complexity of each skill and the level of detail needed for the program evaluation, both of which should be decided by the task force.

Step 5: Field Testing and Revising
the Item Domain

The last step is to try out the items using a sample of students typical of those participating in the educational program. The field test can be used to estimate administration time and to revise poorly constructed or misleading items.

One procedure that can be used in field tests for measuring performance on an item domain is multiple matrix sampling (Shoemaker, 1973; Sirotnik, 1975; Shoemaker, 1977). Since the item domain of an educational program will generally be too large to be administered to any one student, multiple matrix sampling can be used to estimate group performance over the item domain. This technique uses random sampling to divide the item domain into subtests with each subtest administered to a subgroup of students also selected randomly from all students in the program. Although different students take different subtests, the results can be used to estimate how well all students would have performed if they had taken all items. Such a procedure is used by NAEP and several State and local assessment programs (Shoemaker and Shoemaker, 1978a).

The results from the field test can also be used to verify the adequacy of the skills framework. Items should be answered in a manner consistent with the hierarchy proposed; if not, items might be ambiguous or poorly written, or the hierarchy might need revision.

EXAMPLES OF ITEM-DOMAIN CONSTRUCTION

In this section, two examples are discussed to illustrate the use of career education frameworks and the construction of associated item domains.

Department of Defense Dependents Schools (DoDDS)

Department of Defense Dependents Schools (DoDDS, 1976) used a task force of teachers and administrators to define a skills framework to guide (a) the development of career education programs, and (b) the assessment of career education skills. The task force divided the goals of career education into two domains: career development and career preparation. Career development is defined as self- and career-awareness, career exploration, and decision making. Career preparation is defined as the acquisition of academic and vocational knowledge and skills necessary to implement career decisions and plans. Specific program objectives were devised for each goal, and for each program objective specific instructional objectives were identified for four grade levels (K–4, 5–8, 9–12, and 13–A). Instructional objectives included both "enroute" and "terminal" grade-level objectives. Finally, behaviors were given to illustrate proficiency and to serve as a guide for classroom activities—for example:

1. *Program Objective:* Make career choices
2. *Instructional Objective:* Use information sources for solving career decision-making problems
3. *Enroute Objective (grades 9 – 12):* Seek information about occupations in general or about specific jobs
4. *Sample Behavior:* Talks to counselors at schools, employment offices and training centers; uses reference sources to obtain information about occupations

Collectively, this set of objectives serves as the skills framework for DoDDS career education programs. It defines the concept of career education and indicates the target domain of skills for each program. DoDDS is currently planning the development of an associated item domain to be used to assess the worldwide impact of its career education programs.

Texas Career Education
Measurement Series

In 1975 – 1976, the Texas Education Agency conducted a statewide assessment in career education as part of an assessment of student needs. The assessment began with a statewide survey of students, parents, educators, and representatives of business and industry to determine what Texans believed students leaving school should accomplish in career education. This survey identified 177 basic learner outcomes.

To assess these learner outcomes, the Texas Education Agency developed the Career Education Measurement Series (CEMS). The agency noted that the lack of adequate instruments necessitated this development:

> An investigation of available career education measurement instruments was initiated to determine how well these instruments measured student performance in relation to the basic learner outcomes. Because none of the instruments provided adequate coverage of the learner outcomes, it was evident that a new test would have to be developed [Texas Education Agency, 1976, p. 3].

At present, 17 CEMS instruments measure 63 of the 117 basic learner outcomes, which are organized into nine categories of behaviors:

1. Career Planning and Decision Making
2. Career and Occupational Information
3. Job Acquisition and Retention
4. Attitudes and Appreciation for Career Success
5. Skills in Human Relationships for Careers
6. Self-Investigation and Evaluation for Career Success
7. Personal/Work/Societal Responsibilities
8. Economic Factors Influencing Career Opportunity
9. Education/Career Opportunity Relationships

Each category is divided into one or more subcategories, which contain the basic learner outcomes identifed in the survey. Finally, items were written for each of the basic learner outcomes, resulting in an item domain that was divided into 17 different instruments.

Although the instruments are referred to as *objectives based,* they are also criterion referenced, since performance criteria were established for each category. The statewide assessment tested 20,000 ninth graders and 6,500 twelfth graders randomly selected from 396 school districts in Texas. The framework used to structure the item domain was also used to report the evaluation results, which were used to identify those areas of career education needing improvement. The skills framework developed for CEMS continues to affect instruction through *The Selected Activities and Resources Handbook* (no date;

also written by the Texas Education Agency), which is a collection of activities and instructional approaches designed to provide teachers with ideas and resources for helping students achieve the basic learner outcomes. See the appendix of this book for further information about the Texas CEMS.

CONCLUSION

The construction of item domains has been presented here as a procedure for evaluating career education programs. Item domains together with their skills frameworks provide the necessary tools for both evaluation and instruction. Career education does not need more instruments; what it needs is a system for improving the match between what is taught and what is measured. The best way to improve that match is to develop frameworks for use with career education programs. The information needed to create such frameworks exists in the form of stated program goals and objectives, curriculum guides, theoretical papers, and the structure of certain test instruments. What is needed is a sustained effort to develop integrated, theory-based frameworks for career education programs that can be used to guide both program development and the development of associated item domains. The rationale and procedures presented here are a first step toward that goal.

REFERENCES

BAILEY, L. J. (Ed.). *A teacher's handbook on career development for students with special needs: Grades K – 12* (2nd Ed.). Springfield, Ill.: Illinois Office of Education, 1977.

DEPARTMENT OF DEFENSE DEPENDENTS SCHOOLS. *Career education objectives, kindergarten through grade 12.* Alexandria, Va.: circa 1976.

HAMBLETON, R. K., SWAMINATHAN, H., ALGINA, J. J., and COULSON, D. B. Criterion-referenced testing and measurement: A review of technical issues and developments. *Review of Educational Research*, 1978, *48*, 1 – 47.

MILLMAN, J. Passing scores and test lengths for domain-referenced measures. *Review of Educational Research*, 1973, *43*, 205 – 216.

NATIONAL ASSESSMENT OF EDUCATION PROGRESS. *Career and occupational development objectives, second assessment.* Denver, Co.: Education Commission of the States, 1977. (a)

NATIONAL ASSESSMENT OF EDUCATIONAL PROGRESS. *Career and occupational development technical report: Exercise volume.* Washington, D.C.: U.S. Government Printing Office, 1977. (b)

POPHAM, W. J. *Educational evaluation.* Englewood Cliffs, N.J.: Prentice-Hall, 1975.

SHOEMAKER, D. M. *Principles and procedures of multiple matrix sampling.* Cambridge, Mass.: Ballinger, 1973.

SHOEMAKER, D. M. Toward a framework for achievement testing. *Review of Educational Research*, 1975, *45*, 127 – 147.

SHOEMAKER, D. M.   Applicability of item banking and matrix sampling to educational assessment. In D. N. de Gruijter, and L. J. Van der Kamp (Eds.), *Advances in psychological measurement,* New York: Wiley, 1976.

SHOEMAKER, J. S.   Handbook: Assessment of student achievement via matrix sampling. Washington, D.C.: Unpublished manuscript, 1977.

SHOEMAKER, D. M., and SHOEMAKER, J. S.   Applicability of multiple matrix sampling to estimating effectiveness of educational programs. Washington, D.C.: Unpublished manuscript, 1978. (a)

SHOEMAKER, D. M., and SHOEMAKER, J. S.   Constructing item domains for evaluating educational programs. Washington, D.C.: Unpublished manuscript, 1978. (b)

SIROTNIK, K. A.   Introduction to matrix sampling for the practitioner. In W. J. Popham (Ed.), *Evaluation in education: current applications.* Berkeley, Calif.: McCutcheon, 1975.

SUPER, D. T.   *Career education and the meanings of work.* Washington, D.C.: Department of Health, Education and Welfare, 1976.

TEXAS EDUCATION AGENCY.   *Texas career education measurement series: A student needs assessment.* Austin, Tex.: Texas Education Agency, 1976.

WESTBROOK, B. W.   Content analysis of six career development tests. *Measurement and Evaluation in Guidance,* 1974, *7,* 172 – 180.

WISE, R., CHARNER, I., and RANDOUR, M. L.   A conceptual framework for career awareness in career decision-making. *The Counseling Psychologist,* 1976, *6,* 47 – 53.

7

Measurement issues in the national assessment of career and occupational development

RICHARD HULSART and NANCY W. BURTON

National Assessment of Educational Progress

National assessment has been involved in developing measures for assessing career and occupational development (COD) since 1965. The first assessment was completed in 1974; development for the second assessment was begun in 1975. In this paper, we will review the development of the second assessment and our experience regarding the measurement issues involved.

BACKGROUND: NATIONAL ASSESSMENT

The National Assessment of Educational Progress (NAEP) is an information-gathering project that surveys the educational attainments of 9-, 13- and 17-year-olds and occasionally adults (ages 26 – 35) in ten learning areas: art, career and occupational development, citizenship, literature, mathematics, music, reading, science, social studies, and writing. Different learning areas are assessed every year, and all areas are periodically reassessed in order to measure change in educational achievement.

Each assessment is the product of several years' work by a great many educators, scholars, and lay persons from all over the country. Initially, these people design objectives for each area, proposing specific goals that they feel Americans should be achieving in the course of their education. After careful reviews, these objectives are then given to exercise (item) writers, whose task it is to create measurement tools appropriate to the objectives.

When the exercises have passed extensive reviews by subject-matter specialists and measurement experts, they are administered to probability samples from the different age levels. The people who compose these samples are chosen in such a way that the results of their assessment can be generalized to the entire national population. That is, on the basis of the performance of about 2500 9-year-olds on a given exercise, we can generalize about the probable performance of all 9-year-olds in the nation.

Career and occupational development is unique to National Assessment in that the objectives of the area are not the educational goals of any one school subject and do not belong to a single discipline. Rather, the area includes many of the achievements that result from general education and from guidance and counseling. These achievements include accurate self-evaluation, thoughtful career planning, realistic attitudes toward work, employment-seeking skills, effective work habits, and the development of skills generally useful in a variety of occupations.

Specific vocational skills such as typing or carpentering have been purposely omitted from the COD objectives. Instead, National Assessment has sought to measure those generally useful verbal, quantitative, manual, and social skills that are acquired through general educational and work experiences.

THE DEVELOPMENT OF SECOND-CYCLE COD OBJECTIVES

In preparation for development of the objectives for a second assessment of COD, during the spring of 1975 an advisory panel made up of educators familiar with career education reviewed National Assessment's first COD objectives. These objectives, published in 1971, were used as the basis for the nationwide assessment of COD conducted by National Assessment in 1974. On the basis of its knowledge of current directions in career education, this advisory panel suggested extensive additions to the first objectives.

During 1976, these suggestions were reviewed by people familiar with the development of career education concepts in various programs across the country. These reviewers included representatives from various business, community service, educational, industrial, and governmental organizations. The reviewers not only reacted to the suggested changes of the advisory panel but also suggested revisions and additions of their own. A final draft of the revised objectives was published in 1977. This set of objectives will be used as the basis for National Assessment's second assessment of career and occupational development.

The following is a brief outline of the second-cycle COD objectives. A more complete statement of the objectives appears in Table 6-2 in chapter 6.

I. Knowledge, abilities, and attitudes relevant to career decisions
    A. Awareness and knowledge of individual characteristics
        1. Abilities
        2. Interests
        3. Values
    B. Knowledge of career and occupational characteristics
        1. Major duties
        2. Entry requirements
        3. Work conditions
        4. Benefits and employment practices
        5. Social and technological change
        6. Occupational classifications
    C. Making and implementing career and occupational decisions
        1. Individual characteristics and occupational requirements
        2. Career decision making
        3. Career preparation
        4. Career modification or change
        5. Source of additional knowledge
II. Knowledge, abilities, and attitudes necessary for success in a career or occupation
    A. Skills generally useful in careers
        1. Numerical skills
        2. Communication skills
        3. Manual/perceptual skills
        4. Information-processing, problem-solving, and decision-making skills
        5. Interpersonal skills
        6. Employment-seeking skills
        7. Career-improvement skills
    B. Personal characteristics related to career success
        1. Responsibility and initiative
        2. Adaptability to variable conditions
        3. Attitudes and values
        4. Personal fulfillment

MAJOR CHANGES REFLECTED IN SECOND-CYCLE COD OBJECTIVES

General Organization

The original objectives placed considerable emphasis on skills, work habits, and attitudes useful in the world of work. The second set of objectives was designed to provide equal emphasis on developing knowledge, skills, and attitudes relevant to making career decisions.

Individual Characteristics

The reviewers included additional objectives regarding recognition of the effects of abilities, interests, and values on career decisions. The reviewers insisted that the objectives in the area of abilities emphasize the recognition of strengths rather than limitations. In fact, a number of the participants expressed the viewpoint that the school experience often leaves students with a greater knowledge of their weaknesses than their strengths. Therefore, objectives concerned with understanding one's own abilities made specific references to recognizing that abilities may be the result of determination, education, environment, heredity, and practice; that one acquires new knowledge and abilities each year; and that awareness of one's abilities may contribute to feelings of self-worth.

Occupational Characteristics

The reviewers substantially increased the number of objectives relating to the effects of social and technological changes on entry requirements and job responsibilities. They also added objectives dealing with the relationship between careers and life styles and with the benefits and individual rights connected with employment.

Career and Occupational Decisions

The 1977 COD objectives place greater emphasis on the processes of making and implementing career decisions. In addition to objectives concerned with relating abilities, interests, and values to various career opportunities, the reviewers added a series of objectives emphasizing that many deficiencies in career preparation can be overcome by study, practice, and on-the-job experience. The 1977 objectives focus upon the entire process of career decision making, not just upon finding a first job. Thus, the number of objectives dealing with making career changes, and the possible effects of such changes, have been substantially increased. These objectives also place more emphasis on activities leading to an informed perception of career development. Activities include discussing present and future interests, abilities, and career goals with peers, parents, teachers, school counselors, and adults knowledgeable about various careers; taking special tests to identify interests, capabilities, and special abilities; and participating in available career programs and projects.

Skills Useful in Careers

All the major skill areas outlined in the first set of COD objectives were revised to include examples of skills presently important in various careers and occupations (for example, the use of the metric system). In addition to outlining important skills, the reviewers added objectives concerned with knowledge of the importance and application of these skills in various careers. The area of employment-seeking skills was also substantially expanded in the revised objectives.

Personal Characteristics

In the 1977 objectives, a number of separate objectives from the first COD assessment dealing with personal characteristics were combined and included in a section about responsibility and initiative. Objectives in the attitudes and values area were expanded to include identifying and analyzing personal attitudes toward work, evaluating the consequences of these attitudes, and encouraging and assisting others to develop their competencies. The area on personal fulfillment was also expanded to include objectives on the need for personal satisfaction, the establishment of goals that contribute to self-fulfillment, and the acceptance of the diversity of career goals and life styles of others.

ISSUES RELATED TO THE MEASUREMENT OF COD OBJECTIVES

Based on National Assessment's experience with the development of assessment objectives and instruments and the reporting of assessment results, we have identified the following major issues to be considered in planning an assessment in the career area. For each issue there are suggested approaches which, in some cases, need to be further researched.

Citizen Input and the Development of Objectives

Objectives development is often the work of a small number of contributors who have reputations as educational specialists in a particular area. While this approach to objectives development may be appropriate for some kinds of test development, the National Assessment calls for the involvement of many participants outside the field of education: people from business, industry, or social services; legislators; parents and students. This public consensus approach helps to guarantee an assessment that reflects the pluralistic education system in this country; it also helps to assure a broad audience for assessment results. One possible method of obtaining such participation is to have major community organizations nominate individuals to be involved in the development. Another possible method is to obtain a random sample of individuals from the geographic areas covered by the assessment and survey the opinions of this sample regarding the objectives. Whatever method is applied, participants with a variety of life experiences and viewpoints should be involved in the process of objectives development.

The Specificity of Objectives

The objectives can be so broadly stated that the developers of the instruments have great difficulty in determining the precise skills or attitudes that are to be measured. On the other hand, the objectives can be written in such great detail that the document is cumbersome and difficult to use. The National Assessment COD objectives published in 1977 contain major objectives, sub-objectives, and numerous detailed illustrations of the objectives. This level of specificity is necessary for the curriculum or test developer; however, the average lay person might find the document too detailed for general reading. A more useful approach might be to publish both a document containing statements of major objectives and subobjectives for the general public that would provide an overall picture of career development and a more technical document for educators, providing detailed illustrations of objectives and information regarding assessment techniques. The general document, for example, might indicate the importance of using appropriate procedures in seeking employment and provide examples of various techniques, such as obtaining a personal interview. The technical document would go into detail about how these techniques can be assessed.

The Coverage of Content

National Assessment is responsible for measuring achievement on tasks ranging from those that everyone is expected to perform to those that only the most capable can accomplish. Consequently, the assessment is much broader in content coverage than the typical test, which concentrates on skills of medium difficulty that reliably distinguish ability levels.

The COD objectives include more content than any of the other assessment areas. The knowledge, abilities, and attitudes important for career development include those specific to the career area as well as many found in other subject areas. Since COD is not well defined, there is a tendency to include every skill that contributes to a person's ability to function in society. The task of adequately measuring career and occupational development within the limited assessment time is a very difficult problem.

One approach to this problem of coverage is to focus development on only the most critical COD objectives. While this appears to be a simple solution, the task of identifying which objectives are the most critical can be difficult. There may not be agreement even among specialists in the area as to which are the most critical objectives. Some might favor an emphasis on job-specific skills, while others would be far more concerned about skills that are transferable from one career to another. For example, some specialists would like the assessment to emphasize the evaluation of specific skills such as filing and typing. However, others feel that it would be more valuable for the assessment to survey some general communication skills such as the ability of young people to listen to, understand, and give spoken and visual instructions. In addition, since National

Assessment's primary function is to measure change over time, it is impossible to guarantee that objectives identified as being critical at present will still be critical ten or twenty years from now.

The assessment staff has also considered the possibility that some of the COD objective areas, particularly generally useful skills, can be adequately measured in other assessment areas such as mathematics, reading, citizenship, social studies, writing, or science. However, an examination of these areas indicates that the specialists have given very little attention to the practical, career-related aspects of their areas. If this approach is going to be viable, then specialists in these other areas have to become more aware of the COD objectives and how these objectives relate to other subject areas.

Generalized Skills versus
Job-Specific Skills

Career development evaluators have tended to focus on those skills common to broad families or clusters of careers to cut their jobs down to manageable proportions. However, the assessment has had strong pressure from the general public to report on the question, are the schools preparing our children to hold some specific job when they graduate?

To answer that question, in the early 1970s NAEP developed performance measures for seven common entry-level jobs: typist, waiter/waitress, service station attendant, salesperson, carpenter, farm tractor operator, and stenographer. However, the need to screen out students from the national sample who had training or at least some interest in one of these seven common entry-level jobs and the expense of actually administering the performance exercises to individual students increased the cost substantially beyond the assessment's budget. In addition, during the time required to determine if a job-skills assessment was feasible, the importance of some of the skills originally identified had changed. For example, in many areas of the country self-service gas stations were installed, reducing the demand for service station attendants. And the growth of prefabricated construction created a need to revise some of the emphasis in the assessment of carpentry skills.

It appears that the approaches utilized in a nationwide survey such as National Assessment are more appropriate for the measurement of generalized skills. The measurement of job-specific skills is probably better handled by specially designed studies able to target specific populations.

The Development of Instruments
to Measure Process Objectives

The 1977 objectives call for the measurement of career decision-making, problem-solving, and information-processing skills. These skills are particularly difficult to measure because they often involve sequential steps over extended periods of time.

National Assessment did include some process measures in the first assessment. These exercises were primarily concerned with having the students indicate the most efficient ways to solve various problems such as finding a destination on a map or putting together a puzzle. There were no exercises that dealt with the process of making a career decision. Since the respondents were required to solve the problems within limited administration time, the problems had to be narrow in scope, leaving some doubts as to whether the results really could be used in determining the general decision-making ability of students. For other tasks, the respondents recorded the process they used in solving a problem. In these exercises it was sometimes difficult, especially for students who had poor verbal skills, for scorers to determine what steps the respondent had taken in attacking the problem. A third type of presentation involved having the respondent select the best solution from a series of possible solutions. While this simplified the scoring process, it automatically eliminated the possibility of a student coming up with a unique or particularly innovative solution. However, even though the process exercises were not ideal, they did allow the assessment to measure skills not tapped by more conventional methods.

The Development of Instruments
to Measure Affective Objectives

Several COD objectives call for respondents to report on their activities in career preparation and implementation and their attitudes toward various work experiences.

Since many self-report and attitudinal instruments are administered in a school setting, the issue of invasion of privacy is an important consideration. National Assessment has approached this concern by insuring the anonymity of the respondents. The students are randomly selected and their names are never recorded on any materials leaving the school.

Self-report and attitude items present some interpretation problems. Although some research indicates that students tend to be generally honest on self-report items, the nagging doubt persists that results might be affected by differences in accuracy or in perceptions. Consider the results for the following item:

> Seventeen-year-olds were also asked if they had ever taken an aptitude test (of the type that measures mechanical, clerical, etc. abilities). Only 40 percent of the 17-year-olds stated that they had done so, and only 16 percent said that they had discussed the results with someone who could advise them about their career plans [NAEP, 1976, p. 6].

These results leave one wondering whether the respondents remember very accurately, given the national emphasis on testing. It is possible to verify the accuracy of the results of self-reports by observing the behavior of respondents or by verifying the self-reports with parents, teachers, counselors, and employers who are familiar with the respondent's career experiences. However, in the case of National Assessment, this process of observing actual behavior or collecting supporting data is practically impossible since the sample in the assessment is randomly drawn and the names of the respondents are unrecorded. In addition, the assessment does not have the funds available for this type of follow-up research.

The Development of Instruments
to Measure Performance Objectives

Many COD objectives involve specific performances such as completing a job application, filling out an order form, or writing a want ad. The measurement of these skills required a considerable amount of assessment time. In addition, the scoring of performance instruments required the examination of a number of different factors in each response. Though administration of a performance instrument is usually expensive, assessment experience has demonstrated that the expense is often well justified because performance exercises usually hold the greatest interest for the general public.

The results of two rather simple performance items from the first assessment are shown below. The first example is in the mathematics area:

One more sample exercise may shed further light on the "copeability" of our populations in the practical world. Respondents were presented with an exercise requiring the conversion of several units of measurement into other units (e.g., inches to feet, ounces to pounds). The exercise first required the recall of certain unit values and, second, the mathematical process of conversion (multiplication or division).

The exercise as it appeared to the respondents follows:

A. 30 inches   = _____ feet
B. 2 feet   = _____ inches
C. 45 seconds   = _____ minutes
D. 1 minute   = _____ seconds
E. 16 ounces   = _____ pounds
F. 1½ pounds   = _____ ounces

The exercise serves two functions. It can give some indication of people's facility in dealing with daily mathematical demands, either in the home or in the marketplace. It can also reveal proficiency in some basic skills that are required for certain jobs (e.g., clerk, carpenter, warehouse worker).

Over 90 percent of the people in all three groups (13-year-olds, 95 percent; 17-year-olds, 98 percent; adults, 96 percent) correctly answered part D of the item. However, having established the fact that a large number of respondents were familiar with the value of the units involved in the problem (i.e., seconds and minutes), it is significant to note that many of the respondents were not able to work with fractions. Part C asks for a mathematical application of this information, and the success rates fall off sharply (13-year-olds, 41 percent; 17-year-olds, 72 percent; adults, 74 percent).

The same situation holds true for parts A and B and parts E and F. In each case all three ages scored considerably higher in familiarity with the value of the units in question than they did in using this information in a mathematical operation.

Once again, the question does not seem to be how many of the respondents completed the exercise correctly but rather how many did *not*. The types of careers that would require the amount of mathematical proficiency called for in this exercise are not particularly demanding in an academic sense. Most jobs as clerks, check-out cashiers and craft apprentices are entered by persons with a high school diploma or less. What is asked for in these careers is not an academic degree, but a facility with basic skills. Based on this, a significant number of our population could not qualify for these jobs [NAEP, 1977, pp. 9–10].

The second example is in the verbal area:

Below are three ads from the *Help Wanted* section of a newspaper. Read all three ads and choose which job you would like best if you had to apply for one of them.

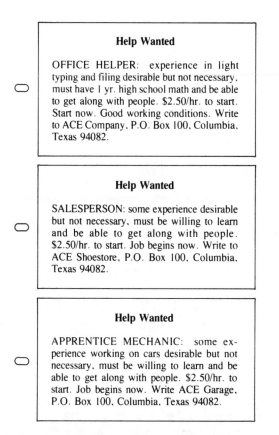

Fill in the oval beside the ONE you choose.
On the next two pages, write a letter applying for the job that you chose. Write the letter as if you were actually trying to get the job. Use the name Dale Roberts.

Several aspects of this item were scored. [The table below] shows percentages of success for each age level on a number of the elements scored.

The table reflects the percentages of respondents who performed two overall operations (first, they thought of the elements to be included in a business letter and, second, they rendered those elements correctly).

Comparing the relative results of the 17-year-olds and adults, it would appear that the older group is more adept in the overall expression of their thoughts in writing: more of them described the job, provided references, requested an interview and gave information about where and how they could be contacted. In these particular "expression" areas, 17-year-old percentages were higher only in the section on job qualifications.

JOB APPLICATION LETTER RESULTS, WRITTEN COMMUNICATION SKILLS, AGES 17 AND ADULT

	17-Year-Olds	Adults
Correct job description	78%	82%
Correct description of qualifications	93	90
Correct provision of references	9	14
Correct approach for interview	16	26
Correct information to make contact by employer possible	36	42
Correct format for return address	20	24
Correct form for date on letter	32	40
Correct format for inside address	33	39
Correct format for greeting	92	88
Correct format for closing	85	82
Signature included in accepted mode	85	85

In the formal areas of the letter there seems to be somewhat of a stand-off between the two age levels: the teenagers did better with the greeting, closing and signature while the adults did better with things such as return address, date and inside address.

A breakdown of the data according to region, sex, race, level of parental education and size and type of community does nothing more than underline the trends that we have seen up to now in these categories: the Southeast region of the country scored consistently below the national average on this type of exercise, females and whites showed more proficiency, respondents from more educationally oriented home environments did better and people from the more affluent neighborhoods showed their usual advantage [NAEP, 1977, pp. 20–21].

The first of these exercises—the math units—could easily have been done in a multiple-choice format. The great advantage of free-response or performance mathematical exercises is to allow us to observe how the students solved the problem—either to identify the process chosen or the errors made. In such a simple conversion problem, no such observation is possible. (Of course, it might well be useful to try this question out in an open-ended format to identify plausible incorrect alternatives to include in the final multiple-choice item.)

The second exercise, however, must be done as a performance item. The actual scoring revealed interesting results; additional scoring could have been designed to touch on the appropriateness of the tone or the grammatical correctness of the responses.

Performance measures often require the completion of sequential tasks. If one of the parts of an instrument is not clear to the respondent, this can interfere with the completion of the other parts. It is essential that the performance tasks be outlined in clear and specific language and that the performance exercise be field tested with a sufficient number of students to assure that the respondents understand the instructions.

Another difficulty is misplaced face validity. Measures involving simulations are often attractive to reviewers, but in the final analysis may not provide any more information than much simpler instruments. In complex exercises such as films or other simulations, the respondent is exposed to a variety of stimuli and may choose to respond to something other than that desired by the designer of the instrument. Again, the solution to this problem is adequate field testing in which samples of the full range of major types of responses are gathered and examined. The field testing should reveal if the performance task requested is not clear or if the criteria for scoring the performance are not adequate.

National Assessment has learned to develop performance exercises only when an objective can be measured in no other way, and only when sufficient time and money are available to develop the exercises adequately and to analyze them fully. Under these conditions, a few well-developed performance exercises can add to the coverage and the interpretability of an assessment. Especially in practical areas such as COD, performance exercises are essential.

Background Information

The results of an assessment are difficult to interpret unless there is information about the environment of the respondents. When the knowledge, skills, and attitudes recorded by the assessment are compared with information about the socioeconomic and educational background of the respondents and the educational practices of their schools, some inferences can be made about conditions that contribute to achievement of various skills and attitudes. This background information can also be used in establishing reporting categories.

National Assessment collects background information from two sources—school principals and the respondents themselves—during the administration of the assessment exercises. The principals' questionnaire provides information on school enrollments, attendance, distribution of students by size and type of community, occupations of parents, numbers of minority students, and types of special funds received by the school. The students answer questions about the education of their parents, their socioeducational status, and changes in their residences. In addition, there are specific questions about curriculum, courses taken, and other experiences related to the area being assessed.

While this information is valuable in reporting assessment results, much specific information about the respondents' home and school life cannot be obtained. In some cases, this is a matter of invasion of privacy, and in other cases the information cannot be obtained without extensive interviews and observations.

Communicating Assessment Results

The results of an assessment will have little impact unless there is communication between assessors and people interested in the assessment results. National Assessment has given a great deal of thought to the problems of communicating assessment results and has found the following approaches valuable:

1. Identification of potential audiences for assessment results very early in the assessment process and involvement of these potential users in the planning, analysis, and reporting of research.
2. Publication of reports that emphasize key findings and important trends and that are written in language appropriate for target audiences.
3. Maintenance of regular contact with and provision of summaries of findings to the media.
4. Supplying of up-to-date information to key decision makers through seminars, telephone contact, individual meetings, and attendance at hearings.

SUMMARY

National Assessment has nearly fifteen years of experience in developing measures of career and occupational development. The second set of objectives maintained the structure of the first but contained major additions in the area of career decisions. The major measurement issues arise from the fact that the skills, knowledge, and attitudes needed in the world of work are numerous and not necessarily academic.

Based on National Assessment's experiences with the development of assessment objectives and instruments and the reporting of assessment results, the following goals appear to require further research:

1. Developing methodology for obtaining greater citizen input into the development of objectives.
2. Developing the kinds of objectives that will facilitate communication between the designators of the objectives and the developers of assessment instruments.

3. Development of instruments that will effectively measure process objectives (for example, career decision-making, problem-solving, and information-processing objectives).
4. Development of instruments that will effectively measure affective objectives (for example, self-awareness, interpersonal relations, attitudes toward work, and personal fulfillment).
5. Development of performance instruments that are clear and specific to respondents and provide responses that can be scored and analyzed.
6. Development of criteria and methodology for determining the validity of instruments.
7. Development of techniques for getting assessment results into the hands of decision makers.
8. Development of techniques for communicating and linking the work of researchers to organizations interested in assessment and evaluation.
9. Development of meaningful background variables (for example, curriculum, work experience, environment) that can be related to cognitive achievement.

REFERENCES

The following is a list of Educational publications about the COD assessment available from the National Assessment of Educational Progress, Education Commission of the States, 1860 Lincoln Street, Suite 700, Denver, Colorado 80295.

Leaflet: Two-page overview of results   N/C

Objectives Booklets
COD, 1971 ED 059119 $ 1.40
COD, 1977 ED 143829   1.90

Kits and Exercise Sets

Basic Life Skills Kit—Six NAEP assessment booklets covering personal finance and consumer protection, health maintenance, interpersonal, family responsibility, and career development skills. Also contains a guide for conducting an assessment using the NAEP exercises. No results included.   17.00

Exercise Sets—Unbound sets of released exercises, documentation, and scoring guides. National results are shown for some learning areas. Sets, which are duplicated and may be reproduced locally, are designed for states and local education agencies interested in reviewing NAEP's released items.

Career and occupational development (1973–74 assessment, results, 472 pages)   21.00

Math resource items for minimal competency testing, a collection of math items for state and local education agencies to draw upon in custom-building their own minimal competency instruments. National results, 1977.   7.40

Reading resource items for minimal competency testing, similar to math above. National results, 1977.   6.80

Consumer Skills Kit consisting of 200 looseleaf pages of exercise items and a 36-page *Guide to assessment of consumer skills*, 1978.   7.80

A 48-page report, *Basic life skills: Results manual* has been produced to go with the BLS kit listed. The manual is $6.15; the total kit is $23.15.

Reports of Results of First Assessment (1973 – 74)

Adult work skills and knowledge: Selected results from the first national assessment of career and occupational development, 1976 (05-COD-01).   3.65

An assessment of career development: Basic work skills, 1976 (05-COD-02).   1.15

The first national assessment of career and occupational development: An overview, 1976 (05-COD-00).   1.60

Career and occupational development technical report: Exercise volume, 1977 (05-COD-20). Released exercises, documentation, scoring guides and national and group results.   25.00

Career and occupational development technical report: Summary volume, 1978 (05-COD-21). Results for selected exercises for 9-, 13-, 17-, and 25 – 36-year-olds about knowledge generally useful in the world of work, knowledge about jobs, self-appraisal skills, work-related experiences, and work-related values.   24.30

Papers

Richard Hulsart, *National assessment's consumer skills assessments,* February 1978, 16 pp.   Free

School and the 17-year-old: A comparison of career development skills of 17-year-olds attending school and those not attending, March, 1978, 38 pp.   1.50

Some possible uses of performance testing in career assessment

CURTIS R. FINCH

Virginia Polytechnical Institute and State University

OVERVIEW

Few can question the need for more meaningful measurement of career education outcomes. Those who have examined the quality and use of career education measures (for example, Thomas, 1977; Shoemaker, 1978; Young and Schuh, 1975) point to numerous shortcomings in this area. Among the more frequently cited problems are lack of appropriate psychometric data, difficulty in administration and scoring, stereotyping, and the difficulty of measuring certain career education objectives.

This chapter serves to raise further questions about career education measurement. It is based on the notion that alternate assessment approaches have the potential to solve some of the more persistent problems in career education measurement. More specifically, the discussion that follows centers on performance testing and the role it may play in assessing career education outcomes. Initially, some basic concerns are presented and the nature of performance testing is discussed. Then follows a brief look at the utility of performance testing in career education. Finally, several recommendations are presented that, it is hoped, will set the stage for future research efforts in this area.

It is appropriate to begin with a definition of the concept. *Performance testing* (also referred to as *applied performance testing*) is "the measurement of performance of some task significant to a student's life outside the school and/or in adult life. Such a task is valued as output for public schools. The testing device must allow for measurement of the task in an actual or simulated performance setting" (Sumida, 1975).

BASIC CONCERNS

When one begins to examine the expansive area of career education assessment, numerous questions come to mind about the various prerequisites to meaningful measurement. At the risk of avoiding certain testing issues, I considered it best to identify certain basic concerns about the area. These include the theory-versus-practice debate, career education objectives, and the fiscal and moral commitment to test development.

Two groups have mutual concern about career development and career education: career development researchers and career educators. The career development researcher seeks to identify a fundamental body of knowledge about the field and carries on this search by developing and utilizing theory-based instruments. This individual's focus is primarily on studying and identifying career development constructs while the applied assessment of career education outcomes in the schools takes a secondary position. The practicing career educator, on the other hand, has as his or her primary concern the determination of how career education programs affect students. While career development constructs are important to the educator, they must always be considered in light of student outcomes. Though rather subtle, we must recognize this difference in emphasis when developing instruments, asking questions about the ultimate purpose of the instrument. Will the instrument, for example, assess a basic concept such as career maturity or deal more directly with the application of career education instruction? While researchers may often develop theory-based instruments that are ultimately used in applied learning settings, few applied measures have been related back to theory. This idea perhaps points to the need for identifying early on what the instrument's purpose is and where it will ultimately be used.

While a whole host of goals and objectives are available for use in establishing career education programs (for example, Center for Vocational Education, 1972; Partners in Career Education, 1976; Bailey and Stadt, 1973), most appear to be "a mixed bag of short range knowledge and skill acquisition objectives, affective objectives, and objectives related to the facilitation of developmental psychological processes" (Asche and Finch, 1978). If student performance is to be measured, we must demand that more tangible, applied career education objectives be identified. Examples of such objectives might be "describe worker qualifications for specific jobs that are related to a particular career choice" or "apply decision-making steps to solve a personal problem and make a career choice." These objectives would most logically be stated in behavioral terms so that their attainment could be assessed in a reasonable manner. We must keep in mind, however, that behavioral objectives are not necessarily applied. Stating an objective in behavioral terms merely means that it is more easily measured, not that it has greater relevance.

A third concern focuses on the basic commitment to performance testing. Anyone who chooses to develop and use performance tests must recognize that assessing performance can require more time and resources than those needed for traditional testing approaches. Performance testing may not always allow for pencil-and-paper formats that can be administered to groups. The administrator could be required to test students in applied settings on a one to one basis. Such a requirement, in itself, would mean a higher administrative cost for performance testing, though, indeed, higher costs could result in greater benefits. The fact that student performance would be assessed more realistically and completely than with conventional tests should serve to justify a basic commitment to the concept of performance testing.

THE NATURE OF
PERFORMANCE TESTING

While performance testing has been with us for some time, the systematic measurement of performance seems to be at least partially based upon the early work of military training researchers. During the 1950s and 1960s, the military made a concerted effort to establish meaningful performance-testing standards and procedures, particularly as they might relate to technical training settings (for example, Wilson, 1962). More recently, the performance-objectives movement and an increased concern about accountability have heightened public educators' awareness of the need for applied performance tests. Agencies that have been most responsive to this need include the Clearinghouse for Applied Performance Testing (CAPT), the Vocational and Technical Education Consortium of States (VTECS), and other, similar groups. CAPT has perhaps been a major catalyst in the performance-testing movement. Located at the Northwest Regional Educational Laboratory in Portland, CAPT has as its mission the gathering and dissemination of performance-assessment information. As the name implies, CAPT serves as a clearinghouse for testing and tests. CAPT maintains a comprehensive library on performance testing and tests, develops bibliographies in the area, and conducts research in the field. VTECS has employed the consortium approach in an effort to meet the increased demand for performance measures in vocational and technical education. Sixteen states have joined the consortium, their purpose being to develop applied performance objectives and criterion-referenced measures in a variety of occupational areas. Materials developed by each member state are distributed to all other states for use by local teachers.

Major projects such as the National Assessment of Educational Progress (NAEP) have attempted to deal with applied performance in a more global fashion (Ahmann, 1977). NAEP surveys the attainments of 9-, 13-, and 17-year-olds and young adults in ten learning areas including career and occupational development. Assessment for the area of career and occupational development has been based upon educational objectives that young Americans should be achieving in the course of their education. Exercises in the form of test items were developed for each age group based upon subdivisions of objectives. This assessment effort is one of the first large-scale attempts to measure career development outcomes of a more applied nature.

Essentially, applied performance testing deals with "the measurement of performance in an actual or simulated performance setting" (Sachse, 1975). Central to this measurement concept is the requirement that an examinee must actually demonstrate that he or she can perform the required task or activity. As noted by Sachse, examples of tasks would be "fill out an application for a job" or "make a budget." Not included would be such vague objectives as "awareness and knowledge of careers and occupations." It would seem that performance testing represents a radical departure from conventional assessment of career education outcomes. Its focus on the ability to *do* rather than just *know* tends to create problems with those who are used to developing and administering conventional instruments.

The characteristics of applied performance tests are quite different from conventional tests. As so aptly described by McKeegan (1975), they include

1. Systematic Measurement
     of
2. Observable Behaviors
     defined in terms of
3. Either Process or Product or Both
     in
4. Real or Simulated Environments
     where
5. Previously Learned Concepts and Skills
     can be Applied in Problem Situations

Systematic measurement basically means that the test design should follow sound measurement principles and practices. Thus, appropriate information regarding test administration and scoring must be documented. Documentation might include the checklists, equipment, supplies, and settings associated with the particular test. Likewise, the measurement of *observable behavior* is important, since performance must not be inferred. While traditional tests typically allow students to consider answers to multiple-choice test items, the performance test relies on demonstration of more realistic behavior. If, for example, the student is to show that he or she can balance a checkbook, the examiner might provide a checkbook, bank statement, deposit slips, and cancelled checks. Observations might include procedures followed, sequence of procedures, and accuracy of calculations.

Behavior may be observed as a *process,* a *product,* or a combination of the two. In the above example, final calculations and balances might constitute the product, whereas sequence of procedures would deal with process. Ultimately, the developer considers which is most important for a given test and constructs observation schemes that account for the relevant behaviors.

Performance tests are carried out in *real or simulated environments.* To do otherwise would leave some doubt about the student's true proficiency. If possible, a real-world setting is used. An alternate choice would be to simulate key elements of the real environment to make the test as realistic as possible. In the case of a test dealing with interviewing for employment, it would probably not be possible to use a real employer. However, the interview could take place in an actual office and be conducted by an experienced personnel officer. These factors would contribute to the test's realism and insure that performance is being measured.

Finally, the performance test deals with *application* in problem situations. Fundamental concepts and skills such as reading, writing, and computation are important only to the extent that they are applied in realistic settings. While basic concepts and skills are extremely important in their own right, the performance test seeks to assess how well concepts and skills are used in applied settings. In determining alternate arrangements for financing a purchase, mathematics decision-making skills are essential. However, the individual with proficiency in these basic skills may not necessarily be able to carry out the process of financing a purchase.

While a detailed discussion of procedures for developing performance tests is beyond the scope of this paper, the reader should note that documents have been written that speak to a number of development as well as management issues and concerns (for example, Finch and Impellitteri, 1971; Sumida, 1975; Osborn, 1977; Perloff, 1980). As a means of further illustrating the nature of performance testing, it may prove useful to briefly describe a test that could be applied in career education settings. Such a test, titled "Complete an Employment Application," focuses on one's ability to fill out accurately various parts of a typical job-application form. The test utilizes an actual form that is similar to those used in many businesses and industries. Each examinee is given a set of directions that he or she would typically receive from an employer and completes the form under controlled conditions. Each person is asked to play the role of a fictitious job applicant and is provided with a vita from which to draw relevant information. In this case, the product (a completed form) is evaluated with attention given to areas such as accuracy and legibility of written information, relevance of information selected for inclusion, and presentation of the applicant's statement (a part of the form). Time is important only insofar as the examinee is allowed a maximum time to complete the form. This test is quite simple to administer, but scoring is time-consuming, since the scorer must consider a number of written statements. While test results reflect a range of performance for each factor, the examinee is merely provided with a hire/no-hire result. Detailed discussion about performance provided on an individual basis can aid persons in improving their skills, since the completed form serves as an example of work. Where future performance testing is required, this may be accomplished by means of different but parallel application forms and vitas.

Thus, we can state that performance testing *can* assist in the realistic assessment of career education outcomes. While traditional testing processes have much value, they tend to be more basic and abstract. Since career education outcomes do include performance in applied settings, performance tests have the potential not only to assess these outcomes but also to assess them perhaps more accurately than conventional instruments.

THE UTILITY OF
PERFORMANCE TESTING

In considering performance testing as a means of assessing career education outcomes, it is perhaps best that we examine some inherent strengths and limitations. The following comments concerning the utility of performance testing merely represent a starting point for further discussion. In preparing this section, I have considered my own successes and failures in developing tests and conducting performance testing in educational settings.

When examining a measuring instrument, one tends to first look at its psychometric properties. As with any other type of instrument, the performance test should clearly reflect adequate validity and reliability. The basic question, however, is how to define *adequate*. Fortunately, performance testing in vocational and technical education, since it has been extensive in these areas, can aid in determining adequacy. Numerous authors have spoken to the rather unique character of performance testing and can provide us with ways of establishing test validity and reliability. For example, as far back as 1954, DuBois and others explored the applicability of four methods of assessing performance-test validity. These include validity by direct judgment, work-sample validity, class validity, and curricular validity.

Validity by direct judgment refers to the degree to which a panel of experts agree as to whether the test will discriminate between the skilled and the unskilled levels. Of course, this method is sometimes cumbersome to use since qualifications of experts are difficult to define, and once standards have been established, few experts may be readily available.

Work-sample validity focuses on the degree to which performance on the sample is predictive of actual work performance. This approach is typically used when a written examination must be given in lieu of a performance test because of high administration costs or difficulty in administration (for example, when medical diagnosis in emergency situations is being tested). This factor is perhaps not as appropriate in the career education area.

Class validity concerns the differentiation between two classes or groups of persons based upon work performance. A performance test would be considered valid in this regard if it differentiated between more proficient and less proficient groups. Obviously, some problems could arise in identifying groups that vary in performance but are equivalent in other areas.

A fourth method, *curricular validity*, appears to be similar to class validity except that the two groups being differentiated are composed of those untrained and those trained in a particular area. When dealing with this method, one makes the assumption that training does effect an increase in performance.

Instrument development represents a great challenge to anyone in the measurement field. Glaser and Klaus (1962) point to several sources of measurement error that are directly related to performance development and administration. These include environmental influences, situational influences, test instrumentation, sampling, behavior complexity, and examinee reactive effects. All these sources of measurement error can be controlled to a certain degree if appropriate effort is put forth during the test development and administration process. Given that students can tolerate only so much variability in the testing environment, there is a point at which certain conditions (for example, weather, distractions) may have adverse effects on test reliability. Thus, it is important that the examiner have adequate control over the environment to the extent that student performance will not be hindered. Situational influences such as instability in equipment, systems, or materials may also contribute to the unreliability of a test. The examiner must make every effort to maintain consistency in this area as well.

Test instrumentation, a third source of measurement error, must be considered as the test is being developed. Thus, the developer must review all parts of the test, including examinee and examiner instructions, checklists, and arrangements for arriving at scores, in terms of their objectivity. Lack of objectivity may result in unsystematic variabilities in scores given by different examiners while incomplete student instructions may affect the student's score in a similar manner.

A fourth source of measurement error is the sampling process by which specific tasks or items are selected for inclusion in the test. It is important to sample a wide enough range of behavior so that potential variability is maximized. Generous sampling, however, must be balanced against test length, since some performance tests take a great deal of time to administer.

The complexity of the behavior being measured constitutes another factor. The test developer should exercise care to insure that items on the test are reasonably homogeneous and thus contribute to a common score. If a test deals with performance criteria such as speed, sequence, and accuracy, then the developer must be sure that each criterion contributes to a common score. Otherwise, criteria would have to be considered as scores for separate performance tests.

A final factor consists of the reactive effects that an examinee might have to the testing situation. Lack of motivation, illness, fatigue, and the pressure associated with being tested may all contribute to low performance from a student who might otherwise be able to perform satisfactorily. Therefore, it is imperative that the student be prepared physically and emotionally for a performance test.

Unlike most conventional tests, the administration procedures for performance tests are typically quite elaborate (Finch, 1980). While these procedures are certainly necessary in order to insure reliability, they place certain limitations on the test administrator. Classroom pencil-and-paper tests are relatively easy to schedule: Students are brought into a classroom, situated at different desks, and given tests to complete. In performance testing, however, students are typically tested individually or in small groups in applied settings. These requirements often place a heavy burden on the examiner, since arranging acceptable test schedules and supervision may be difficult.

While conventional tests tend to focus on a particular type of objective (cognitive, affective, psychomotor) as Shoemaker described in chapter 6, applied performance tests typically combine—rather subtly—several types of objectives. In fact, if we adhered to using separate types of objectives for individual performance tests the result might be, as Popham (1975) so aptly put it, domain poisoning. If, for example, we were developing a test to measure a person's job-interview skills, it would be most difficult (if not impossible) to separate out the various cognitive, affective, and psychomotor components. In this case, knowledge about jobs, hiring practices, and interview procedures would combine with one's basic attitudes and values toward work to produce some overall behavior during the interview process. This is not to say that we completely ignore what Bloom (1956) and others have told us about objectives. Rather, it means we must merely recognize that real-world performance reflects a blending of elements, often so subtle a blending that a test consists of a global experience rather than merely a consolidation of statements from different areas.

SOME RESEARCH RECOMMENDATIONS

While it is clear that numerous research ideas will emerge as career education receives further scrutiny, we can address several questions immediately. These questions, which follow, apply to testing within the context of measuring career education outcomes.

1. Can performance outcomes actually be specified for all career education areas?

2. To what extent can performance testing be utilized in the measurement of career awareness, knowledge, and exploration?
3. Do the benefits of performance testing outweigh its apparently high administration costs?
4. To what extent might the administration costs of performance test be reduced?
5. How well do local education-agency personnel (particularly teachers) accept the notion of career education performance testing?
6. How will students react to performance testing in relation to the content of career education and learning experiences?

Implicit in these questions is the idea that exploratory ventures to develop and try out career education performance tests may give us a clearer picture of this alternate assessment approach. It is apparent that performance testing has the potential to serve as a useful means of assessing career preparation outcomes. Now is perhaps the best time to realize this potential.

REFERENCES

AHMANN, J. S.   Assessing the job knowledge and generally useful skills of young Americans. *Journal of Vocational Education Research*, 1977, *2* (2), 1–15.

ASCHE, F. M., and FINCH, C. R.   Designs for evaluating career education programs: Status and prospects. Paper presented at the American Educational Research Association Annual Meeting, Toronto, March, 1978.

BAILEY, L. J., and STADT, R.   *Career Education, new approaches to human development*. Bloomington, Illinois: McKnight, 1973.

BLOOM, B. S. (Ed.).   *Taxonomy of educational objectives, handbook I: Cognitive domain*. New York: David McKay, 1956.

CENTER FOR VOCATIONAL EDUCATION.   *Developmental goals for the comprehensive career education model*. Columbus, Ohio: Ohio State University, 1972.

DuBOIS, P., TEEL, K. S., and PETERSON, R. L.   On the validity of performance tests. *Educational and Psychlogical Measurement*, 1954, *14*, 605–616.

FINCH, C. R.   Considerations in the implementation of performance testing. In J. E. SPIRER (Ed.), *Performance testing: Issues facing vocational education*. Columbus, Ohio: National Center for Research in Vocational Education, 1980, pp. 139–148.

FINCH, C. R., and IMPELLITTERI, J. T.   The development of valid work performance measures. *Journal of Industrial Teacher Education*, 1971, *9* (1), 36–49.

GLASER, R., and KLAUS, D. J.   Proficiency measurement: Assessing human performance. In R. GAGNE (Ed.), *Psychological principles of system development*. New York: Holt, Rinehart and Winston, 1962, pp. 419–474.

McKEEGAN, H. F.   Essential characteristics of applied performance testing. *CAPT Newsletter*, 1975, *2* (1), 3–5.

OSBORN, W. C.   *Essential dimensions of performance testing*. Alexandria, Va: Human Resources Research Organization, 1977 (ERIC Document Reproduction Service No. ED 137 372).

PARTNERS IN CAREER EDUCATION.   *Matrix of basic learner outcomes for career education*. Arlington, Texas: Partners in Career Education, 1976.

PERLOFF, E.   Technical considerations: Validity, reliability, efficiency, and observer/rater reliability. In J. E. Spirer (Ed.), *Performance testing: Issues facing vocational education.* Columbus, Ohio: National Center for Research in Vocational Education, 1980, pp. 53–66.

POPHAM, W. J.   *Educational evaluation.* Englewood Cliffs, N.J.: Prentice-Hall, 1975, p. 61.

SACHSE, T. P.   What is applied performance testing? *CAPT Newsletter,* 1975, *1* (5), 3–5.

SHOEMAKER, J. S.   Measuring career education outcomes: A federal perspective. Paper presented at the American Educational Research Association Annual Meeting, Toronto, March, 1978.

SUMIDA, J. (Ed.).   *Guidelines for evaluation of applied performance test materials and procedures.* Portland, Ore.: Clearinghouse for Applied Performance Testing, 1975.

THOMAS, H. B.   Use of instrumentation in career education. Paper presented at the American Educational Research Association Annual Meeting, New York City, March, 1977.

WILSON, C. L.   On-the-job and operational criteria. In R. Glaser (Ed.), *Training research and education.* Pittsburgh: University of Pittsburgh Press, 1962, pp. 347–377.

YOUNG, M. B., and SCHUH, R. G.   *Evaluation and educational decision-making: A functional guide to evaluating career education.* Washington, D.C.: Development Associates, 1975.

9

Measuring the quality of career decisions

JOHN D. KRUMBOLTZ
Stanford University
DANIEL A. HAMEL
Harvard University
and DALE S. SCHERBA
California State University,
Dominguez Hills

We frequently hear people making evaluations of the quality of their own or others' decisions—for example, "My decision to buy Xerox stock in 1954 was the best decision I ever made" or "I made a terrible decision when I accepted the position with the XYZ Company." It is clear that decisions are evaluated, but on what basis are these evaluations made? There appear to be two primary methods, process and outcome evaluation.

EVALUATION METHODS

Process Evaluation
One way of evaluating a decision is to determine whether "proper" procedures were followed in order to reach that decision. Many legislative, executive, and judicial decisions are evaluated on the basis of whether all the appropriate procedures for making those decisions were followed. But what *are* the procedures that should be followed? In legal cases, precedents have been

159

established and codified specifying the appropriate procedures. In career decision-making, various self-appointed authorities have prescribed procedures for making decisions. Some procedures have been adapted from the scientific method; others are based on procedures used by "successful" people. Thus, one may ask whether the particular set of procedures being advocated is really the best set of procedures. Could a better decision have been made if some alternative set of procedures had been used? To answer such a question, we need some criteria against which to evaluate the competing sets of procedures. The best decision-making procedures would yield decisions that met what criteria? ease of use? low cost? popularity of outcome? decider's satisfaction with outcome?

People make decisions because they desire certain outcomes and must take action to achieve them. A decision involves a choice of a certain course of action to the exclusion of certain other courses of action. But in the case of career decisions, the deciders may not know what they want from their decisions. Some high school students might decide that they want the prestige, money, and security that go with being a physician without realizing that doctors must also listen to peoples' complaints and deal with stressful situations. Only after they enter medical school might they discover that they actually prefer less stress, fewer complaints, and less money and prestige. So values can change as a result of experience. But the basic question still remains: How can one best achieve one's values—new or old?

Outcome Evaluation

When we compare sets of procedures for decision making, we are actually using the second method of evaluating the quality of decisions— outcome evaluation.

Any decision can be judged on the basis of outcomes attributed to it. However, a number of questions arise when we attempt to evaluate decisions on the basis of their consequences:

1. Is the consequence attributed to a decision really the result of that decision or of some other decision, event, or circumstance?
2. What criteria are to be used in evaluating the decision? Every decision has multiple outcomes, only some of which may be favorable.
3. Who is to evaluate the quality of the decision? A decision may yield favorable consequences for some people and unfavorable consequences for other people. The desirability of a decision is thus a function of the person making the judgment.
4. When is the decision to be evaluated? Outcomes of a particular decision may be favorable at Time 1, become unfavorable at Time 2, and turn out favorable at Time 3.

In career decision making (CDM), some possible outcome measures would include the following:

1. Self-rated happiness with the decision
2. Other-rated estimates of success
3. Judgments of the extent to which one has achieved one's maximum potential
4. The extent to which one has achieved one's own values
5. The extent to which one may have achieved the values unknown at the time the decision was made but learned subsequently

In the procedures to be described, we have opted for the fourth alternative—a *values-congruence definition* of quality. We acknowledge that achieving one's own values is only one possible way to evaluate a decision. We have chosen it because of our own counseling orientation and a personal commitment to help people achieve the kind of lives that they desire for themselves.

The instrument we have developed enables us to measure the quality of a person's simulated career decision when the following assumptions hold true:

1. Each decider determines which values are important to achieve. It is not necessary for any two deciders to agree on the values they want.
2. Attainment of the values is attributable to the decision.
3. The decision can be evaluated objectively by the extent to which the decision achieves the values specified by the decider.
4. The values of the decider are determined in advance of the decision. They could also be ascertained subsequent to the decision. A judgment about the quality of a decision could be different depending upon the set of values against which it is judged.

In summary, a good decision was defined as one yielding consequences consistent with the values of the decider. The problem then became one of designing an instrument to measure the extent to which persons could make decisions consistent with their own values.

THE SIMULATION OF DECISION MAKING

The process of making occupational choices has been described by some authors as assuming different occupational persona to explore various alternatives. In this process, people imagine themselves in a number of occupations while evaluating the consequences they believe may follow from each (Kaldor and Zytowski, 1969). If this picture of career decision making is accurate, then simulation may be an appropriate assessment device. Simulation requires that the deciders take on roles, imagine themselves in different situations, act out how they might respond, and experience how they might feel in those situations.

Simulations have been shown to be good devices to measure complex human behavior in that they require the person performing them actually to demonstrate the behavior being assessed. There is some evidence that interviews and paper-and-pencil tests do not accurately tap decision-making skills

(Tallman and Wilson, 1974). These more conventional assessments test cognitive rather than behavioral indicants of the skill. By building several variables into the simulation task, a designer can allow for the assessment of actual decision making under lifelike conditions: time pressure, lack of information, uncertainty, and conflicting values (Boardman and Mitchell, 1977).

Our goal was to create an analog device that would capture as many of the complex dimensions of CDM as possible and also yield objective measures of CDM efficacy.

We determined that a simulation device was needed that would meet the following specifications:

1. Provide an objective, standardized procedure for assigning a numerical value to the outcome of a subject's job decision—that is, a "degree of goodness" score
2. Represent real-life CDM as closely as possible—that is, have high face validity
3. Deal with a variety of personal work-value dimensions
4. Provide a recording system for tracking a person's decision-making behavior —that is, both record and preserve the cumulative sequential information on how the simulation was used
5. Be noncompetitive and compatible with independent use—that is, require only one subject's participation at a time
6. Be possible to complete with a reasonable amount of effort within a two-hour time limit
7. Be self-contained
8. Be stimulating, easily understood, and unbiased with regard to age, race or sex.

Although both the Life Career Game (Boocock, 1967) and SOC (Katz, 1976) contained features attractive for this research project, neither simulation adequately met all the above specifications. Thus, it became necessary to design and construct an appropriate device.

THE DEVELOPMENT OF THE CAREER
DECISION SIMULATION (CDS)

The basic rationale of the CDS is that good decision makers interpret information accurately and are able to make decisions that yield consequences consistent with their own values. Subjects were allowed up to two hours to pick one of twelve fictitious occupations that most nearly satisfied their values. Some 333 separate bits of information organized into ten different information sources were available on cards or audio tapes. The information was so designed that for each of 1680 possible value preference configurations generated by a forced values-rating task, the "goodness" rank order of the simulation's twelve fictitious occupations could be quickly determined.

Subjects could adopt any particular type of decision style and still be able to make a good choice. They could impulsively or fatalistically choose their preferred occupation immediately without surveying any of the occupational information, or they could spend up to two hours searching and thinking.

The *values-congruence score* was based on the "degree of fit" between the actual values inherent in a subject's chosen occupation and that subject's own work-value ratings. As already mentioned, the rationale here was that good decision makers choose alternatives consistent with their expressed value preferences. The scoring system was also based on the assumption that it is most important to match high values, somewhat less important to match medium values, and least crucial to match lowest rated values. A scoring system was devised for translating the "degree of fit" between the work values of an occupation and a subject's value preferences. This scoring system produces raw scores that are then transformed into standard scores to indicate the degree to which subjects chose the occupations most similar to their value preferences (70 = best possible choice; 30 = worst possible choice).

The self-rated confidence score represented how confident subjects were that their chosen occupation represented the best one for them among the twelve available. They rated their confidence on a $0-10$ scale (10 = very confident) immediately after choosing an occupation.

To use the simulation, players began by reading a card labeled "Start Here," which acquainted them with their purpose and directed them to listen to further orientation and instructions on the Directions tape. The "Start Here" card contained this information:

START HERE

You are about to make a major career decision—but only as part of a simulation exercise. You will find the process both educational and fun.

You are to pretend that you want to decide on your life's work, or at least the job you want to try next. Try to approach this task in the way you would really decide on a career.

This simulation exercise is self-explanatory. Your next step is to find the cassette tape labeled "Directions" above Tape 1 in the Casette Tape Holder. Insert this tape in the tape player, push the "Play" button and follow the directions you will hear.

The Directions tape elaborated further on the purpose of the CDS and provided an overview of the components of the device and how they were to be used. In addition to explaining the mechanics of using the CDS, the tape provided all subjects with a uniform orientation.

Subjects were asked to specify their own work values, rating the nine given values (Katz, 1976) as either high, medium, or low. Value ratings were recorded on the Personal Work Values Rating Form, a wooden strip with indentations next to the nine labeled work values used in the CDS. Subjects were provided with color-coded, wooden pegs labeled *H* for high (blue), *M* for medium (red), and *L* for low (yellow), which were placed into the indentations.

An added restriction on this task was that subjects were to rate three of the values high, three medium, and three low.

Subjects were acquainted with procedures for using the following nine informational resources:

1. Book or Magazine: A wide variety of books and magazines
2. Career Handbook: Occupational dictionaries and career guidebooks
3. Career Speaker: Speeches given at local "career night" presentation or classroom
4. A Friend: Conversation with friends
5. Horoscope: Horoscopes written for the examinee's astrological sign on the day of the simulation
6. Newspaper Ad: Classified advertisements or want ads from a daily newspaper
7. Personal Experience: Personal experiences with jobs and careers
8. Radio or TV: A variety of radio or television programs and commercials
9. Worker Interviews: Interviews with persons actually working on various jobs

Subjects were also told that the information contained in these sources was organized by occupations and a set of work values. These work values are almost identical to those used by Katz (1973) in his work on SIGI, and are listed below:

> Early Entry
> Helping Others
> Income
> Independence
> Leadership
> Leisure
> Prestige
> Security
> Variety

The Directions tape went on to point out that a set of Value Definition cards was available to players who wished to clarify the meaning of any of the CDS's nine personal work values. Both sides of one Value Definition card are reproduced in Figure 9-1.

The subjects were repeatedly informed that the object of the CDS was to pick one of the available occupations that would give them most of the things they really want in a job.

To record the subject's actions, we required subjects to place each card they read into the Card Return Box. Thus, for each CDS participant, data on the amount, particular kind(s), and sequence of information used in making a simulated career decision were available for subsequent analysis.

Subjects terminated performance on the CDS whenever they wished,

FIGURE 9-1.
**THE FRONT AND BACK OF A VALUE
DEFINITION CARD**

```
What does the value of "Independence" mean?




328                                    234000
```

```
Independence is the extent to which you make your

own decisions and work without supervision or

directions from others.

If your occupation offers high independence, you

would be your own boss.

Low independence would mean working under close

supervision carrying out the decisions of others.
```

up to the two-hour time limit. They ended the actual performance by writing the name of the selected occupation on the Job Decision Card, and, as with all other cards, placing this card in the Card Return Box.

Information about the fictitious occupations was organized within each of the nine sources described earlier. Each source contained information about three different values for all twelve occupations. Thus, a subject had a total of 324 separate pieces of occupational information from which to choose, or thirty-six pieces per information resource. For six of these sources (Book or Magazine, Career Handbook, A Friend, Horoscope, Newspaper Ad, and Personal Experience) the information was written on 3″ × 5″ index cards. The cards were contained in separate boxes for each source, indexed alphabetically by job, and indexed alphabetically within each job by the three different values represented there. Both sides of two representative cards are reproduced in Figures 9-2 and 9-3.

FIGURE 9-2.
**THE FRONT AND BACK OF A CARD
SHOWING INFORMATION FROM THE
SOURCE LABELED "A FRIEND"**

```
 A Friend          Breandist        Independence




 109                                 101344
```

```
"A friend tells you that one of the character-

istics of breandists is that they are able to

run their own affairs, make their own decisions,

and 'sink or swim' based upon the decisions they

make.  He says they are not closely supervised."
```

There were also $3'' \times 5''$ index cards arranged in the same fashion for the three "audio sources:" Career Speaker, Radio or TV, and Worker Interview. However, these cards referred the subject to the appropriate cassette tape containing information for that particular source, occupation, and value. The entire set of cassette tapes was housed in two conveniently labeled, revolving carousel storage units that held 108 job-information tapes (36 per information source) and the Directions tape.

A computer-assisted calculation of the CDS scoring key for values-congruence scores resulted in a computer print-out on ninety-five $8\frac{1}{2}'' \times 11''$ pages. This key provided a handy way for the administrator to determine quickly a subject's values-congruence scores on the CDS. It displayed the 1680 different ways a subject could assign three high, three medium, and three low values from a set of nine different work values and for each of these configurations, it provided a values-congruence score for each of the twelve fictitious occupations.

FIGURE 9-3
**THE FRONT AND BACK OF A CARD
SHOWING INFORMATION FROM THE
SOURCE LABELED "PERSONAL EXPERIENCE"**

```
Personal Experience     Deptician    Leisure




220                                    102367
```

```
"While working at the Big Blue Sky Resort area
last summer, you had a chance to meet and talk
with many of the vacationing guests. You were
struck by the large number of depticians spend-
ing their vacations there. You also learned
that many of these depticians visited the
resort 2 or 3 times a year, and usually for
several weeks at a time."
```

The CDS administrator could look up a subject's standard score in the print-out simply by knowing that subject's ratings on the Personal Work Values Rating Form and the name of the occupation that subject wrote on the Job Decision card. Standard scores, ranging from 30 to 70, represented the relative "goodness" of the choice regardless of the amount of information needed to make it.

EXPERIMENTAL TRIAL

Subjects

In the first systematic use of the Career Decision Simulation, one hundred female and forty-eight male subjects from three California community colleges cooperated. Although the subjects' average age was in the mid twenties, the range of age was considerable. Fifty-one percent were between 17 and

20 years old, but another 28 per cent were age 31 or older. These subjects were taking part in an experiment that has been reported elsewhere (Krumboltz, Scherba, Hamel, Mitchell, Rude, and Kinnier, 1979).

Preliminary Data

What were the most important values reported by these community college students? As Table 9-1 indicates, the most important job value reported was Income, followed closely by Independence, Variety, and Security. The least important value was Early Entry—an occupation requiring a minimum amount of training. Other values receiving low ratings included Prestige, Leadership, and Leisure. The value of Helping Others occupied the midpoint.

What fictitious occupations were chosen by the subjects? Table 9-2 reveals that every one of the twelve fictitious occupations was chosen by someone. Zampic was chosen as the most popular occupation, but the names of the occupations have little meaning since they do not correspond to any real occupation.

Table 9-3 represents data related to actual use of the CDS. Subjects were told they had a maximum of two hours to complete the entire process. However, the first twenty minutes were used for giving directions on how to use the CDS. The average subject took 79.2 minutes to complete the process. Four subjects took longer than the allotted two hours and seven subjects took exactly two hours. All others finished well within the prescribed time limit.

Subjects scattered their search for information over a wide range of jobs and used a wide range of information sources. On the average, they investigated 10.2 jobs out of the possible 12 and searched 7.6 of the possible 9 information sources. They used an average of 44.8 information cards out of 324 that were available. Even the one subject who used 173 information cards did not come

TABLE 9-1
**MEANS AND STANDARD DEVIATIONS OF VALUE
PREFERENCES (N = 148)**

VALUE	MEAN	SD
Income	2.45	.67
Independence	2.34	.72
Variety	2.32	.76
Security	2.32	.71
Helping Others	2.04	.85
Leisure	1.82	.79
Leadership	1.63	.74
Prestige	1.58	.74
Early Entry	1.49	.64

Note: 3 = high value, 2 = medium value, 1 = low value

TABLE 9-2
**PERCENT OF SUBJECTS SELECTING EACH FICTITIOUS
OCCUPATION AS FINAL JOB CHOICE (*N* = 148)**

FICTITIOUS OCCUPATION	PERCENT CHOOSING
Breandist	8.8
Deptician	10.1
Geebist	7.4
Hister	12.2
Jepist	8.1
Kralician	8.1
Onician	2.7
Plinder	9.5
Quentic	8.8
Splacker	2.7
Tasindic	2.7
Zampic	18.9
	100.0

close to exhausting the total supply of available information. In this respect, the CDS was successful in simulating the fact that no one can possibly gain access to the total range of occupational information that is available. Only 30 percent of

TABLE 9-3
**MEANS, STANDARD DEVIATIONS, AND RANGES
ON SELECTED VARIABLES OF THE CAREER
DECISION SIMULATION**

VARIABLE	RANGE						
	Planned		*Actual*				
	MIN.	MAX.	MIN.	MAX.	MEAN	SD	N
Number of minutes to finish	15	120	22	161	79.2	24.3	147
Number of information cards used	0	324	7	173	44.8	23.4	148
Number of information sources used	0	9	4	9	7.6	1.8	148
Number of jobs checked Raw score on "goodness of choice"	0	12	1	12	10.2	2.7	148
	−219	360	22	295	184.4	48.7	148
Standard score on "goodness of choice"	30	70	30	70	58.0	12.4	148
Self-rated confidence in choice	0	10	0	10	7.6	1.9	146

the subjects actually checked out all twelve occupations; 12.8 percent checked all nine information sources.

How "good" were the choices? It was very clear that subjects were responding in a nonchance way with a tendency to make choices consistent with their own values. The raw score was derived from a table in which the maximum number of points was assigned to subjects who picked an occupation possessing values that they themselves had stated earlier as their own values. The more similar the occupation was to one's own values, the higher was the raw score. However, we adjusted the raw score by subtracting the number of information cards accessed. The CDS attempted to simulate that information costs something to obtain. In order to motivate them to try their best, we paid subjects a fee for cooperating in the study. They were paid a base rate of $3.00, regardless of their score, plus one cent for every point in their raw score above that. Thus, the maximum that each subject could earn was $3.00 plus another $3.60 for a total of $6.60. If subjects picked an occupation that perfectly matched their values, they could achieve a maximum score of 360 points. Even the minimum score of 105 points could be achieved by the worst possible mismatch; however, if subjects used all 324 information cards to make a totally inadequate choice, the subtraction of the 324 cards would produce a minimum score of negative 219. As Table 9-3 indicates, the average subject scored 184.4.

We derived the standard scores from the raw scores before subtracting the number of information cards. In other words, the standard score represented the absolute quality of the choice regardless of how much information had been collected to achieved it. Subjects could state their values in 1680 possible ways. The quality of their job choice depended upon what values they had selected. For example, Zampic might have been the best possible choice for an individual who valued Income, Independence, and Variety. But, Zampic might have been the worst possible choice for an individual who valued Early Entry, Prestige, and Leadership.

The actual mean of the standard scores was 58.0. The distribution was considerably skewed: 27 percent of the subjects selected the best possible occupation out of the available twelve but only 4.1 percent of the subjects selected the worst possible occupation. The subjects' general success in selecting occupations congruent with their values was reflected in their self-rated confidence. On a scale ranging from 0 to 10, the average subject recorded a self-rating of 7.6. A total of 62 percent rated themselves as 8, 9, or 10 on the scale.

IDEAS FOR FURTHER RESEARCH

A number of problems became evident through our experience with the CDS, and a number of possibilities have been suggested to improve the instrument. Owing to its very structure, the CDS virtually teaches a rational process of decision making. For example, the job strips (devices for recording judgments about value ratings for specific jobs) fit alongside the Personal Work Value Rating Form in such a way that a grid is formed that can be used systematically to compare each job with the previously stated work values. Such a grid-building mechanism is very instructive but it not generally available to people making real-life career decisions. Future experimentation might eliminate these artificial aids to enhance the lifelike quality of the instrument.

No studies have yet been done to assess the reliability of the values-congruence score. Also, since collecting one measurement of values congruence takes two hours, no study has yet been done to check the test-retest reliability.

How well does the quality of choice measured here compare with other assessments of decision-making ability? One big problem is defining other measures of decision quality. It would be difficult to validate the present values-congruence score against any other criterion since it would be hard to define any single other criterion that purports to measure decision quality. However, one might expect generally positive correlations between the CDS values-congruence score and measures of satisfaction with other career-decision outcomes, extent of career-exploratory behaviors, and success in other problem-solving activities.

Work remains to be done. The CDS must be made easier to administer; in fact, computerizing the directions and administration might well be attempted. More fundamentally, we still need some way to evaluate the quality of decisions if we are to determine the best procedure to follow in making decisions. The CDS was a first approximation, but other efforts are needed if we are ever to generate scientific evidence on the best way to make a career decision.

REFERENCES

BOARDMAN, R., and MITCHELL, C. R.   Crisis decision-making and simulation. In P. J. Tansey (Ed.), *Educational aspects of simulation.* London: McGraw-Hill, 1971, pp. 228–245.

BOOCOCK, S. S.   The life career game. *Personnel and Guidance Journal,* 1967, 45, 328–334.

KALDOR, D. R., and ZYTOWSKI, D. G.   A maximizing model of occupational decision-making. *Personnel and Guidance Journal,* 1969, 47, 781–788.

KATZ, M. R.   Simulated occupational choice: A measure of competencies in career decision-making. Final Report, National Institute of Education (DHEW), Washington, D.C., February, 1976 (ERIC Document Reproduction Service No. ED 121 841).

KRUMBOLTZ, J. D., SCHERBA, D. S., HAMEL, D. A., MITCHELL, L., RUDE, S., and KINNIER, R.   *The Effect of Alternative Career Decision-Making Strategies on the Quality of Resulting Decisions.* Final Report, U.S. Office of Education Grant G007605241, August, 1979 (ERIC Document Reproduction Service No. ED 195 824).

TALLMAN, I., and WILSON, L.   Simulating social structure: The use of a simulation game in cross-national research. *Simulation & Games,* 1974, 5 (2), 147–167.

PART FOUR
PRACTICAL PROBLEMS OF EVALUATORS

How does all the talk about historical origins, theory, technical requirements, and alternative assessment methods affect the people "out there" actually doing the evaluating? The ultimate goal of theory building, instrument development, and research studies is to provide useful information that will guide the delivery of improved career education practices. We should not lose sight of the fact that practitioners face many practical problems in implementing and evaluating career development programs.

The three chapters in this part provide a small sampling of the "nitty-gritty" problems career educators are attempting to resolve. Programs are often difficult to evaluate even when a curriculum is grounded in a strong theory base, the learner objectives are clearly specified, and the program is adequately staffed and funded. Questions arise regarding the degree to which (and the consistency with which) the goals of the program have been implemented, which measures, if any, are most appropriate for evaluation purposes, and ways in which new instruments can capture objectively what investigators can sense and observe about actual career education and career development training programs.

173

In chapter 10, Owens and Haenn address the problem of how to determine program fidelity. The practical necessity of ascertaining just what constitutes the program and the degree to which the intended training has been implemented is too frequently ignored. Even if the instruments used satisfy all the psychometric requirements discussed in part II or represent some of the more novel assessment procedures described in part III, they have no change to measure if the treatment interventions did not actually occur.

As Owens and Haenn point out, evaluators are not the only professionals interested in the degree of program implementation. Program staff members need to know which goals and objectives they have been most successful in covering and which components need further attention. Furthermore, policy makers and administrators are eager to learn how difficult or expensive it is to conduct various aspects of an intervention. Only by assessing which concepts, which behavioral objectives, and which materials have actually been used, and to what extent, can we make useful modifications of the instruments and render overall judgments about cost-effectiveness and outcomes.

Owens and Haenn describe two "degree-of-implementation" instruments and the data they generated in assessing twenty-one Experience-Based Career Education (EBCE) programs around the country. One measure, the EBCE Essential Characteristics Checklist, assesses the goals and philosophy of a given program. The other instrument, the EBCE Process Checklist, is designed to identify the actual operational procedures used at various sites. Both checklists are capable of assessing the degree to which a range of program components have been implemented, generating a profile rather than a single score. The instruments are also reliable, easy to administer, and capable of measuring program changes over time.

We think that Owens and Haenn have succeeded not only in identifying a crucial issue for those concerned with formative evaluation, but also in developing several promising measures that can serve as models for further instrument development. Adapting implementation measures to the goals of local career development programs can help identify variations in philosophy and teaching that are likely to be reflected in outcome-measure scores.

The challenges facing evaluators trying to assess the outcomes of local, often idiosyncratic, and occasionally misguided career education efforts are covered in chapter 11 by Bonnet. Bonnet provides readers with a hypothetical anecdote that succinctly portrays many of the exasperating difficulties career education evaluators encounter in the field. Her observations are a clear statement of the sometimes glaring discrepancies between the academic, theoretical, and textbook notions of how career development assessment "should" be done and what practitioners can realistically hope to accomplish.

Among the problems described by Bonnet are some discussed by several other contributors to this volume. For example, Bonnet's lament about the scarcity of measures "with respectable evidence of reliability and validity or with norms based on decent samples" underscores concerns expressed earlier by both Borow and Cole. Bonnet's frustration at the lack of tests providing data on key career development outcomes for many grade levels desired by school officials sounds familiar. Hulsart and Burton's chapter 7, on the Career and Occupational Development exercises and Finch's chapter 8 on performance testing address some of these same issues.

Bonnet suggests that when professional evaluators are consulted by educators to do an evaluation project, local environmental factors often produce formidable constraints. Inadequate budgets, unrealistic expectations, poorly trained staffs, and partially implemented program goals all make assessment difficult, especially for an "outside" consultant. However, she also points out that even under the best conditions, much of the difficulty lies in adapting existing measures to a unique set of local objectives. Here one encounters a large number of problems: tests where subjects' reading level is either too high or too low, tests that require too much reading (see chapter 5, by Westbrook), test batteries that include only one or two appropriate instruments, and tests that contain only a small percentage of items pertaining to a local program's particular objectives.

It is interesting to note that in concluding her chapter, Bonnet suggests several solutions discussed by other volume contributors. Her wish for "easy access to an item bank" that would help evaluators tailor their evaluation instruments to fit program objectives is at least partially addressed in chapter 6, by Shoemaker, on evaluating career education programs by using item domains. Bonnet's final point is that if evaluators simply asked the right questions, the frequent claims that career education really works would be validated.

In chapter 12, Brickell suggests an elaborately tested procedure for helping evaluators to ask those "right" questions. He tells the story of a large-scale career education evaluation effort. Brickell and his associates were hired to test the career education learning they had observed occurring in classrooms across the state of Ohio. State officials had first invited evaluators to visit classes, talk with teachers and students, and look for evidence of career learning. Having found it, these same officials then asked for testing evidence. Brickell and his colleagues then did the logical thing: they constructed multiple-choice test items based on a review of the objectives contained in the state's curriculum guides. After testing 6000 program and nonprogram students, they found no significant differences between the two groups.

Incredulous, teams of observers were sent out once again. Their reports that career learning was in fact taking place led the evaluators to reconsider their assessment strategy. The decision to develop field-based tests—ones based on what teachers were teaching and what students were learning rather than the stated program objectives—generated the hoped-for significant differences between program and nonprogram students. Thus, Brickell and his associates finally succeeded in measuring what they had seen, but the difficulties and frustrations the team experienced during this effort suggest a new strategy for developing career development assessment measures.

The success of Brickell's field-based testing in Ohio provides support for the controversial concept of goal-free test development. This concept argues for developing test items by looking at specific treatments and instructional processes rather than intended objectives and learner outcomes. Brickell makes a strong case for career education evaluators to spend more of their time observing career development instruction and training prior to developing items or selecting appropriate outcome measures.

Together these three chapters are a sobering reminder of the many tough challenges facing career development evaluators, but they are encouraging in suggesting that creative responses are possible and sometimes successful.

10

Assessing the degree of implementation of experience-based career education programs

THOMAS R. OWENS

Northwest Regional Educational Laboratory

and

JOSEPH F. HAENN

RMC Research Corporation

A common problem in evaluating career education programs is that of identifying precisely what constitutes the program and determining the extent to which the intended treatment is being implemented. Charters and Jones (1973) have addressed the issue of appraising "nonevents" in program evaluation. They indicate that often the lack of significant differences in student outcomes between experimental and control or comparison groups may be owing to the fact that certain program treatments have never actually occurred. Leonard and Lowery (1979) have developed a specific quantitative procedure for verifying different treatments in classroom teaching methods. This problem of appraising "nonevents" is especially crucial in career education because this subject often is offered by means of an infusion mode, where career education content is infused into the existing school curricula rather than treated as a separate course.

This paper was developed while both authors were employed by a private, nonprofit corporation. The work upon which this publication is based was performed pursuant to *Contract No. NE-C-00-4-0010 of the National Institute of Education*, 1978. The paper does not, however, necessarily reflect the views of that agency or of NWREL.

Even in cases where career education is a separate course or program, its components need to be well documented, since no universal agreement exists as to the meaning of career education.

The need to assess the degree of program implementation affects not only evaluators but also policy makers, administrators, program staff members, and curriculum developers. Policy makers need to know if a proposal to adopt an existing model of career education is first accepted and then actually implemented. Administrators are often interested in knowing what components of a model have been found to be the easiest or most difficult to implement so that they can anticipate trouble spots. Program staff are usually interested in knowing how effective they have been in implementing each of the components of a program and in identifying areas that need improvement. Finally, developers of program models need feedback on how their programs are implemented and what changes and adaptations are made in school districts to fit local needs. Such feedback is important in assessing the effectiveness of curriculum design materials and the training and technical assistance that they may have provided. It also allows the developers to see how realistic and adaptable their model is for varying local conditions.

This chapter describes the background, development, and usage of two measures of program implementation that have been helpful in the evaluation of Experience-Based Career Education.

BACKGROUND

Experience-Based Career Education (EBCE) is a fundamentally unique type of education for secondary students. While students in traditional high school programs attend classes all day, EBCE students spend a major portion of their time working on learning projects in the community. EBCE activities are tailored to individual needs, abilities, learning styles, and goals, and students are guided in their learning by working adults in the community.

Through their interactions with community members, EBCE students learn about careers, other people, themselves, and life in general. They also learn basic skills of critical thinking, science, personal and social development, functional citizenship, and creative development, and gain competence in the skills adults need to function effectively in a technological society. They learn responsibility by helping to design their own learning activities and by following a set of accountability standards that parallel those standards working adults are expected to maintain on the job.

Perhaps most importantly, EBCE students learn how to learn: how to plan learning activities, how to find and use community resources, and how to build on experience. They begin to see learning as a lifelong process with rewards directly related to each individual's personal goals.

The (CE)₂ Program

Since the fall of 1972, a model EBCE program, funded by the National Institute of Education (NIE) and sponsored by the Northwest Regional Educational Laboratory (NWREL), has been operating in Tigard, Oregon.[1] This version of EBCE is a full-time educational alternative for high school juniors and seniors. The pilot program serves about 10 percent of the eligible student body at Tigard High School.

The majority of student learning takes place at sites in the southwest Portland metropolitan areas. When students are not pursuing community learning activities, their home base is the (CE)₂ learning center. Center staff are not teachers in the traditional sense, but rather facilitators of student learning who help students design and follow individualized learning plans within a prescribed curriculum. Volunteers at community sites serve major support roles in student learning. Policies for (CE)₂ were determined by a board of directors composed of students, parents, employers, labor leaders, and school district representatives. When students leave (CE)₂, they receive a unique portfolio displaying their program experiences and accomplishments; upon completion of program requirements they receive a standard diploma from Tigard High School.

Pilot Sites

The NWREL EBCE program was developed and refined over a three-year period at the (CE)₂ demonstration site in Tigard, and then tried out in five school districts in the Northwest. Each program was operated by the local district, with NWREL providing training, technical assistance, and program evaluation for two years. The pilot sites—located in Colville, Washington; Hillsboro, Oregon; Jefferson County, Colorado; Kennewick, Washington; and Kodiak, Alaska—funded their own program operations using local district funds. Evaluation of the (CE)₂ demonstration site was intended primarily to determine whether EBCE was an effective program for students. Evaluation at the pilot sites was designed to determine how well EBCE programs could operate in school districts under local funding conditions and without the direct supervision of the developer.

Part D Sites

In 1975, guidelines were issued regarding applications for funding under Part D of the Vocational Education Act. These guidelines gave high priority to proposals that would implement EBCE. Through Part D funding from the U.S. Office of Education, approximately fifty new EBCE sites were created, twenty-three of which proposed to use the NWREL version of EBCE. These

[1] EBCE programs also have been developed, pilot tested and disseminated by the Appalachia Educational Laboratory, Inc., in Charleston, West Virginia; Far West Laboratory for Educational Research and Development in San Francisco, California; and Research for Better Schools, Inc., in Philadelphia, Pennsylvania.

twenty-three Part D projects, which represented fourteen states, were generally funded for a three-year period and involved high school or college students. These programs varied in the degree to which they planned to implement EBCE. Regulations governing Part D projects required that each be evaluated by a third-party evaluator. For these projects, both the program operation and the evaluation were independent of NWREL.

INSTRUMENT DEVELOPMENT

The Rationale for Measuring
Program Implementation

Since the development of EBCE at the demonstration site was under the direct control of NWREL, the program was planned and implemented to fit the laboratory's design for EBCE. However, there was less NWREL influence on the pilot sites than at the demonstration site and even less on the Part D sites. Thus it became important to know the extent to which the pilot and Part D sites were implementing EBCE as prescribed in the five EBCE handbooks[2] and in the NWREL EBCE staff training. After discussion with the NWREL EBCE development staff, it became clear that we should be examining the extent to which sites adopted the EBCE philosophy as well as the extent to which the sites used the various EBCE program components.

In our opinion, the belief that greater program fidelity will result in more positive student and program outcomes is fallacious. This myth assumes that the demonstration model being replicated is the ideal. In reality, no demonstration model is perfect; at best, a model is only a working guide based on procedures that were demonstrably effective in one or more testing sites. Therefore, there can be no assurance that high-fidelity implementation will yield any better results than those obtained from a less faithful site. What can be hypothesized, however, is that high-fidelity implementation will yield student and program outcomes more consistent with those obtained in the prototype site.

A review of the literature on measurement of program implementation (Owens and Haenn, 1977) suggests four important criteria in developing implementation instruments. The program implementation instruments should be able to

1. Assess the degree to which each program component has been implemented
2. Generate a program profile
3. Measure program changes over time
4. Provide reliable information and be easy to administer

---

[2] Built on (CE)₂s experiences. NWREL has compiled a set of five handbooks on the operation of an EBCE program. Each handbook is devoted to a particular area of program operation: *Management and Organization, Curriculum and Instruction, Employer/Community Resources, Student Services,* and *Program Evaluation.*

It is important to assess the degree to which each prespecified program component has been implemented. Evaluators must work closely with developers to identify the essential program components and to determine the best indicants of the level of proper component utilization.

The instruments should be capable of generating a profile of program components rather than a single score that attempts to capsulize the innovation. Profiles should allow for natural variation so that local sites can adapt or implement a program at different stages.

The instruments should also be able to measure changes in the program over time. Although most people realize that programs at replication sites evolve over time, few have considered that typically adopting all the features—even all the essential features—of a given program is impossible. Replication sites often initiate implementation with the most compatible and easiest-to-implement components; then, over time, they add or refine components. This process affords replication sites immediate visibility with minimal local resistance to totally new procedures. However, unless the degree-of-implementation instruments are capable of measuring these fine differences, it may be difficult to gain an accurate picture of this gradual adoption strategy. This criterion also implies the open-endedness needed in the instrument to identify new components or features that are added to the system at local sites.

Degree-of-implementation instruments should be reliable but easy to administer. An on-site checklist verifiable by observation and records examination is recommended. The checklist should cover both structural and behavioral program features as well as the objectives and philosophy of the program.

Given the above four criteria, we felt that two separate EBCE implementation instruments would be needed: one to assess the philosophy and goals of the program (EBCE Essential Characteristics Checklist) and one to examine the operational aspects (EBCE Process Checklist). The first instrument assesses fidelity to the model, while the second examines degree of local adaptation. Both instruments were pilot tested at several EBCE sites and revised for completeness and ease of administration. Each of these instruments is described in the following sections. The checklists themselves are reproduced in full at the end of this chapter.

The EBCE Essential
Characteristics Checklist
Program developers and the evaluation staff felt that the essential characteristics of EBCE could be circumscribed within five descriptive areas:

- EBCE is an individualized program.
- EBCE is community-based.
- EBCE is experience-based, incorporating the daily activities of adults.
- EBCE has its own identity and is comprehensive and integrated.
- EBCE places a major emphasis on students' career development.

An Essential Characteristics Checklist was developed to measure the degree of implementation within each essential area. Each area contains four or five essential characteristics. The individulization area contains five characteristics:

- On-going assessment of student needs, interests and abilities
- Active student participation in the assessment process
- Projects negotiated between a student and staff
- Individual assessment and accountability integrated with a student's learning plan
- Flexibility in student accountability standards

These characteristics are rated on a scale of 1 to 5, with prespecified anchor points.

EBCE is a community-based program and should have the following characteristics:

- Community input into program planning and operation
- Role of the program advisory board
- Involvement of community members in student learning
- Provision for training of community instructors

In regard to the experience-based nature of EBCE, the desired characteristcs are these:

- An active mode of learning
- Responsibility taken by students for budgeting their time and managing their daily activities
- Priority utilization of primary resources (such as community organizations and experts in a field) over secondary resources (such as textbooks)
- Attention to adult activities in the community as a primary context for learning
- Systematic analysis of the learning potential of the local community

As a comprehensive and integrated program, EBCE determines:

- Whether student learning plans are based on EBCE requirements rather than regular high school course requirements
- The extent to which program-completion requirements are clearly defined and consistent with program goals and local requirements
- Whether the curriculum structure includes experiences in basic skills, life skills, and career development
- Whether performance-based survival competencies are present in the program
- The degree of emphasis on interrelated curriculum areas in student learning activities

As a program that places a major emphasis on students' career development, EBCE:

- Provides for different types and levels of learning situations at employer/community sites
- Emphasizes use of employer sites for learning about careers rather than earning money
- Involves students in gathering information about themselves and the world of work and applying this information in career decision making
- Encourages students to reflect on their community experiences and evaluate their own strengths and weaknesses, and their own progress

A checklist-examiner's guide explains the purposes of the checklist and describes special considerations for each essential characteristic. Anchor points have been set so that 5 represents perfect program fidelity, while 1 represents an antagonistic concept unacceptable within the framework of the NWREL EBCE model. Thus, 2 would represent a highly questionable concept, 3 a somewhat less questionable concept, and 4 an approximation of the intended concept, that lacks perfect fidelity. This instrument takes about fifteen minutes to complete.

The EBCE Process Checklist

While the Essential Characteristics Checklist measures fidelity to basic policy and philosophical characteristics of an EBCE site, the Process Checklist is designed to identify natural local variations in procedures used to operate an EBCE program. This initial process checklist consists of four sections:

- EBCE objectives
- Management and organization processes
- Curriculum and instruction processes
- Student service processes

The objectives section contains a response format in which the project director checks the degree of usage—for all, some, or no students—for each of the initial NWREL EBCE student outcome objectives in career development, basic skills, life skills, and experiential learning. The project director is also asked to write in any additional objectives used at his or her site. The section on management and organization processes contains items determining whether the EBCE project had been approved, in writing, by the local school board and the state department of education, and whether it meets all, most, or none of the fair labor practice requirements. This section also determines which actual staff roles are used. The section on curriculum and instruction processes determines whether each of the EBCE competencies and student projects is required of students, is an optional activity, or is not used, and also whether these competencies and projects are used differently from the methods described in the EBCE handbook. Again, a place is provided for identifying other competencies and student projects that are developed locally. Specific information is also collected regarding the number of student projects, career explorations, and learning levels required of students, and the average number of hours that students spend on each. A checklist section containing specific curriculum materials and forms used at some EBCE sites provides the opportunity for project directors to indicate whether these are used with all, some, or none of their students. The student services section contains questions dealing with student-recruiting strategies; types of students enrolled; student guidance functions; student accountability systems; and policy regarding student course enrollment in the local high school, at postsecondary institutions, and at employer sites.

Two additional sections have been added to the EBCE Process Checklist to be used with EBCE sites completing their third year of Part D funding. One deals with funding sources and the other with the program's future. Funding questions look at the percentage of funds from local, state, and federal sources for the current year and for those anticipated in the next year. The section on the program's future contains questions on whether the program will continue beyond the three-year Part D federal funding, on the changes anticipated in program operations and on reasons for program termination (where applicable). The EBCE Process Checklist takes about twenty-five minutes to complete.

Evaluating the Checklists

As Proper (1979) has indicated, no single approach to implementation measurement can cover every situation. In our opinion, the two checklists previously described have several advantages:

- Both instruments can be completed by a knowledgeable staff member untrained in evaluation.
- The checklists are specific and cover all the important aspects of EBCE
- Completing both instruments takes less than forty minutes.
- The instruments provide a profile of a program rather than a single overall score.
- The EBCE elements contained in the NWREL EBCE handbooks are covered by the instruments.
- Each instrument can be verified by program observation and documentation.

There are two perceived limitations of the checklists. First, they rely on self-report data by a project staff member and thus are subject to bias. Second, as Proper (1979) has noted about these two checklists, they do "not provide direct observation of individual behaviors, and thus information about process and interaction may be lost" (p. 190).

FINDINGS FROM THE CHECKLISTS

This section reports findings from the two checklists completed by project directors of the NWREL EBCE sites receiving funding through Part D of the Vocational Education Act. These checklists were completed at the end of the first and third years of the program's operation. In 1976, experiences from the demonstration and pilot sites indicated that a high degree of correspondence existed between ratings on these forms completed by project directors and those completed independently by the NWREL evaluators, who had conducted three visits a year to each site. Thus, the practice of having project directors complete the forms is considered credible, especially since the project directors were told their findings would not be identified by site name. This credibility is enhanced since these directors were willing to rate certain programs areas low and the pattern of high and low ratings from the Part D sites was consistent with the pattern generated by the evaluators at the pilot sites.

In May 1977, the EBCE Essential Characteristics Checklist and EBCE Process Checklist were sent to the project director of each NWREL EBCE site receiving funding through Part D, VEA. After one follow-up letter from NWREL, responses were received from all twenty-three sites. These twenty-three sites involved both full- and part-time programs for junior high, senior high, and college students in fourteen states. Of the twenty-three sites, sixteen applied to use a full EBCE program, five decided to integrate EBCE with a work-experience program, and two chose to adapt EBCE to fit a careeer-clusters approach.

In May 1979, project directors at twenty-one of these twenty-three sites again completed the two instruments. (One site did not return the forms and personnel at the remaining site informed us that they had switched from the NWREL model of EBCE to one developed by another laboratory.) Of the twenty-one sites, eleven were full-time programs and ten were part-time programs. One site involved only junior high students, sixteen involved senior high students, three sites had both junior and senior high students, and one site involved senior high students and adults. There were from two to nine staff members per site, with an average of five. The number of students ranged from 10 to 648, with an average of 104.

EBCE Essential Characteristics
Checklist Results

The EBCE program characteristics receiving the highest and lowest ratings in 1977 and in 1979 are displayed in Table 10-1. It is interesting to note that the three areas rated highest in 1977 remained so in 1979. The pattern for characteristics rated lowest also remained stable over the two years, with an increased rating in all areas in 1979 except for the use of basic skills, life skills, and career development in the curriculum and the active role of the advisory board. Some sites in which students are involved in EBCE for only part of a day have emphasized the career development objectives but not the other two areas, resulting in a decreased rating. The slight decrease in involvement of advisory board members occurred because some sites indicated they used the advisory board to set up policies primarily at the start of the program. In general, most Part D sites were adhering to the NWREL EBCE model despite wide variation across sites on some characteristics.

TABLE 10-1
**HIGHEST AND LOWEST RATINGS ON THE EBCE
ESSENTIAL CHARACTERISTICS CHECKLIST
FOR PART D SITES**

HIGHEST RATED AREAS	1977 MEAN (N = 23)	1979 MEAN (N = 21)
1. Emphasis on using community sites for learning about careers rather than on paying students	4.70	4.86
2. Provision for different types and levels of learning situations at community sites	4.66	4.81
3. Students gather information about themselves and the world of work and apply this in career decision making	4.62	4.62
4. Curriculum includes experiences in Basic Skills, Life Skills and Career Development	4.56	4.14
5. Students reflect on their experiences and evaluate their own strengths, weaknesses and progress	4.50	4.62
LOWEST RATED AREAS		
1. Provision for regularly scheduled community instructor training	2.54	2.67
2. Interrelated curriculum areas demonstrated through student learning activities	3.26	3.45
3. Program requirements determined by student learning needs more than by regular high school requirements	3.41	3.68
4. Program advisory board takes an active role in direction of the program	3.50	3.43
5. Students play an active and involved role in the assessment process	3.62	4.20

EBCE Process Checklist Results

Findings from the EBCE Process Checklist over the two-year period are very interesting and are summarized below.

There are fifteen NWREL EBCE student objectives, covering the areas of career development, basic skills, and experiential outcomes. Several of these objectives were used in all or all but one project. Two objectives are used at all sites: (1) students will increase their knowledge of their own aptitudes, interests, and abilities and apply this understanding to their potential career interests; and (2) students will broaden the range of sources they use in gathering information for work and decison making. All fifteen of the objectives are being used with all or at least some students at 90 percent or more of the EBCE sites.

Seven potential staff roles were identified in the checklist as being potentially useful in an EBCE project. The roles of project director and learning manager are most frequently used in EBCE (91 percent of the projects), followed by employer relations specialist (73 percent), aide (41 percent), learning resource specialist and student coordinator (14 percent each).

Thirteen original student competencies are described in the NWREL EBCE training manual. Each of these thirteen competencies is required of students in at least half of the EBCE projects except for maintaining good physical health, participating in the electoral process, and operating and maintaining an automobile. The latter three are required of students in at least 40 percent of the projects. In the case of most competencies, these competencies are used significantly more in full-time than in part-time projects. Competencies added by local sites include consumer education, survival swimming, use of public transportation, real estate, oral and written communication, time management, and use of community resources.

Both predesigned and individually created projects are advised in the areas of Creative Development, Critical Thinking, Functional Citizenship, Personal/Social Development, and Science. Except for the predesigned science projects, which are used at 71 percent of the sites, all the NWREL student project areas are used, at least on an optional basis, at 80 percent or more sites. The individually designed projects are each used at significantly more full-time than part-time sites. Students are required to complete an average of eight projects, although the requirements range from one to twelve projects.

When EBCE students visit an employer site to explore a certain career, it is suggested that they complete a record of the exploration. Career-exploration packages are required of all students at 79 percent of the sites and are required of some students at 16 percent of the sites. Students are required to complete six explorations on the average, although the requirements range from three to ten explorations across the sites. These explorations take an average of 12 hours to complete, although they range from two to twenty-five hours to complete across sites.

After students explore a site or several sites it is recommended that they go on-site for an extended period to learn more about the career(s) of interest. Completion of learning levels is required of all students at 44 percent of the sites, is required of some students at 6 percent of the sites, and is optional for students at 44 percent of the sites. Programs that require learning levels average 1.5 learning-level activities per semester. These activities take 56 hours to complete, on the average.

An optional activity of the NWREL EBCE program is the opportunity to obtain a degree of proficiency within a given skill area. Skill-building levels at employer sites are required of all students at 12 percent of the sites and are optional in 83 percent of the projects.

In order to better describe and record their experiences, each EBCE student is advised to maintain a journal of activities. Student journals are required of all students at 85 percent of the sites, are required of only some in a few cases (5 percent), or are optional (5 percent). The journals are used primarily to help students know themselves better (45 percent), to develop communication skills (30 percent), and to develop trusting relationships with an adult (15 percent). Students are most frequently required to write journal entries on a weekly basis (74 percent).

Students at 95 percent of the EBCE sites can be enrolled in regular high school courses while they are in EBCE. Students in EBCE also can be enrolled in postsecondary classes at 65 percent of the sites and in classes offered at employer sites for 57 percent of the projects. This latter option differs significantly between full-time EBCE programs (where it can occur in 91 percent of the sites) and part-time programs (where it is allowed in only 20 percent of the sites).

Of twenty-one EBCE sites, eighteen indicated that they would continue in the next year. This indicates at least an 86 percent continuation rate. Two of the three sites that are not continuing are part-time projects; one site has operated as a school class, one as an infused curriculum, and one as a program within the regular school building. One project serves junior high only, one senior high, and the third both groups. Lack of funding and administrative support were the reasons given for the programs not continuing, although in all three cases the project directors felt it would have been desirable for EBCE to continue. In one of the three sites, certain project elements will be infused into the science, math, and English curricula and into the counseling program of the regular high school.

Using the Results

The most obvious application of any degree-of-implementation instrument is in assessing program fidelity. This fidelity can be viewed in terms of both congruence between a model and the plans of a project and congruency between a project's plan and its actual operation. However, we have identified additional uses for the essential characteristics and process checklists used with the NWREL EBCE program. First, these instruments provide the potential adopter with a good orientation to the characteristics and processes of the EBCE program. In fact, NWREL EBCE Implementation Technical Assistance Staff personnel have found these instruments to be effective tools for planning in helping to define EBCE.

These instruments are also valuable in establishing initial priorities. Implementation sites that cannot immediately adopt all processes and characteristics can use these instruments to focus their initial implementation efforts and guide future revisions. Moreover, the instruments can be used to assess initial efforts, to pinpoint weaknesses, and to set the stage for future implementation.

Furthermore, the instruments help stimulate discussions among site staff personnel regarding program strengths and weaknesses. As a result of such discussion, staff members may formalize plans to revise or complete program implementation.

In addition, these instruments could be used to evaluate program changes during the course of a school year or over several years. NWREL EBCE evaluation staff personnel have found this application useful in identifying areas of implementation that were incomplete at the beginning or middle of the year, but that had reached completion by the end of the year.

Finally, one function of implementation instruments not yet realized in EBCE is correlating the degree of program implementation with student- and program-outcome measures. Using the instruments in this way would require some common outcome measures across sites. Although this process may be complex, it would allow those interested in career education to learn what program features are associated most closely with program success. Such research is recommended in the future.

SUMMARY AND CONCLUSIONS

In this article, we have attempted to sketch a rationale, description, and use for two measures designed to assess the degree of implementation of NWREL Experience-Based Career Education Programs. The data provided by these two instruments were found useful in identifying variations in program implementation across twenty-one nationwide EBCE implementation sites over a two-year period. Significant differences were found between full-time and part-time EBCE programs on use of decision-making skills, individualized student projects, and access to student participation in courses offered at employer sites. Project ratings of various components were found to be stable over the two-year period, and 86 percent of the EBCE projects planned to continue after federal funds terminate.

The two program-implementation measures were found to be useful in a variety of settings. In proposal writing and initial program design, the checklists helped to define the key elements of an EBCE program. During the early period of program operation, the checklists allowed project staff to review their progress and to identify areas of program implementation they had not yet fully developed. Toward the end of the first and following years of program operation, the checklists served as a measure of program change and as documentation of the program treatment. Finally, the checklists have documented ways in which the EBCE concept has been implemented and modified by school districts around the country after the initial development and pilot-testing period at NWREL.

Although the implementation checklists described in this chapter are based solely on the NWREL model of EBCE, the general criteria and procedures described in this chapter can be adapted by local educators to document and describe their own career education programs. This adaptability becomes especially important for districts where a career education program or model is operating in various schools, so they can determine the extent of variation that may exist in the philosophy and actual processes used.

REFERENCES

CHARTERS, W. W., JR., and JONES, J. E.   On the risks of appraising non-events in program evaluation. *Educational Researcher,* 1973, *2* (11), 5–7.

EVANS, W. J., and SHEFFLER, J. W.   Degree of implementation: A first approximation. Paper presented at the annual meeting of the American Educational Research Association. Chicago, April 1974.

EVANS, W. J., and SHEFFLER, J. W.   Assessment of curriculum implementation. *Planning and Changing,* 1976, 80–85.

FULLAN, M., and POMFRET, A.   Review of research on curriculum implementation. Prepared for U.S. National Institute of Education, Career Education Program, NIE-P-74-0122, April 1975.

GEPHART, W. J.   Problems in measuring the degree of implementation of an innovation. Paper presented at the annual meeting of the American Educational Research Association, San Francisco, April 1976 (ERIC Document Reproduction Service No. ED 124-584).

LEONARD, W. H., and LOWERY, L. F.   Was there really an experiment? A quantitative procedure for verifying treatments in educational research. *Educational Researcher,* 1979, *8* (6), 4–7.

OWENS, T. R., and HAENN, J. F.   Assessing the level of implementation of new programs. Paper presented at the annual meeting of the American Educational Research Association, New York, April 1977.

PROPER, E. C.   Documentation of program implementation. In T. Abramson, C. Title, and L. Cohen (Eds.), *Handbook of Vocational Education Evaluation,* Beverly Hills, Calif.: Sage Publications, 1979, pp. 179–194.

ROGERS, E. M., and SHOEMAKER, F. F.   *Communication of innovations:* A cross-cultural approach. New York: Free Press, 1971.

STUFFLEBEAM, D L., ET AL.   *Educational evaluation and decision-making.* Itasca, Ill.: Peacock Publishers, 1971.

EBCE ESSENTIAL CHARACTERISTICS CHECKLIST

(3,4)* **Site** _____

(5,6) **Respondent** _____ **Date** _____

For each area, rate the project on a five-point scale using the anchor points indicated for each area. Place the number 1 to 5 that most clearly represents your opinion in the box by each area.

I. EBCE is an individualized program.

A. Ongoing staff assessment of student needs, interests and abilities in Basic Skills, Life Skills and Career Development:

(7) □

|1| There is no ongoing assessment in two or more of these areas.

|5| Student needs, interests and abilities are continually assessed.

B. Participation in assessment:

(8) □

|1| Students play a passive role in the assessment process.

|5| Students play an active role in the assessment process.

C. Individual negotiation:

(9) □

|1| All student projects are preassigned and not subject to negotiation.

|5| All student projects allow for negotiation between student and staff.

D. Integration:

(10) □

|1| Student projects are not integrated with a student's prior experiences.

|5| Individual assessment and accountability are integrated with program learning strategies when learning plans are negotiated.

E. Accountability standards (a set of learning and behavioral expectations for students as members of the EBCE 'community'):

(11) □

|1| There are few if any accountability standards.

|5| Clear accountability standards exist and give students the necessary flexibility to meet basic program expectations.

*Please ignore the numbers in parenthesis. These numbers are for data processing purposes only.

191

II. EBC is a community-based program.

   A.   Community input into program planning and operation:

(12)

        [1] No mechanism currently exists for obtaining community input.

        [5] A systematic mechanism exists for procuring and utilizing community input.

   B.   Role of the program advisory board:

(13)

        [1] There is no program advisory board.

        [5] The program advisory board takes an active role in direction of the program by providing program input.

   C.   Community members and student learning:

(14)

        [1] Community members are not involved in student learning activities.

        [5] Community members serve as resource instructors and certifiers of student learning.

   D.   Provision for community instructor training/development activities:

(15)

        [1] There are no community instructor training/development activities.

        [5] There are at least four regularly scheduled community instructor training/development activities each year.

III. EBCE is an experience-based program and is built from the career activities of adults.

   A.   Mode of learning:

(16)

        [1] Students are instructed in a passive or school-like mode.

        [5] Active, realistic, lifelike learning activities are provided for all students.

   B.   Student activity:

(17)

        [1] Students have little or no role in planning and scheduling their activities.

        [5] Students have the responsibility for budgeting their time and managing their daily activities.

   C.   Utilization of resources for learning:

(18)

        [1] Secondary resources (textbooks, courses) are given priority.

        [5] Primary resources (people, institutions such as libraries and museums, events) are given priority.

D. Community learning activities:

(19)

☐   1   Adult activities in the community are not utilized in student learning.

     5   Adult activities in the community serve as the primary context for student learning.

E. Reference population:

(20)

☐   1   Teachers and school work are the primary referent.

     5   Adults in the world of work are the primary referent.

F. Community learning potential:

(21)

☐   1   No analysis is made of the learning potential of the local community.

     5   There is systematic analysis that enables staff and students to take full advantage of the learning potential of the local community.

IV. EBCE must have its own identity and must be comprehensive and integrated.

A. Program requirements and processes:

(22)

☐   1   Regular high school requirements and processes are used to determine student learning plans.

     5   EBCE program requirements and processes determine student learning plans.

B. Program completion requirements:

(23)

☐   1   Program completion requirements are vague, unspecified or not differentiated from the regular high school requirements.

     5   Program completion requirements are clearly defined and consistent with program goals and local requirements.

C. Curriculum:

(24)

☐   1   The curriculum structure includes experiences in no more than one of the following areas: Basic Skills, Life Skills, Career Development.

     5   The curriculum structure includes experiences in all of the above areas.

D. Survival competencies:

(25)

☐   1   There are no performance-based survival competencies in the program.

     5   There are at least ten performance-based survival competencies in the program.

193

E. Interrelatedness of curriculum areas and student learning:

(26) ☐

1 Curriculum content areas, such as chemistry, are emphasized separately.

5 Emphasis is on interrelated curriculum areas and this is demonstrated by the student learning activities.

V. The EBCE program places a major emphasis on the career development of students.

A. Types of community learning situations:

(27) ☐

1 There are no employer/community learning sites.

5 Provision is made for different types and levels of learning situations at employer/community sites.

B. Emphasis at learning sites:

(28) ☐

1 Students are paid for their contributions on employer/community sites.

5 Students are on employer/community sites for learning about careers, not to earn money.

C. Career decision making:

(29) ☐

1 Students are not encouraged to improve their career decision-making processes.

5 Students are required to gather information about themselves and the world of work and apply this information in career decision making.

D. Reflections on student experiences:

(30) ☐

1 There are few or no opportunities for student self-evaluation.

5 Students are encouraged to reflect on experiences and evaluate their own strengths, weaknesses and progress.

194

EBCE PROCESS CHECKLIST

(3,4)* **Site** _____

(5,6) **Respondent** _____ **Date** _____

I. OBJECTIVES

For each objective listed below please check whether it applies to all, some, or none of your EBCE students. Also list any additional student outcomes that your project may have. (Please note that the Life Skills curriculum area is not included here because it is addressed in Section III B.)

	All Students	Used With: Some Students	No Students
Career Development			
1. Students will increase their knowledge of their own aptitudes, interests and abilities and apply this understanding to their potential career interests. **(7)**	_____	_____	_____
2. Students will increase their knowledge of social, governmental and economic issues and trends in the world of work. **(8)**	_____	_____	_____
3. Students will develop the general skills of job finding, job application, on-the-job negotiation and dependability necessary in daily work interactions. **(9)**	_____	_____	_____
4. Students will analyze potential careers for financial and psychological inducements, preparation needs and preparation programs available. **(10)**	_____	_____	_____
Basic Skills			
5. Students will improve in their performance level of fundamental basic skills (reading, writing, oral communication and mathematics). **(11)**	_____	_____	_____
6. Students will be able to perform applied skill tasks related to careers of interest to them. **(12)**	_____	_____	_____

*Please ignore the numbers in parentheses. These numbers are for data processing only.

195

			Used With:	
		All Students	Some Students	No Students

Basic Skills (continued)

7. Students will become aware of the level of basic skills needed to enter careers of interest to them and will understand the relationship of that level to their current basic skills

(13) proficiency. _____ _____ _____

8. Students will demonstrate an increased willingness to apply basic skills to work tasks and to everyday

(14) problems. _____ _____ _____

Experiential Outcomes

9. Students will broaden the range of sources they use (people, events, institutions, laws, books, etc.) in gathering information for work and

(15) decision making. _____ _____ _____

10. Students will demonstrate the ability to conduct conversation with an adult that reveals the student's self-confidence and understanding of the other person's message and

(16) feelings. _____ _____ _____

11. Students will demonstrate an increase in self-initiated behaviors and in assuming responsibility for carrying out and evaluating tasks

(17) which they agree to complete. _____ _____ _____

12. Students will demonstrate an increase in behaviors that reveal a tolerance for people and institutions having different values, ideas or background than themselves; an openness to change and a willingness to trust others

(18) when circumstances warrant. _____ _____ _____

13. Students will include data from their total sensory system as part of their input into their decision-

(19) making processes. _____ _____ _____

196

		Used With:	
	All Students	**Some Students**	**No Students**

Experiential Outcomes (continued)

(20) 14. Students will be able to assume adult responsibilities and relationships in a positive and self-confident manner. _____ _____ _____

(21) 15. Students who select a career area to pursue will acquire specific job skills while at employer sites related to their career area. _____ _____ _____

(22)
(23)
(24)
(25)
(26) 16. Other outcomes *(please list)* _____ _____ _____ _____
_____ _____ _____ _____
_____ _____ _____ _____
_____ _____ _____ _____
_____ _____ _____ _____

II. MANAGEMENT AND ORGANIZATION PROCESSES

Please check the appropriate response that describes the current status of your project on each of the following dimensions.

1. Has the district school board approved the project?

(27) ☐ 1. Approved in writing   ☐ 2. Verbally approved   ☐ 3. Not approved

2. Has the state department of education approved the project?

(28) ☐ 1. Approved in writing   ☐ 2. Verbally approved   ☐ 3. Not approved

3. Does the project meet all legal and fair labor practice requirements?

(29) ☐ 1. Yes   ☐ 2. Meets most requirements   ☐ 3. No

(If you select "meets most requirements" or "no," please explain.)

4. Are the following staff roles being used? *(Check those roles actually defined and used.)*

(30) ☐ Project director   (34) ☐ Student coordinator

(31) ☐ Learning manager   (35) ☐ Learning assistant

(32) ☐ Employer relations specialist   (36) ☐ Aides

(33) ☐ Learning resource specialist   (37) ☐ Others *(list)* _____
_____

197

III. CURRICULUM AND INSTRUCTION PROCESS

A. Competencies

Of the following competencies check those, if any, that are part of your program. List any competencies your site may have added. Indicate if they are required of all students or are optional. If your site uses competencies differently than as described on pages 331-407 of the NWREL EBCE Curriculum & Instruction *handbook, please explain the differences on the back of this sheet.*

		Required	Optional	Used Differently Than in the Handbook	Not Used
(38)	1. Transact business on a credit basis	_____	_____	_____	_____
(39)	2. Maintain checking account	_____	_____	_____	_____
(40)	3. Provide adequate insurance for yourself, family and possessions	_____	_____	_____	_____
(41)	4. File state and federal taxes	_____	_____	_____	_____
(42)	5. Budget time and money effectively	_____	_____	_____	_____
(43)	6. Maintain good physical health and make effective use of leisure time	_____	_____	_____	_____
(44)	7. Respond appropriately to fire, police and physical health emergencies	_____	_____	_____	_____
(45)	8. Participate in the electoral process	_____	_____	_____	_____
(46)	9. Understand the basic structure and function of local government	_____	_____	_____	_____
(47)	10. Explain personal legal rights	_____	_____	_____	_____
(48)	11. Make appropriate use of public agencies	_____	_____	_____	_____
(49)	12. Make application for employment and successfully hold a job	_____	_____	_____	_____

198

		Required	Optional	Used Differently Than in the Handbook	Not Used
(50)	13. Operate and maintain an automobile	_____	_____	_____	_____
(51) (52)	14. Other competencies (please list) _____	_____	_____	_____	_____
		_____	_____	_____	_____
		_____	_____	_____	_____

B. Student Projects

1. *Check those projects, if any, that are part of your program. List any student projects your site may have added. Indicate if they are required of all students or are optional. If your site uses student projects differently than described on pages 189-273 of the NWREL EBCE* Curriculum & Instruction *handbook, please explain the differences on the back of this sheet.*

		Required	Optional	Used Differently Than in the Handbook	Not Used
(54)	1. Creative development predesigned project	_____	_____	_____	_____
(55)	2. Creative development individual project	_____	_____	_____	_____
(56)	3. Critical thinking predesigned project	_____	_____	_____	_____
(57)	4. Critical thinking individual project	_____	_____	_____	_____
(58)	5. Functional citizenship predesigned project	_____	_____	_____	_____
(59)	6. Functional citizenship individual project	_____	_____	_____	_____
(60)	7. Personal/social development predesigned project	_____	_____	_____	_____
(61)	8. Personal/social development individual project	_____	_____	_____	_____
(62)	9. Science predesigned project	_____	_____	_____	_____
(63)	10. Science individual project	_____	_____	_____	_____

199

		Required	Optional	Used Differently Than in the Handbook	Not Used
(64)	11. Others _____	_____	_____	_____	_____
(65)		_____	_____	_____	_____
(66)		_____	_____	_____	_____

(67,68) 2. How many projects is each student expected to complete each year? _____

3. On individually prepared Life Skills projects, who generally does the following? *(Check responses that apply):*

(69)   1. Selects the topics   ☐ 1. Students   ☐ 2. Staff   ☐ 3. Both

(70)   2. Determines the objectives and activities   ☐ 1. Students   ☐ 2. Staff   ☐ 3. Both

(71)   3. Evaluates the results   ☐ 1. Students   ☐ 2. Staff   ☐ 3. Both

C. Exploration Package

(72)   1. Are the exploration packages—

      ☐ 1. Required of all students

      ☐ 2. Required of some students

      ☐ 3. Optional for students

      ☐ 4. Used differently than described on pages 105-185 of the NWREL EBCE Curriculum & Instruction handbook. If so, please explain the differences.

(73-74) 2. How many explorations, if any, are required of students in your program? _____

(75)   3. Who selects the exploration sites for an individual student?

      ☐ 1. EBCE staff

      ☐ 2. The student

      ☐ 3. Staff and student jointly

      ☐ 4. Other *(please specify)*

(76-77) 4. What is the average length of each exploration in hours? _____
(80=1)

D. Learning Level Process

(7)   1. Are learning levels—

      ☐ 1. Required of all students

      ☐ 2. Required of some students

200

☐ 3. Optional for students

☐ 4. Used differently than described on pages 277-327 of the NWREL EBCE *Curriculum & Instruction* handbook. If so, please explain the differences.

(8)   2. How many learning level experiences, if any, are required of students in your program? _____

(9-10) 3. What is the average length of each learning level in hours? _____

E. Student Journals

(11)   1. What are the primary purposes served by the journals?

☐ 1. Analyzing and integrating career awareness information

☐ 2. Developing communications skills

☐ 3. Helping students know themselves better

☐ 4. Developing trust relationships with an adult

☐ 5. Other *(please list)* _____

(12)   2. Are student journals—

☐ 1. Required of all students

☐ 2. Required of some students

☐ 3. Optional for students

☐ 4. Used differently than described on pages 411-451 of the *Curriculum & Instruction* handbook. If so, please explain the differences.

(13)   3. Approximately how often are students required to *write* journal entries?

☐ 1. Daily ☐ 2. Weekly ☐ 3. Biweekly ☐ 4. Monthly ☐ 5. Other

(14)   4. How often are students requried to *turn in* their journals to a staff member?

☐ 1. Daily ☐ 2. Weekly ☐ 3. Biweekly ☐ 4. Monthly ☐ 5. Other

F. Student Seminars by Employers

(15-16) 1. Approximately how many seminars with employer or community resource people have you held for students or do you plan to hold this school year? _____

G. Skill Building Level

(17)   1. Will skill building levels at employer sites be—

☐ 1. Required of all students

☐ 2. Required of some students

☐ 3. Optional for students

☐ 4. Used differently than described on pages 277-327 of the NWREL EBCE *Curriculum & Instruction* handbook. If so, please explain the differences.

201

2. If skill building levels are an intended part of your program, have any students begun them yet?

(18) ☐ 1. Yes ☐ 2. No

H. Special Placements

(19) 1. Are "special placements" of students at employer or community sites for Life Skills or Basic Skills an option within your program?

☐ 1. Yes ☐ 2. No

2. If "special placements" are a part of your program, have any students begun them yet?

(20) ☐ 1. Yes ☐ 2. No

I. Specific Curriculum Materials

Please indicate which of the following materials are used by students in your program.

		All Students	*Used By: Some Students*	*No Students*
(21)	1. Individualized Learning for Adults (ILA) Basic Skills materials	_____	_____	_____
(22)	2. Career Information System (CIS)	_____	_____	_____
	3. Other materials *(please specify)*			
(23)	_____	_____	_____	_____
(24)	_____	_____	_____	_____
(25)	_____	_____	_____	_____

J. Program Completion Requirements

(26) 1. Does your project have written program completion requirements that are clearly defined?

☐ 1. Yes ☐ 2. No

(27) 2. If yes, are the requirements like those described on pages 52-53 of the NWREL EBCE *Curriculum & Instruction* handbook?

☐ 1. Yes ☐ 2. No

If no, please describe the differences.

IV. STUDENT SERVICES

A. Student Recruitment

(28) 1. Has student recruitment been aimed at a cross section of local high school students?

☐ 1. Yes ☐ 2. No

202

(29)   If no, what types of students have been recruited? _____

(30)   2.   What recruitment strategies were used?

(31)   3.   When were students recruited?

(32)   4.   What types of students actually entered the program? *(Indicate only if different from type of student recruited.)*

     B.   Classes

(33)   1.   Are students allowed to take classes at the local high school?

        ☐   1.   Yes   ☐   2.   No

(34-35) 2.   If yes, how many students are taking such classes? _____

(36)   3.   Are students allowed to take classes at community colleges or other institutions?

        ☐   1.   Yes   ☐   2.   No

(37-38)   If yes, how many students are taking such classes? _____

(39)   4.   Are students allowed to take classes or courses at employer sites?

        ☐   1.   Yes   ☐   2.   No

(40-41)   If yes, how many students are taking such classes? _____

     C.   Guidance

     1.   Is the guidance function shared by all professional staff members?

(42)   ☐   1.   Yes   ☐   2.   No   If no, how is the function handled?

(43)   2.   Do staff members conduct student staffing sessions regularly to discuss the progress of each student?

        ☐   1.   Yes   ☐   2.   No

        If no, how do staff share information about students?

     D.   Accountability System

(44)   1.   Does your project utilize a student accountability system with clearly defined expectations and consequences?

        ☐   1.   Yes   ☐   2.   No

(45)   2.   If yes, does your accountability system work like that described on pages 77-91 of the *Curriculum & Instruction* handbook?

        ☐   1.   Yes   ☐   2.   No

        If no, please describe the differences.

     E.   School Year Action Zones

     1.   How many, if any, school year action zones for students are utilized by your project?

(46-47)   If none, write "0." _____

(48) 2. If you have action zones, are they organized like those described on pages 81-84 of the NWREL EBCE *Curriculum & Instruction* handbook?

☐ 1. Yes ☐ 2. No

If no, please describe the differences.

F. Assessment Forms

Listed below are a number of EBCE forms or instruments sometimes used. Please indicate which forms are required, optional or not used. Also indicate if they are revised or different from those developed or used by NWREL.

			Required	Optional	Not Used	Revised or Different From the Handbook
(49)	1.	CTBS Reading & Arithmetic Subtests (C:27,54)*	_____	_____	_____	_____
(50)	2.	Basic Skills Prescription Pad (C:635)	_____	_____	_____	_____
(51)	3.	Self Directed Search (C:116, 145, 640-41)	_____	_____	_____	_____
(52)	4.	Student Attitude Questionnaire	_____	_____	_____	_____
(53)	5.	Semantic Differential	_____	_____	_____	_____
(54)	6.	Psychosocial Maturity Scale (Student Opinion Scale)	_____	_____	_____	_____
(55)	7.	Parent Opinion Survey	_____	_____	_____	_____
(56)	8.	Employer Opinion Survey	_____	_____	_____	_____
(57)	9.	Student Application Form (S:69-75)	_____	_____	_____	_____
(58)	10.	Staff Questionnaire	_____	_____	_____	_____
(59)	11.	End-of-Year Student Questionnaire	_____	_____	_____	_____
(60)	12.	Learning Site Analysis Form (C:72-75)	_____	_____	_____	_____
(61)	13.	Skill Development Record (S:108-109)	_____	_____	_____	_____
(62)	14.	Student Performance Review (by employers) (S:112-113)	_____	_____	_____	_____

*This form is shown or discussed in the designated NWREL EBCE handbook on these pages. (C = *Curriculum & Instruction*; S = *Student Services*) Those not referenced will be found in the *Program Evaluation* handbook.

204

			Required	Optional	Not Used	Revised or Different From the Handbook
(63)	15.	Student Evaluation of Learning Site (S:110-111)	_____	_____	_____	_____
(64)	16.	EBCE Record of Student Performance (S:265-297)	_____	_____	_____	_____
(65)	17.	EBCE Student Experience Record (S:102-104)	_____	_____	_____	_____
(66)	18.	Weekly Time Reports (S:90-91)	_____	_____	_____	_____
(67)	19.	Student Profile Sheet (S:98-99)	_____	_____	_____	_____
(68)	20.	Accountability Write-Up Form (S:118-119)	_____	_____	_____	_____
(69)	21.	Learning Site Utilization Form (S:106-107)	_____	_____	_____	_____
(70)	22.	Maintenance Visit Record (S:130-131)	_____	_____	_____	_____
(71)	23.	Zone Debriefing Form (S:116-117)	_____	_____	_____	_____
(72)	24.	Predesigned Projects (C:196)	_____	_____	_____	_____

2. *Please list any additional forms or instruments your project uses and attach a copy of each to this checklist.*

(73) _____
(74) _____
(75) _____
_____
_____

(80=2)

V. FUNDING SOURCES

1. What is/are the *current* funding source(s) for your project (i.e. local district, state, federal)? If more than one funding source, list the approximate percentage of project funds provided by each source.

    local district _____ (7-8)   state _____ (9-10)   federal _____ (11-12)

(13-14)   other *(specify)* _____

2. What funding source(s) do you anticipate *for next year?* If more than one funding source, list the approximate percentage of project funds provided by each source.

    local district _____ (15-16)   state _____ (17-18)   federal _____ (19-20)

205

(21-22)   other *(please specify)* _____

(23-24)   _____

VI PROGRAM FUTURE

1. Will your EBCE program continue next year? Yes _____ No _____ **(25)**
    If yes, go to question 2; if no, go to question 3.

2. a) If your EBCE program will be continuing next year, what changes in operations will occur? b) In what ways will these changes affect the number of staff or students, the scope of the program, etc.?

(26-27)   _____
(28-29)   _____
(30-31)   _____
(32-33)   _____

3. If your EBCE program will *not* not continue next year, what are the reasons for its termination?

    lack of funding _____ **(34)** lack of district interest and support _____ **(35)**
    lack of community support _____ **(36)** lack of student interest _____ **(37)**
    lack of staff interest _____ **(38)**
(39,40)   other *(please list)* _____

    _____

4. If EBCE will terminate, will any components of it continue in some other form?
(41)   Yes _____ No _____ If yes, please describe.
(42-43)   _____
(44-45)   _____

5. Do you feel that it would have been desirable for EBCE to have continued?
(46)   Yes _____ No _____
(47-48)   Why? _____
(49-50)   _____

(51-52) 6. What actions do you feel have helped to keep EBCE from terminating?

(53-54)   _____

(80=3)

206

11

Choosing career education measures: the evaluator's plight

DEBORAH G. BONNET

New Educational Directions, Inc.

You have just been hired to evaluate the student impact of a career education program. We will be realistic and assume that your budget is too small, that you were hired too late, that evaluation is not the number one priority of your clients on the staff of the career education program (nor should it be). We will also assume that the staff has no authority to force the schools to do anything or, if it does, has good reason to refrain from exercising it unless absolutely necessary.

You probably face a lot of challenges—for instance, determining how much and what kind of career education activities take place and gaining the cooperation of comparison groups. But the principal task at hand is to come up with some instruments or techniques for measuring the program's impact on student learning. You're lucky—you have a full month before the pretesting.

You believe that outcome evaluations should deal with the program's own objectives, so you start by asking what the objectives are. Any of several things may happen at this point. For example, the program may not have specific grade-level objectives yet. Or it may indeed have stated objectives buried in a funding proposal written a year ago. You discover that the writer is no longer around to translate the proposal rhetoric into English and to sort out the promises funders like to hear from the results the grantees realistically hope to deliver. You discover that the program staff members are new to career education and unprepared to develop good objectives on the spot. Therefore, though you know it is not your role to define objectives, because you have a job to do you compromise by suggesting ten or so program goals, asking staff members to pick the ones they most want to evaluate. The staffers love them all. You wonder how they could possibly accomplish ten objectives when they would be doing well if their kids got an hour of career education a week. However, the staff's planning efforts have not progressed to a point where they can specify priorities, so you agree to do your best with all ten objectives. You just hope they end up resembling the curriculum actually being developed.

Alternatively, you might be presented with a list of objectives that covers an entire wall. You can see a good three hundred person-hours of your client's efforts in it, so you muster up all the tact within you and distribute a few warm fuzzies before mentioning that some of the objectives cannot be measured. You add that immeasurable means neither unimportant nor unachievable, and that you hope they will not be discouraged from working toward these noble outcomes. You suggest that although their system of grouping specific objectives together into larger concepts or goals works well for the purposes of curriculum development, it fails to correspond to the kinds of domains tests tend to encompass. You offer to help them identify a half-dozen or so outcomes to use for the evaluation. Staff members are cooperative, but understandably disappointed that the evaluation results will not fit each cell of their matrix, or even all of its columns and rows.

On the other hand, you might get just what you have in mind when you ask for the program's objectives: a manageable number of outcomes for each of several grade levels whose key words are something like "good work habits," "career planning skills," and "awareness of a variety of occupations." Also, program staff members, it is hoped, will be able to tell you exactly what they mean by these phrases. If you're lucky they'll have on hand a list of more specific attitudes, facts, skills, and behaviors composing each objective.

One way or another, you will have managed to get a pretty good idea of the outcomes your evaluation should address. The last time you did an evaluation like this you chose the measures yourself. When the final results showed no impact, everyone blamed the tests, charging that the questions had nothing to do with what staff members were trying to teach. They were probably right, so this time you plan to propose some measures, asking a committee of program staff members and other school representatives to help you make the final choices.

For several of the outcomes, you have some neat ideas for direct behavioral measures. One of them requires teachers to make in-class observations, but to do so teachers would have to be trained first, which in this district means paying for either stipends or released time. Your budget is incapable of handling such a cost and the project director wants to use all of her training budget for teaching teachers how to *do* career education—not how to evaluate it. Besides, you taught a class once and don't recall having had a lot of extra time to observe and record reliably specific student behaviors. Reluctantly, you drop your favored measure. Budgetary concerns also lead you to reject several other behavioral measures—several that require a number of judges and others that require only one, but for long observation periods. You hope you might be able to afford one of these measures if you use a small sample.

One of the measures you have in mind should not be expensive, since schools keep the data it measures on file. If the files are complete and you can work out an acceptable system for gaining access to them without coming up against the school's confidentiality policies, you'll be in good shape.

Some of your other measurement ideas call for open-ended questions. Using interviews would be expensive, and too few kids can write coherently enough to use the paper-and-pencil approach. Either way, scoring will be costly. But you decide to propose one of your ideas and hope that it will measure something besides verbal skills. And for the rest of the outcomes you'll have to go with paper-and-pencil forced-choice tests.

Fortunately, you make a habit of maintaining an updated file of available career education tests. (For suggested tests, see the Appendix of this volume.) Without this file you could forget about ordering specimen sets, reviewing them, and still getting multiple copies before the pretest date. You look in your file now. Here is what you find:

- No tests at all for some of the outcomes, or none that are appropriate for the grade level you want to test.
- Few test with respectable evidence of reliability and validity or with norms based on decent samples.
- Tests where the reading level is too high.
- Tests with a low reading level—but at the sacrifice of clarity. (Which is worse—a question poor readers won't understand, or one that good readers will find ambiguous?)
- Tests that require too much reading—they would be fatiguing to take and you wonder whether a 100-word test item is needed just fo find out whether kids know what an anthropologist does.
- Tests designed to measure personality traits, such as self-esteem or locus of control, which career education seeks to influence in a given direction. For their intended purposes, these are good tests. But you can tell by examining the items that the optimal score from a career education point of view is neither the highest nor the lowest, but somewhere between the middle and one of the extremes. This problem would seriously complicate your evaluation design unless you were willing to overlook it, toss out the items you considered too extreme, or avoid the test altogether.
- Tests containing items which, in your career-educated opinion, are incorrectly keyed.

- Test scales composed of items addressing more than one outcome as defined by your program. Under the test developer's construct, the items may hang together nicely. But you want to make a distinction between awareness of the nature of specific occupations and knowledge of the economic system in a more general sense.
- Tests that, according to their authors or their titles, measure an outcome you want to evaluate but that upon closer examination are not concerned with the same attitudes toward school or decision-making skills that your program hopes to develop. In one form of this problem, the test measures (or appears to measure) only a very small segment of the domain you hoped to tap. In another, only a small number of the items relate to your program's objectives, the rest remaining unaffected by career education instruction.
- Test batteries from which you want only one or two scales.

In spite of these problems, you find several available measures that look as if they will do. But when you add up the testing times and the prices, you are horrified to find that for these measures you would need four hours and $5.00 per student. It was all the program director could do to get the school to agree to one class period for testing; worse, the cost of the tests would be more than the entire evaluation budget. So you must decide either to use small samples for each measure by administering only one or two tests to each available student or to ask your review committee to prioritize the outcomes to evaluate.

At the instrument-review committee meeting you are reminded that the public (including many educators) has been misled and has reached two faulty conclusions: first, that the state of the art of measurement is considerably more advanced than it really is, and second, that test selection is strictly a matter of looking at the numbers in the technical manual.

You might make the unfortunate mistake of beginning to explain that there are no tests or other feasible means of evaluating one of the committee's favorite objectives. Several committee members find this hard to believe and one of them mentions a wonderful test he knows for that outcome. The test turns out to be one of the instruments you rejected because you found practically nothing to support the lavish claims implicit in its title and impressive packaging.

When you say that you have several evaluation measures to suggest, the first two questions will almost certainly be "Are they valid?" and "Are they standardized?" You get the impression that you are expected to produce a yes or no answer to the first question and that most of the group thinks that the second question is identical to the first. You explain that, no, some of your suggested measures are not standardized, but that it doesn't really matter because your evaluation design does not rely on national norms. You summarize the reliability and validity evidence, but stress that even if all the *r*'s are in the nineties, an evaluation tool is useless unless it measures the attributes targeted for evaluation. Until the day when a consensus is reached on a set of career education objectives that everyone interprets in precisely the same way, and until we have measures for each objective that are proven valid in every sense of the word, we will have to rely largely on our best judgment in deciding whether tests measure what we want to evaluate. Most of the committee members seem satisfied with your explanation and even pleased to learn that measurement is not quite as mystical as they had believed. But one hard-core skeptic in the corner is drafting a plea to the school board to withdraw your contract.

You ask the committee to evaluate the proposed tests with two criteria in mind: (1) Do the items represent attitudes or information the committee hopes to convey to youngsters through career education? and (2) Are the vocabulary and syntax appropriate for their students? Assuming members are knowledgeable about career education and thoroughly grasp their own objectives, most of them will be able to evaluate the tests once they understand why the process is needed.

In the process of their evaluation, you will probably find that you were a little off in your understanding of the program's interpretation of some of its objectives. You have mixed feelings when the group starts recognizing some of the inadequacies you found—pleased that they noticed and nervous about whether they will accept any of the tests (or, if they do, whether they will accept the evaluation results).

Group members will have a few problems in identifying the concepts underlying test items and in evaluating how well the items of a test scale cover the objective. One teacher will say repeatedly, "My kids don't know this!" but eventually will realize that the question is whether they can and should learn it. With all the talk of accountability, it's no wonder people forget that low pretest scores are okay.

Sometime during the meeting, someone will ask when teachers will get the test results. You were hoping this question wouldn't come up, because you would really prefer not to give them individual student scores. When your own faith in the measures as program evaluation tools is guarded, how can you put students' scores on attitudes toward school, self-esteem, and work attitudes into the hands of teachers? After all, you know that at least some of the teachers will try to use the results for individual diagnosis regardless of warnings against it. You wouldn't admit it to just anybody, but there have been times when you've caught yourself conjuring up images of people based solely on their scores on perfectly awful measures. If *you* can't resist this temptation, why should people who don't understand all the arguments against it? You dodge the question for the time being and recall with relief that at least the tests you will use don't come with norms. Perhaps in return for the class time teachers will be devoting to testing, you can satisfy their desire for something instructionally useful by giving them group item data. Or you may use a complex coding system and hope that teachers' interest in individual scores will be dampened by the chore of decoding.

After much discussion and many compromises, the committee agrees on some measures. Nobody is really happy with them, least of all you. You make a mental note to order the commercial tests the first thing in the morning and wonder whether they'll arrive in time.

Most aggravating of all is your certainty that you could develop more suitable tests for the program yourself. Oh, well; maybe next time. Of course, developing new tests would take a while, and you would have to suffer your colleagues' criticisms for using unvalidated measures. You may wonder why it's generally considered preferrable to use tests that have data to prove how mediocre they are than to use ones that look better but have yet to be subjected to the proper statistical gyrations. Perhaps it's because we lost sight of the differences between *validated* and *valid*. Do we find ourselves believing that validity does not exist until we measure it?

You wish for easy access to an item bank with lots of psychometric data on each item. That would alleviate the problems of time and critics and would enable you to construct tests to fit the program's students and its objectives. If you asked the right questions, the answer might be that students really *do* learn from career education—just as everybody claims, but hardly ever demonstrates.

POSTSCRIPT

Since I wrote "The Evaluator's Plight," some changes have occurred—in the career education movement, the evaluation profession, and the public's attitudes toward testing. It is necessary to add some components to the scenario.

Since the program you are evaluating can afford your services, it is less likely to be K – 12 and school-based and more likely to be CETA-funded and targeted for disadvantaged youth. The term *career education* might not even be used, at least not in public; *employability skills* or *transition skills* are probably used instead. But your clients may nevertheless be seasoned veterans of the career education movement, or at least have advisors who are.

The task of picking outcomes to evaluate should be a little simpler. The program's objectives are probably more explicit and more realistic. But if you have time, you might decide to ignore the written objectives anyway, starting instead with a goal-free investigation of what participants experience and how the program affects them. (See chapter 12 for a rationale and description of a more "goal free" approach.) That approach is quite chic these days. You might be able to get away with stopping there, but we'll assume that a traditional streak compels you to treat your goal-free findings as hypotheses for empirical testing. So on you go with your search for measures.

Since the program involves only teenagers, you are spared the special challenges of finding instruments for the elementary level. On the other hand, the reading and writing skill limitations of youths are harder to ignore, since the program you are evaluating is only for the disadvantaged.

The national item bank you longed for never materialized, although you may have compiled a modest one on your own. You've kept your file of commercial tests current, but it's grown very little in the last two years. You've kept in close enough touch with your colleagues to gather that individual researchers have been busy developing and testing new instruments and some exciting alternatives to paper-and-pencil tests. Unfortunately, though, no one has indexed this recent work into a central reference tool.

In developing your proposals for the review committee, you find yourself slower to reject "nontest measures" than you use to be. Some of the program's objectives beg for straightforward behavioral measures; some, like postprogram employment status, are even required by the program's funder. You've learned more about collecting and analyzing unobtrusive, observational, and self-report data, and the program involves extended youth contact with employers, giving you a rich new data source. Just sprinkling the final report with words like "naturalistic" and "responsive" will get you off the hook regarding validation with many of your colleagues.

You may still propose a test or two, but you steer clear of the old stand-by career development batteries. The reading difficulty on those tests is just too obvious, and the program directors have told you they want nothing to do with them, having already experienced the consequences of their insensitivity to instruction. Perhaps this time you'll develop a customized test, since criticism of this approach seems to have subsided in the literature. Maybe you could come up with something in an audiovisual format.

The review committee is remarkably receptive to your suggestions. Your paper-and pencil-test is the least popular. They remind you that "these kids are turned off by tests," but agree that half an hour of testing is tolerable. This time they are relieved to learn that the tests are not standardized; Ralph Nader and company may have gotten carried away, but exposing shortcomings of testing is still a necessary public service.

They are delighted that you plan to talk to the kids ("Maybe the evaluators will finally find out that we really are doing something for youth"). Asking employers to report their observations of the program's effects also gets approval ("Employers carry a lot of weight"). Particularly popular are your most unusual approaches ("We would like our evaluation to be a little different"). Your simulation exercise may be time-consuming, but that's okay as long as it's instructional ("It has good intuitive appeal"). The only serious reservations concern the measures that require additional record-keeping. Paperwork is still a problem, as is the cost of the measures they want.

You leave the meeting wondering why, after ten years of career education, choosing evaluation measures has not yet evolved into a perfunctory task, like choosing a reading-achievement test once was. Pulling something off the shelf would surely be easier and cheaper than this. But it might be less fruitful, and certainly less fun.

12

Needed: instruments as good as our eyes

HENRY M. BRICKELL

"All right. Pick up your yellow pads; pack your suitcases; get on the plane to Ohio. And don't come back. Not until you have an instrument that can measure as well as your eyes, ears, noses, and throats."

I was tired. And frustrated. Why couldn't they measure what they could see? If career education in Ohio was as vivid as they said—if teaching was as career-flavored—if student learning was as apparent—why couldn't our evaluation staff measure it? Why couldn't we have hard evidence to match soft evidence: test scores to match classroom observations?

MERCURY BETWEEN THE FINGERS

We had been at it in Ohio for three solid years already. Teams of observers could see it, or so they said. Not only career teaching. Career learning. They could see it. But they couldn't pick up the evidence and bring it back to

This paper, originally published in the *Journal of Career Education,* Winter 1976, *2* (3), 56–66, is reprinted by permission of the *Journal of Career Education.*

New York. Palpable as mercury but just as elusive: independent observers could agree the silvery globules were there yet not one of them could pick one up and hand it over to another observer, or to us, or to Ohio officials, or to Ken Hoyt, or to America.

Thousands of students taught by hundreds of teachers in dozens of schools; interviewed, watched, and tested. All kinds of teachers, young and old, good and bad; all kinds of students, bright and dull, black and white; all kinds of schools, urban and rural, rich and poor. Learning, learning everywhere but not a statistical difference.

Thorndike echoed across fifty years: ". . . if it exists, it exists in some quantity and can be measured . . ." or something like that. Easy enough for you to say, E.L. If you were here, I'd give you a yellow pad and put you on the plane to Ohio. See what you could do. It exists, all right. Go measure it!

FOUR YEARS AGO:
OBSERVE IT

Four years ago, we hadn't been sure. Back then, Ohio had issued a career development curriculum guide in three volumes, very impressive: Career Motivation for K−6, Career Orientation for 7−8, Career Exploration for 9−10. Our mission as external evaluators: try to find it in the classrooms.

Out went our teams, hardheaded people, skillful observers, familiar with the ways of career education, out across the old Northwest Territory, following the State guides. They coursed down the Ohio to Cincinnati, up the Miami to Dayton, up the Scioto and along Paint Creek to Paint Valley, up the Muskingum to East Muskingum, over land north to Akron and still further along the Cuyahoga to Cleveland. The teams sat with project staffs, looked at materials, talked with teachers, visited classrooms, watched students. In time, the word worked its way back East.

"We have found it: project staffs explaining careers, teachers teaching careers, even students learning careers—especially in K−3, a bit less in 4−6, still less in 7−8, and least in 9−10. It cannot be found everywhere and it differs according to habitat and natural surroundings, but its range is statewide."

At year's end, we told the State officials in Ohio. They were pleased with what their $25 per pupil had accomplished in the K−10 pyramids of project schools—K−6 feeding into 7−8 and on into 9−10. We were happy; they were happy.

Then they said the words that have destroyed many happy marriages between friendly observers and friendly program people: "Test it."

THREE YEARS AGO:
TEST IT

Easy. We knew exactly how to do that. Take the State Curriculum guides, thumb to the objectives, write multiple-choice test items to match, show them to State and local officials as a face validity check, pilot test the items to make sure the difficulty level is right, and compile final tests for grades 3, 6, 8, and 10—the natural terminal points of major program segments. We did all of that.

Then we administered those tests to 6,000 students—students in the program and students not in the program—in four representative cities, cities our teams had visited. And then we analyzed the results. What did we find?

No significant difference. None. Not in cognitive learning. Not in affective learning. Not in item clusters. Rarely in individual items.

Mercury

Of course, we were not alone. Soon the nation would have spent $10 billion in ESEA Title I since 1965. $10 billion while 10,000 teachers and specialists and observers insisted that something good was happening: teachers were teaching, paraprofessionals were tutoring, students were learning. But Jim Coleman said "No significant difference." And Christopher Jencks seemed to agree. Very familiar. Too familiar.

The Ohio officials were not pleased. That year's finding cancelled the previous year's finding. Then you saw it, now you don't. Magic. Magic that makes the client's money disappear, leaving nothing. No findings. Not even an explanation.

How could this be? How could our independent observers have gone out, seen nothing, and called it something? They were too good to be wrong; they had observed the way they were supposed to. Still, our tests were too good to be wrong; we had made them the way we were supposed to.

What were we to believe: the evidence of our eyes or the evidence of our instruments. And how, as supposedly-skilled evaluators, could we explain the conflict?

Four explanations occurred to us. One assumed that our instruments were right; one assumed our eyes were right; two assumed both were right. Here were the possibilities:

Interpretation 1: No career education is taking place. Our observers are blind—or hallucinating. Our tests are right.

Interpretation 2: Non-career curricula teach career content. Program teachers are teaching it and program students are learning it, but so are non-program teachers and students. Our observers and our tests are both right.

Interpretation 3: Non-school sources teach career content. Career information is so important that the home does not leave it to the school. Family, friends, and TV teach the content to non-program students. Our observers and our tests are both right.

Interpretation 4: Program students cannot fully demonstrate their learning on our tests. Career education is taking place. Our observers are right; our tests are wrong.

We knew that Interpretations 2 and 3 were right. Non-program students scored well on the tests, tests that Ohio local and State officials said fit their curriculum. Somebody in school or out of school was teaching career concepts to non-program students.

But what about Interpretation 1 versus 4? We decided to go back to Ohio, look at those classrooms, and double check our impression not only that teachers were teaching but that students were learning.

TWO YEARS AGO:
OBSERVE IT AGAIN

Out went the observer teams again, down the Ohio, up the Miami, along the Cuyahoga. This time they went to seven sites—a good cross-section. We waited for their report.

When it came, it sounded stunningly familiar, completely reassuring, and deeply disturbing.

"We have found it again: project staff explaining careers, teachers teaching careers, even students learning careers—especially in $K-3$, a bit less in $4-6$, still less in $7-8$, least in $9-10$. It cannot be found everywhere and it differs according to habitat and natural surroundings, but its range is statewide."

Thanks a lot! I guess.

So they were not blind. Or at least they hallucinated consistently. But how could we prove that they were not seeing mirages, illusions rising from the hot enthusiasm of project staff, teachers, and students eager to show the Wise Men from the East what they had come so far to see—and eager to keep their $25 per pupil? That is where last year's story began.

ONE YEAR AGO:
TEST IT AGAIN

We were back in New York, reviewing the evidence. We had seen it once, seen it twice, but we couldn't make a test to show it at all. Not even with tests our own staff had built to match the Ohio curriculum—tests the local and State officials had endorsed.

Let's look again at Interpretation 4 and go over it once more, this time slowly. Let's see: program students are learning something but they can't show it on our tests. Hmmm . . . okay . . . adopt that interpretation . . . try to prove it.

"All right, staff. Pick up your yellow pads; pack your suitcases; get on the plane to Ohio. And don't come back until you can measure what you can see. Pick up the mercury. Bring it home. Somehow."

"Try this. Leave those three Ohio curriculum guides in your offices here in New York. When you get on site, walk past the project staff, walk past the principal's office, slip past the teachers and sit in the backs of the classrooms."

"Watch the learning. Don't watch the teaching. If you ever see a student or a class learn something about careers—anything about careers—take out your yellow pad and write a test item she could pass. Wait a minute. Now, this could be critical for us: make it an item no other student could pass unless she had been in that same class. Or in an equivalent career education class across the hall, across the town, across the county, or across the state. That's it: we want items not only for the rooms where they were written; we want items that will work statewide. We want items career students can get right but other students can't—items that show the special things only career students are learning."

"Write the item on the spot, if possible; at least write notes for it. Polish the items that night in your motel rooms."

"Ideally, we ought to administer those items to students the day we write them, or the next day. In fact, we shouldn't even bring items out of the classroom where they were written, if students can't pass them. We'll get items like that when you thought you saw learning, but didn't. However, we can't work that fast.

"So instead, as soon as the items are written, polished, edited, and printed, we'll administer them not only in that class but in other program classes in the same city—and to non-program classes as well."

"Take along three big canvas bags: a green one for items that discriminate in favor of program classes, a red one for items that discriminate against program classes, and a grey one for items that don't discriminate. We'll give gold stars for green items."

"Now that is one way to write items. But only one. Let's think up others. How else can we get items that will let the career students show their stuff?"

The conversation went on and on and on. When it was over, we had thought of eight more. A total of nine ways to pick up mercury. Before the teams came home, they would need them all.

FIELD-BASED TEST DEVELOPMENT

We were out to find whether tests developed in the field rather than in the office—tests to measure what teachers were teaching rather than what program designers planned for them to teach, tests to measure what students were learning rather than what program designers intended them to learn, tests that were classroom-sensitive rather than curriculum-sensitive—whether such tests could distinguish between program students and non-program students. That is, we were out to find whether we could measure what we could see. And the technique would be simplicity itself. We would make the instruments where we had seen the learning—in the classrooms. We would build the tests to match the learning.

The item-writing teams spent the winter in the river valleys of Ohio, picking their way through the white snow and the brown slush, going from school to school and room to room, moving along the rows, picking an item here and an item there, filling their green bags and their red bags and their grey bags one item at a time.

It was slow work. A few of the nine methods worked; most didn't. Teachers weren't very good item writers; students weren't either; our writers weren't either. They strained hard to find career learning in grades 9 – 10. They strained harder to find affective learning—the much-hoped-for program out- come, according to State and local officials—at any grade. Maybe affective learning is as ephemeral to the eye as it is to an instrument.

They wrote over 1,000 usable items, leaving hundreds more in the wastebaskets of Ohio motels.

Each item was piloted with hundreds of program and non-program students in grade 3 or 6 or 8 or 10. Each was piloted with students in the city where it was written and in three other cities.

THREE BAGS FULL

The writers brought three bags of tested items home to New York. We had to help them carry the grey bag, sagging with non-discriminating items. The green bag was much lighter. The red bag was, happily, the lightest of all.

We dumped out the contents of the grey bag and the green bag and compared them. The teams had had to write 5 cognitive items to produce one discriminating in favor of the program and 9 affective items to produce one discriminating in its favor. Hard work, picking up mercury.

"Save all the items. Each one is equally valuable, equally diagnostic. We'll go over each one with the State officials in Ohio. We have to tell them— even if they won't be happy to hear it—where the program is strong, neutral, and weak—the green items, the grey, and the red." What was it Ohio State wore to the Rose Bowl this year—red and grey. We could have told them.

We took the greenest of the green items and compiled them into four tests—one each for grades 3, 6, 8, and 10—each with cognitive items and affective items.

We shipped them off to seven sites: some where we had written items; some where we had piloted them; some where we had neither written nor piloted them. We administered the tests to 12,000 students—some in the pro- gram and some not in the program, the two groups as comparable as we could make them under natural field conditions.

SIGNIFICANT DIFFERENCES AT LAST

The new test results demonstrated the superiority of program students to non-program students on every test in every grade. They were ahead on the cognitive tests and on the affective tests; they were ahead at grades 3 and 6 and 8 and 10. Statistically significant differences at the .01 level in statewide results on every test in every grade (except grade 10 affective learning, where both our observers and our item writers had found the atmosphere thin).

Our eyes had been right. Our original instruments had been wrong. And we knew why.

But there was more. The results showed the program was working best in K–3, a bit less in 4–6, still less in 7–8, and less in 9–10—but it clearly was working at every grade. Exactly what our observers had said!

And more. The program was working in most grades in most cities but not in all and it varied in scope and success. What had our observers said? "It cannot be found everywhere and it differs according to habitat and natural surroundings, but its range is statewide."

And more. The test items written in one program classroom worked in many other program classrooms—across the hall, across the town, across the county, across the state. So there was much commonality statewide along with the diversity. It meant teachers were teaching similar things, even though not necessarily the things in the State curriculum guides. It meant that State officials had issued a common message, that local officials had heard it, that classroom teachers were listening to it.

Checking Validity

Before we scored the tests and analyzed the results, we asked the State and local officials in Ohio to rate each item in each test as measuring "important" or "neutral" or "unimportant" career knowledge and career attitudes in grades 3, 6, 8, and 10. Making their judgments independently, the officials rated an average of 87 percent of the test items as "important," 9 percent as "neutral," and 4 percent as "unimportant." So much for validity. That was the best we could do that year.

Checking Reliability

After we had scored the tests, we computed split-half reliability coefficients for each test using the Kuder-Richardson 20 formula. *Affective* test reliabilities ranged from .52 to .68; *cognitive* results good enough for individuals.

Using Spearman-Brown, we found that we would have to lengthen the 20-item affective tests to 80 items to make them as reliable as the 40-item cognitive tests. Not surprising. Feelings are more subject to variation from time to time than knowledge; thus our affective tests would have to be longer than our cognitive tests to be equally reliable.

Checking Item Difficulty

Both State and local officials in Ohio had wanted the test items to be made easy enough so that students could demonstrate clearly what they were learning. Many teachers echoed that concern. Our analysis showed that the final tests were indeed rather easy, with students averaging 60–70 percent of the items correct.

Checking Test Coverage

The Ohio career development program has seven divisions—world of work, economics, decision-making, etc. Our analysis showed that the greenest of the green cognitive and affective items came from all seven divisions, demonstrating that the program students were able to show their superiority across the entire program spectrum.

CONVERGENCE AT LAST

We could measure what we could see at last. The evidence of our eyes converged with the evidence of our instruments. And now it was easy to see why. Evaluators use their eyes to see what is there, whether it is intended or not. But they use their test instruments to measure what is intended, whether it is there or not. Like other evaluators, we had made field observations of the in-fact curriculum as it was being taught. And like other evaluators, we had originally written test items in the office to match the official program intentions.

We had achieved convergence by moving our item development out of the office and into the same locations as our observations. That suggested another route to convergence: train our observers to see as little as our tests. Train them to look only for what is intended and to ignore everything else that is accomplished. Just like our current tests.

Of course, it is important to know whether intentions were accomplished. But it is equally important to know what was accomplished, intended or not. Our Ohio curriculum-based tests measured intentions; our field-based tests measured accomplishments.

Indeed, the finished field-based tests themselves profiled the superior learning of the program students. The items themselves actually mirrored their learning. Say that again. What mirrored the learning—what? The items—the silvery test items spread on flat sheets. Exactly. The mercury at last. We had it. A mirror as good as our eyes.

We need such instruments. As evaluators, we need to be able to say to program directors and classroom teachers: "Yes, we can measure what you can see." Otherwise, we may look irrelevant or incompetent or dangerous.

Evaluators have been broadening their repertoire of instruments for years: curriculum-embedded tests, observer checklists, audiotape recorders, videotape recorders, unobtrusive measures, the critical incident technique, situational tests, peer ratings, projective tests, criterion-referenced tests, and on and on. Developing tests in field situations promises to enrich our repertoire still further.

The notion of field-based testing blends nicely with some recent and current thinking about alternatives to testing the declared objectives of a program.

GOAL-FREE TEST DEVELOPMENT

Unthinkable. Until you think about it. Michael Scriven suggests somewhere that the difference between main effects and side effects are in the eye of the beholder. Scriven says the program person calls what she intends main effects and what she does not intend side effects. The liberated goal-free evaluator, on the other hand, might call them "unifects." The goal-free evaluator's entire business is effects, not intents; outcomes, not goals; the target hit, not the target set.

But how could the evaluator ever develop a test? Well, she could look at the treatment rather than at the objectives. Since the treatment so often loses sight of the target anyway, she could ask "Where are you shooting?" rather than "Where are you aiming?" That is, she could start at the muzzle, and predict the trajectory, and go to the other end of that arc—rather than standing out there beside the official designated target, waiting for the holes to appear.

We are talking about developing test items by examining instructional processes rather than stated goals and objectives. And we are saying they might be a better source. Better in the sense that the evidence of the evaluator's instrument might more closely match the evidence of the evaluator's eyes. Better in the sense that they would report whatever is going on. Better in the sense that they would give us significant differences. Better in the sense that they would be firmer guides to the evaluator than the kind of "official" pious overstated goals and objectives loaded like so much ballast into proposals to get them through the heavy seas of the review process, then dumped overboard.

Theory-Based Test Development

Theory-based evaluation should be employed where an instructional program aims toward distant or intangible outcomes . . .

Remoteness and inconcreteness of objectives seem, in fact, to be particularly characteristic of the humanistic trend in education . . .

The evaluation question becomes: Have the variables which theory indicates are crucial to the program actually been operationalized? . . .

This is what Carol Tylor Fitz-Gibbon and Lynn Lyons Morris said in the June, 1975 issue of *Evaluation Comment* (UCLA Center for the Study of Evaluation). Making a case for theory-based evaluation, they suggested that both

formative and summative assessment should be guided by the theory on which
the program is based.

> One cannot measure or observe or report on everything about a program;
> inevitably, one selects . . .
>
> The choice of variables to study need not remain a matter of opinion. . .
>
> When a theory-based evaluation is planned, the variables selected for study
> are those which a theory indicates are crucial. . .

Fitz-Gibbon and Morris talk mostly about process variables but they
suggest that the same reasoning applies to outcome variables.

If they are right, how does one develop a test? Well, the theory underlying the program is—to put it oversimply—a set of cause-and-effect statements
about what processes will lead to what outcomes. It follows that a program based
on that theory—irrespective of whether the program knows what theory it is
using—is likely to produce certain outcomes whether it intends them or not.
Presumably, those are the outcomes a skilled observer would detect with his
eyes and ears. And those are the outcomes a skilled evaluator would create
instruments to measure. Then, happily, the evidence of the observer's eyes and
evaluator's instruments would converge.

"Don't bother to declare your objectives. We'll just check your program
vehicle, decide which theoretical road it is designed to travel, draw a finish line
across the end of the road, and wait there for you to arrive." Thus speaks the
pure theory-based evaluator. The finish line is of course the criterion level and
the ribbon stretched across the road above it is the instrument.

FIELD-BASED EVALUATOR, MEET
GOAL-FREE EVALUATOR AND
THEORY-BASED EVALUATOR

F. B. Evaluator and G. F. Evaluator and T. B. Evaluator can get along
well together. None of the three is much interested in intended outcomes. All
three predict the outcomes—F. B. from observing learning, G. F. from observing processes, T. B. from identifying theory. None of the three would design
instruments to measure the intended objectives exclusively.

And all three would hopefully produce hard evidence that would coin-
cide with soft evidence.

PROTECTING CAREER EDUCATION
FROM FALSE CONCLUSIONS

How good it might be for the evaluator to watch what career educators
are doing, determine where that will take the students, and design tests to

measure how far they get. Beyond that, evaluators might keep career education out of undeserved danger by telling project directors things like: "No. We won't test academic learning to see whether your one-day values-clarification workshop for teachers last summer raises students' scores on the Iowa achievement tests next June. The treatment is too weak for that objective. In fact it isn't even worth trying. If you're going to clarify values all year, we're going to test values clarification."

As evaluators, we ought to get our values clarified about that.

PART FIVE

FUTURE DIRECTIONS: FUNDING AND RESEARCH

The volume concludes with several chapters that offer practical information and suggestions for future evaluation and research efforts. The budgetary, technical, and practical problems facing career development assessment are addressed in some detail. This material will be of particular interest to those seeking funding sources and priority areas for conducting research studies.

In chapter 13, Robert Wise, a program officer at the National Institute of Education, discusses his views of the emerging federal priorities for career education and career development research. He urges researchers to become aware that changing national economic policies will result in the more careful targeting of research dollars and to look to state and local government agencies as well. His message implies that successful research proposals will be less theoretical and more relevant to immediate problems and the policies instituted to alleviate them.

Wise has also provided readers with descriptions and addresses of agencies within the Departments of Education and Labor that presently support a range of research and evaluation areas related to career education. Wise adds to the usefulness of these listings by elaborating on the particular concerns and mandates of each funding agency. He urges researchers to make direct contact with the appropriate offices for up-to-date information on proposal requirements and application deadlines.

The final chapter, by Hamel and Krumboltz, is a synthesis of the major themes and recommendations posed by contributors to this volume and others in the field. The goal was to define some high priority research and evaluation studies of particular interest at this time. The list of issues is by no means exhaustive, but it does represent a range of topics that must be addressed in the near future if we are to achieve substantive progress in assessing career development outcomes.

13

Opportunities for funding research on education and career development

ROBERT I. WISE
National Institute of Education

My purposes in this chapter are two: (1) to share some unofficial views on evolving federal research priorities related to education and career development and to urge researchers to become more policy-relevant in a time of fiscal constraint and competition; and (2) to point to possible sources of funding for research, development, and program demonstration to improve the contribution that education is making to career entry and progression.

National interest in education for career development is entering a new phase in the decade of the 1980s. Until the 1970s the relationship between schooling and work has been popularly understood to be real and direct. Most Americans have believed a good education would lead to a good job, and indeed data have consistently shown that number of years of schooling is positively correlated with income and job status. Also, since the second decade of this century, vocational education has been offered to a significant number of youth who wanted a direct but nonacademic educational route into the work-

This article was written by Robert Wise in a private capacity. No official support or endorsement by the National Institute of Education or the U.S. Department of Education is intended or should be inferred.

place. In good economic times, the labor market has offered a sufficient number of jobs at professional, technical, and managerial levels to accommodate all students who have continued schooling beyond the compulsory age. But in hard economic times, when there are not enough of these jobs to keep pace with the number of college graduates, extra years of schooling do not automatically bring that expected good-paying job.

In the 1970s, several publications appeared arguing that the economic returns of higher education were declining and that for the foreseeable future a college graduate could not necessarily expect to get that better job (Berg, 1971; Freeman, 1976; O'Toole, 1975). And the public in general, experiencing unsatisfactory unemployment and inflation rates, became more concerned about the career payoffs for their educational investments. These new circumstances made the 1970s a time of serious questioning of the long-accepted relationship between schooling and career development. Simultaneously, the policy-makers became more sensitive to a range of existing problems—for example, that vocational and career graduates were failing to get the jobs they trained for, sex-role stereotyping was having a limiting effect on career development, and that many youths were lacking knowledge about the world of work and about career options. These conditions may have existed in the earlier part of the century, but they had not been viewed with much concern. The 1970s, therefore, became a period of questioning and attempting to repair the relationship between education and career development.

Career education has been a widely supported educational response to these problems. A major strategy of career education has been to infuse information about occupations into all curriculum subjects in all grade levels, K through 16, and to teach students to relate their educational plans to career options and benefits. This strategy was viewed as responsive to other perceived educational problems in the 1970s, such as students' lack of basic academic skills and the lack of adequate roles for parents and community in educational policy formulation (Herr and Cramer, 1977). Organizing education around career development, it has been argued, would motivate student learning by showing its value in the world of work, and it would overcome the isolation of schools by putting them in touch with the world of work in their local communities. A decade of school reform under the career education banner has seen activity at practically all levels of schooling in every state in the nation. The decade has also seen congressional intent evolve from demonstrating the possibilities of the concept of career education to implementing career education as a well-developed educational approach. This shift from development to implementation carries the implication that career education has completed the conceptual challenge of linking education to career development with its focus on the school curriculum, and that it has answered the questions it posed for itself as to how work-related goals can be infused into existing educational programs. If true, what remains for career education is the refinement and dissemination of these answers.

FEDERAL RESEARCH PRIORITIES

What will emerge in the 1980s as the new formulation of national concern for education and career development? There is no sign that such concern is diminishing, but in the years ahead it will probably be dominated by concerns for strengthening the economy and the United States' economic position in the world. National economic policy will probably emphasize controlling inflation and unemployment, improving productivity, strengthening high technology fields, and modernizing aging industrial plants and equipment. Education may be increasingly viewed as having a role in economic development primarily to reduce unemployment, increase worker productivity, and retrain segments of the workforce to meet changing occupational needs. In developing the education and work agenda of the 1980s, two forces will continue to be significant in federal decision making—the pursuit of the national goal of educational equity and the need to hold down federal spending. The latter force has to do with the necessity of allocating scarce resources; the former, with insisting that those resources go to those most in need. In the next decade, the process of determining who has the greatest educational need will be more difficult than ever.

That we are in the midst of difficult economic times is not represented simply in current efforts to cut back federal spending or to balance the federal budget. Economic and other forecasts indicate that formal education will experience severe financial strain in the next decade, in large degree because we seem to be approaching the point at which education's piece of the nation's fiscal pie will have attained its maximum size. At present, education is labor-intensive rather than capital-intensive—that is, schools use people rather than machines to teach, and salaries tend to rise faster than capital costs. As ceilings are put on public spending, formal education will be caught in a particularly serious squeeze if it cannot increase its share of the pie relative to other economic sectors. These economic circumstances are unfamiliar to educators, and it is very uncertain how the financial tradeoffs will be made.

The force for educational equity is not unfamiliar, however. It has been embodied in a twenty-year national policy concern that included education in the fight to end discrimination and eliminate poverty. As the dominant education and work theme in the 1970s, career education was not conceived primarily as an educational strategy in the fight against poverty; rather, career education addressed itself to the career development needs of all students. However, within its concern for increasing the chances of all students for success in school and work, career education did pay special attention to sources of educational inequity. It sought to avoid sex and race bias in its methods and materials, trained teachers to counteract sex-role stereotyping, and developed classroom materials for handicapped and other populations in order to more fairly distribute career education opportunities. In the education and work agenda of the 1980s, this general interest in all students will probably give way to more concentrated focus on selected populations of learners most in need. This targeting of resources will occur not simply as a result of budget-cutting pressures, but because different populations have different career employment needs and because populations with special needs will require more explicit responses to their needs.

As an example of targeting resources for career development, consider the youth population. A Democratic administration considered new youth employability legislation in 1980. This legislation was aimed at low-income youth, those with the highest unemployment rates and whose employment needs have refused to give way to more general educational strategies. This proposed legislation authorized funds to the Department of Education and the Department of Labor to increase the employability of youth ages 12 to 21 in low-income communities. The Department of Labor would support efforts by their prime sponsors to provide employment, training, and educational opportunities to out-of-school youth, including summer work experience, career exploration, occupational information for 14- and 15-year-olds, part-time work, vocational training, day care, transportation, career guidance for 16- to 18-year-olds, and basic skills training, vocational training, and on-the-job training for 19- to 21-year-olds. The Department of Education would support basic skills instruction and employability training for in-school youth. Grants would be given to local school districts in areas with high concentrations of poor students to develop programs in junior high, senior high, and vocational schools. Program activities might include basic skills training, employability skills training, career counseling, and work experience for junior and senior high students, with additional occupational training for senior high students, and vocational and basic skills training provided in alternative programs. The proposed legislation required that a percentage of the monies for both Labor and Education programs be used to carry out programs under joint agreements at the local level between schools and DOL prime sponsors.

Now, under a Republican administration, a different approach to targeting resources for youth is emerging. The federal government is seeking to return control of the identification and solving of national problems to local communities so that each community can find its own best solutions; and ways are being sought to encourage local institutions, especially business and industry, to use their own resources and take the initiative to meet local needs. The notion is to leave dollars at the local level to be used for local innovation rather than to tax the local community and then to return tax dollars to the community for federally regulated innovation. The notion that the federal government could always find a solution has given way to the notion that federal government solutions always cost more than their benefits are worth.

An example of using federal tax incentives to spur local youth employment initiative might be permitting tax writeoffs to industries that locate a plant in a high unemployment urban area and hire and train unemployed youth and adults. Or a local vocational education program might offer to provide a fully trained and work-ready labor force to an industry that moves into the local community. Even with these very different strategies for targeting resources for youth employment, there will still be a concern for improving the basic skills needed for learning a job, improving the career expectations and work knowledge of youth, and improving the pre-employment skills of job-seeking, interviewing, and work habits and attitudes. The federal role will probably become one of disseminating information about successful local innovations rather than funding them.

Research on education and career development should take a cue from this shift away from the nontargeted career education strategy of the 1970s and likewise concentrate its efforts on selected populations. Research will be increasingly asked to explain its contributions in terms of national economic priorities and problems, and, with limited resources, research will have to concentrate on selected target populations where new knowledge can make the greatest contributions to overall national goals. The implication here is that research will need to learn how to be problem-relevant and policy-relevant, rather than simply theory-relevant. Theory building is never finished; thus it will always be the case that more needs to be known about career development. But researchers would do well to learn to extract practical implications from what research is available at any given time, rather than to postpone looking for implications until more research is done. In designing research studies, researchers would also do well to think in terms of having an impact after two or three years rather than five or ten years or longer, and to see that *each* study contributes something to policy and practice. Research synthesis and utilization should become more integral to the research process. The youth-employability problem, for example, is a rich area for career development research, but the literature currently does not have a lot to say about what affects the employability of low-income youth and what can be done; it could. It could have a lot to say, also, about education and career development for other segments of the population that are not well-represented in the labor market or are not being well served by schools. The economic challenges of the 1980s will continue to call for career-related education. Research will remain vital and find more receptive audiences if it can be linked to education's response to these national challenges.

FUNDING SOURCES FOR CAREER
DEVELOPMENT RESEARCH

To carry out my second purpose in this chapter, I will describe the offices in the Departments of Education and Labor that currently have funded projects related to increasing knowledge about education for career development. Deciding which agencies to include here is largely influenced by what is meant by "career development research." I have interpreted the phrase broadly in the interest of the several different audiences that will be reading this and have listed seven offices and agencies that support various types of research activities in this area. These offices and agencies are, in the Department of Education, the Office of Career Education, the Office of Vocational and Adult Education, the

Office of Special Education, the Women's Educational Equity Act Program, the National Institute of Education, the Fund for the Improvement of Postsecondary Education, and, in the Department of Labor, the Employment and Training Administration.

Writing about these offices and agencies as future sources of funds for research is to write without assuredness, because the Congress is in the process of making major changes in legislation and/or funding for most federal programs. Nearly all of the Department of Education's 150 congressionally mandated programs are now feeling a squeeze in the form of either reduced funding or legislative and organizational changes. Indeed the Department of Education itself is slated for reorganization, although it is not clear what the new organization will look like; whatever its new form, it will be smaller. The Department of Labor is not slated for major reorganization, but changes may be made in some internal units.

Although the organization of the Department of Education is uncertain at this time, there is reasonable clarity about legislation affecting educational programs. For the federal fiscal years 1982 and 1983, the main thrust of legislative changes is to consolidate a number of programs into block grants to states and to permit states to determine which programs will be funded. This will in effect shift funding decisions from the federal to the state level for those programs included in the block grants. A state will have complete discretion in how block-grant funds will be allocated and is not obligated to fund all programs included in the block grant. Of the six Education offices and agencies mentioned above, only the Career Education program is included in the new block-grant program. Vocational Education, Special Education, and the Women's Educational Equity Act Program will continue as separately funded federal programs. The research and demonstration functions of the National Institute of Education and the Fund for the Improvement of Postsecondary Education will probably continue, although at a reduced level of funding and, possibly in a different organizational form.

In the remainder of this chapter, the six offices and agencies that have funded projects related to increasing knowledge about education for career development are listed and briefly described. They are ordered more or less along a continuum from basic research through applied research and development to program demonstration. It is hoped that this permits all readers to find the funding sources appropriate to the type of research they do. The reader should be reminded that, in these uncertain times, it is very important to contact federal and state offices directly to get up-to-date information on a program, its priorities, and its funds.

The National Institute of Education (NIE)

As the federal research arm of the Department of Education, NIE sponsors basic and applied research on education and work as one of several priorities. NIE was created by Congress in 1972 to help solve or alleviate critical problems of American education through research and development. The stress on research and development should be noted. NIE does not fund demonstration projects, nor does it contribute to the operating costs of schools or school-related programs. As the primary federal agency for educational research and development, the institute's mission is twofold: to promote educational equity and to improve the quality of educational practice. The institute's program initiatives grow out of a variety of activities that invite views from educators, researchers, policy makers, parents, and other citizens on nationally significant educational issues. In this regard, research projects related to education and work have been a priority area in the institute since its beginning. At present, projects are located throughout the institute and are concerned with dissemination, policy, and teaching and learning processes. An annual plan for the institute describes all its current priorities and is available from the Publications Office, National Institute of Education, Department of Education, Washington, D.C. 20208. The institute's intention to support new work is generally announced through either a grants competition or a request for proposals, although unsolicited proposals are also accepted.

NIE's early projects in the education and work area were program development efforts closely related to career education at that time. More recent research projects have focused on the career decision-making process, occupational mobility and transferrable skills, the effects of sex bias and sex role stereotyping in career development, what is learned in work experience, alternative ways to mix school and work, and new ways to assess occupational competencies. Some of these directions will continue while others may give way to focused emphases such as youth employability and adult education and training in the corporate sector. To get more specific information about current funding opportunities, contact the National Institute of Education, Department of Education, Washington, D.C. 20208.

The Employment and Training
Administration (ETA)

In the Department of Labor, the Employment and Training Administration sponsors and supports many programs to help youths and adults get jobs. The Office of Research and Development in ETA sponsors research on a wide variety of topics, including labor-market processes; the factors contributing to unemployment and underemployment; the causes of disadvantagement; the strengths and weaknesses disadvantaged persons bring to the work force; and the transitions from school to work, from job to job, and from work to retirement. Much of this research is designed to enhance the effectiveness of Comprehensive Employment and Training Act (CETA) programs, the Work Incentive program, unemployment insurance and employment service operations, and activities of the Bureau of Apprenticeship and Training.

The office also supports experimental and development projects that test innovative ways of serving workers with particular job-related needs for services such as placement, orientation, training, upgrading, or counseling. Many projects focus on the needs of specific target groups—for example, older workers, veterans, minority group members, offenders, and women. Project findings often help institutions improve delivery of employment and training services.

A free annual volume lists, by subject matter, ongoing and recently completed research. The projects book tells who did or is doing each project and lists sources for detailed final reports, which are sometimes issued as R&D monographs or are summarized in ETA publications. A compendium, covering the first sixteen years of the R&D program, is also available at no cost. For information about funding opportunities and priorities, contact the Employment and Training Administration, Office of Research and Development, Patrick Henry Building, 601 D Street, N.W., Room 9100, Washington, D.C. 20213.

The Office of Vocational and Adult Education (OVAE)

The Division of National Vocation Programs in the Office of Vocational and Adult Education (OVAE) administers the vocational education discretionary applied research programs. Research activities under the division's Programs of National Significance were initiated in 1978 to act as a catalyst to improve access to vocational education for the handicapped, minorities, and women. In recent years, among other projects of national significance, a number of awards were made to develop and disseminate materials for new and changing occupational areas and to produce information for policy-making purposes at the state and national levels. Contracts for these projects are awarded competitively and range from one to three years. The foci of these projects include youth entrepreneurship, serving older adults, competency measures for vocational skills, guidance for students with special needs, displaced homemakers, services for the handicapped, basic skills in vocational education, and a number of policy and curriculum projects.

Future priority areas will probably focus on energy conservation and production, increasing work productivity, and using vocational education to improve economic development in urban and rural areas as well as a strategy for using the vocational education delivery system at the secondary, post secondary, and adult levels to assist in the reindustrialization of the United States through close cooperation with business and industry. In addition, these discretionary funds will be used to improve training in inner-city and rural areas, to improve career guidance systems, and for vocational education staff development. Information about research funded by OVAE may be obtained from the Division of National Vocational Programs, Office of Vocational and Adult Education, Department of Education, Room 5052, FOB-3, Washington, D.C. 20202.

The Office of Special Education (OSE)

Within the Office of Special Education and Rehabilitative Services, this office sponsors a program of research in education of the handicapped and has been doing so for over fifteen years. The program is intended to support applied research and research-related activities such as research training, curriculum development and research dissemination. The basic objectives of this support are to (1) identify, study, and demonstrate solutions to problems related to the education of handicapped children; (2) develop and disseminate innovative support systems and techniques to those who serve the handicapped; and (3) create the broadest possible diffusion and utilization of the products of research and development. To achieve these objectives, OSE attempts to identify critical problems that appear to be susceptible to solution through research and development and then solicits proposals to address those problems.

In 1980, OSE included youth employment as one of eleven priority areas that it will focus on in the future. Each fiscal year, a subset of these eleven priorities will be selected for funding. The youth-employment research priority will probably be one of the higher priorities in the near future. There is significant concern about the transition of handicapped individuals from school to work and about the role of the school in increasing the employability of handicapped youth. Further information can be obtained from Research Projects Branch, Office of Special Education, Department of Education, Room 3165, Donohoe Building, Washington, D.C. 20202.

The Office of Career Education (OCE)

The Office of Career Education, in the Department of Education, administers the two Career Education Programs authorized by the Career Education Incentive Act of 1977 (Public Law 95-207). The two programs were authorized through 1983 and include a small discretionary program and a larger state plan/state allotment program. Under the state plan/state allotment program, each state desiring to participate submitted a State Plan for Career Education for approval by the U.S. Commissioner of Education. Then the funds appropriated by the Congress each fiscal year were divided among the participating states. The state educational agency in each participating state utilized the funds, in accordance with its approved State Plan for Career Education, to further the implementation of career education in the elementary and secondary schools of the state. Under the discretionary program, OCE awarded discretionary grants and contracts to support (1) model demonstration projects dealing with career education at the elementary and secondary levels; (2) demonstration projects dealing with career education at the postsecondary level; (3) dissemination of information about federal sources of occupational and career information; (4) dissemination of information about exemplary career education programs already in operation.

Of the research programs discussed in this chapter, only the Career Education program will be included in the new fiscal year 1982 federal block-grant program. Under the Education Consolidation and Improvement Act of 1981, more than twenty previously funded separate programs, including the Career Education Incentive Act, will be consolidated. Funds for these programs will be awarded to each state in a lump sum, and each state will decide how much each program should get. The implication of this change is not that the Career Education program is being phased out (although it is being phased out as a *categorical* program), rather that career educators will have to seek funds within their own states for research and innovation instead of applying to the Office of Career Education in the federal government. Persons desiring additional information should contact the Office of Career Education, Department of Education, Room 3100, FOB-3, Washington, D.C. 20202.

The Fund for the Improvement of Postsecondary Education (FIPSE)

Located in the Department of Education, the Fund for the Improvement of Postsecondary Education (FIPSE) has as its general mission reform, innovation, and improvement in postsecondary education. The fund's primary funding strategy is to provide "seed money" to projects that respond to locally defined problems. Grants have averaged $70,000 per year for one to three years; 70 percent of all grants are awarded to colleges, universities, and other postsecondary institutions; 30 percent are awarded to associations, state agencies, professional organizations, libraries, museums, labor unions, community organizations, and other agencies that have significant roles in the provision of postsecondary education and services.

Projects addressing education and work issues represent one category of fund projects and constitute approximately 20 or 30 percent of the total portfolio each year. Projects serve young people in colleges as well as employees in work settings. Themes of the projects include attempts to develop curricula for future professions, experiential learning for undergraduates, and career counseling and educational programs for full-time workers. A central feature of these projects is collaboration between faculty at postsecondary institutions, learners, and employers.

Interested parties should contact the fund to receive further guidance regarding deadlines and program information. In addition, the fund issues annually a publication entitled *Resources for Change, A Guide to Projects,* which contains project descriptions and listings for contact persons for all active projects. The fund's address is Fund for the Improvement of Postsecondary Education, Department of Education, 400 Maryland Avenue, S.W., Room 3123, FOB-6, Washington, D.C. 20202.

The Women's Educational Equity Act Program (WEEAP)

The Women's Educational Equity Act was enacted in 1974 as part of the Special Projects Act of the Educational Amendments of 1974 (P.L. 93-380) to respond to the need for legislation designed to promote educational equity for women and girls. In order to achieve its goal, the Women's Educational Equity Act authorized the then Office of Education to provide grants and contracts for developmental, demonstration, and dissemination projects of national, statewide, or general significance. A program of small grants, not to exceed $15,000 each, was established to support innovative approaches to the achievement of educational equity for women. In 1978, the act was reauthorized by Congress through 1983.

The reauthorized act established a new, second program in addition to the original program. This new program provides grants for projects of local significance to assist individual school districts and other institutions in their attempts to meet the requirements of Title IX of the Education Amendments of 1972. This activity is dependent however, upon the amount of the appropriation for the program. Five priorities have been established since the program has been reauthorized: (1) model projects in compliance with Title IX of the Educational Amendments of 1972; (2) model projects on educational equity for racial and ethnic minority women and girls; (3) model projects on educational equity for disabled women and girls; (4) model projects to influence leaders in educational policy and administration; (5) model projects to eliminate persistent barriers to educational equity for women. Under the Education Consolidation and Improvement Act of 1981, WEEAP will continue to be a separate program with its own funding authorization. For information on current funding and guidelines, contact Women's Educational Equity Act Program, Department of Education, 1100 Donohoe Building, 400 Maryland Avenue, S.W., Washington, D.C. 20202.

REFERENCES

BERG, I. *Education and jobs: The great training robbery.* Boston: Beacon Press, 1971.

FREEMAN, R. *The over-educated American.* New York: Academic Press, 1976.

HERR, E., and CRAMER, S. *Conditions calling for educational reform: An analysis.* Monographs on Career Education. Washington, D.C.: U.S. Department of Education, 1977.

O'TOOLE, J. The reserve army of the unemployed. *Change,* 1975, 7 (4), 16–33, 63; 7 (5), 26–33, 60–62.

The agenda ahead: research priorities

DANIEL A. HAMEL
Harvard University
and JOHN D. KRUMBOLTZ
Stanford University

In bringing together the viewpoints represented by this volume's authors, we gained a heightened awareness of the complexity that characterizes efforts to assess career development and career education outcomes. Even though many of the most problematic assessment and evaluation issues remain unresolved, the contributors to this volume have helped us generate an agenda of priorities for the immediate future. Our recommendations are organized under three major headings: research objectives, career development outcomes, and methodology.

RESEARCH OBJECTIVES

- Research should examine the fundamental presuppositions of the career education movement.

Career education differs from most other movements in education in several respects, the most prominent of which is its emphasis upon "infusion."

As Bailey points out in chapter 1, the infusion model is only one of the models that have been advocated over the years, but it is the one advanced most often by current leaders in career education (Hoyt, 1975). The basic idea is that career education concepts should not be taught as separate courses or units but should be integrated with other subject matter, infused into the regular curriculum. Thus, mathematics teachers would not merely teach such topics as solving quadratic equations, but would also show how knowledge of mathematics is useful in a variety of occupations. Social studies teachers would not merely teach about the law of supply and demand, but would help students learn about the career opportunities for economists, sociologists, psychologists, historians, and political scientists.

The career education movement seeks to involve every professional educator in making education more relevant to preparation for the world of work. In contrast, vocational education seeks to train people in specific occupational skills and advocates that specially trained vocational education teachers be assigned this responsibility. Consequently, there are a large number of vocational education teachers whose sole responsibility it is to teach specific occupational skills and whose livelihood and professional identification rest upon vocational education. Career education, however, has little "grass roots" support. The mathematics teacher is identified as a mathematics teacher, not as a career educator. The social studies teacher teaches social studies, not career education. As a consequence, relatively few people have a vested interest in advancing the cause of career education.

An interesting series of research studies might compare the infusion model with the discrete-curriculum model. The infusion model involves a reform of the entire education profession. To what extent is it possible to make such a massive change in the commitments of millions of educators? Have such changes in commitment been accomplished in the past? The massive curriculum-improvement projects of the 1960s involved millions of educators. What factors promoted these changes? Certainly more was involved than the launching of Sputnik. But even these massive movements failed to have a long-range impact. A number of research questions are suggested by this experience. How have major reforms in the education profession been achieved? What cultural and social factors have been important in producing these changes? How can similar forces be marshalled in the cause of career education? What would be the effects of experimenting with an alternative approach in career education, namely, developing and promoting specific courses or units of study to achieve specific career education objectives? What are the best procedures for introducing new courses into the curriculum? Evaluation criteria might include not only the impact of the two alternative teaching models on student outcomes but also the extent to which the career education activity itself becomes self-generating.

- Research and measurement in career education should serve multiple purposes.

IMPROVING ACCOUNTABILITY TO FUNDING AUTHORITIES

Perhaps the most pressing reason for conducting evaluation studies is to provide accountability to funding authorities. There is much current conjecture and debate about the benefits of teaching career development concepts and skills in a variety of educational settings. Issues regarding the identification and definition of relevant career development outcome domains, the most appropriate grade-level content and modes of instruction, and the best procedures and instruments for assessing career education curricula remain largely unresolved. Despite massive federal, state, and local expenditures on the career education enterprise during the past half decade, we know relatively little today about the practical short-term and long-range consequences of this substantive effort. Answers to fundamental questions being asked by the consumers of career development programs remain elusive.

Indeed, this nation's passion for career education programs has visibly waned. The honeymoon is over, and as many education budgets begin to shrink, accountability looms as a dominant concern. In testimony before a House subcommittee on education, Ken Hoyt suggested that the day of reckoning has arrived for career education when it will be judged "by its deeds rather than by its words" (Hoyt, 1977). Furthermore, a more recent position paper by a program officer of the National Institute of Education stressed that "the demonstration of the impact of career education programs on students, as indicated through evaluation, is critical for continued federal, state, and local support" (Shoemaker, 1978). The message is clear. Empirical validation of the assumptions underlying our models and practices is urgently needed. But why have evaluation efforts lagged so far behind the widespread implementation of career education and guidance programs?

A number of factors contribute to the dismal assessment record of career development enthusiasts and interact to make the problem particularly challenging. First, historically, educational and vocational guidance practitioners have placed little emphasis on the evaluation of methods and materials (Super and Hall, 1978). Even the best work in this area tends to be correlational rather than experimental, and most often it takes the form of exploratory field trials (almost never replicated) that hint at the impact of local programs and curricula but provide few clues as to the efficacy of a particular methodology or the validity of a particular construct.

However, beginning in the early 1970s, initiatives by the U.S. Office of Education, and later the National Institute of Education, resulted in increased interest in evaluation, often making research funding contingent upon explicit assessment provisions. Another encouraging trend has been the growing attention to important experimental design and psychometric considerations.

Perhaps no problem has hampered progress in assessing career development outcomes so severely as the absence of theoretically and technically sound evaluation instruments. Inadequate instrumentation, the need to refine the validity and reliability of existing measures for assessing certain variables, and the equally pressing need to develop new, innovative tools to tap other variables or skills, is by now an irritatingly familiar refrain to serious students of the subject. Finally, a lack of consensus on the meaning of basic terminology and a bewildering array of basic learner objectives and outcome domains (with considerable conceptual overlap) further confound the evaluation picture.

Beginning with Bailey's description in chapter 1 of specific federal legislation, such as the Career Education Incentive Act of 1977, it has been clear that accountability to funding authorities is a major concern of this volume. That concern was reflected particularly in the chapters by Borow on instrumental outcomes; Hulsart and Burton on the National Assessment's evaluation goals; Krumboltz, Hamel, and Scherba on measuring decision quality; Brickell on field-based testing; and Wise on sources of funding for career development research. All these authors offered specific recommendations for research and development that, if implemented, should go a long way toward meeting the accountability requirements of funding authorities.

IMPROVING THEORETICAL UNDERSTANDING

Vocational psychology is a nascent field, and theories about how career development does or should occur are largely untested. Yet despite the obvious need for controlled studies, very little research is being done. Borow observed in chapter 2 that his review of several volumes of professional periodicals such as the *Journal of Counseling Psychology* and the *Journal of Vocational Behavior* yielded a very small percentage of articles that dealt with career development theory in a substantive way.

In chapter 4, Stenner and Rohlf discussed some of the potential pitfalls of construct development and definition. Clearly, their concerns are worth heeding. Westbrook's attempt to validate the construct of career maturity (chapter 5) is a good illustration of the kind of careful research needed to clarify our assumptions about the integrity of various career development concepts.

An improved understanding of theoretical constructs has the advantage not only of lending more rigor and credibility to all of career education, but of improving the technology for measurement and evaluation as well. The technology is available for refining the meaning of such key constructs as career awareness, career decision making, and work adjustment.

Another advantage likely to accrue from improved construct definitions is uniformity in the delivery of career education treatments. Such implementation measures as those described by Owens and Haenn in chapter 10 will be needed to insure this uniformity. Although local program variations will still occur, appropriate assessment devices or particular items can be used to measure different objectives without damaging efforts to conduct comparative studies.

IMPROVING THE DIAGNOSIS
OF INDIVIDUALS' PROBLEMS

In researching career development outcomes, we should be looking for ways to help people with vocational problems. We would like to know what treatments or learning experiences work best for which people and at which points in their lives. Assuming that career development can be construed as a set of cognitive, affective, and performance skills with useful operational definitions, how can we begin to isolate and specify those variables that contribute unique variance to the measurement of such skills?

Little is known about the nature of career education practices that lead to better outcomes. Few comprehensive training programs or models have been rigorously evaluated. Progress has been limited by the lack of sound measures yielding criteria useful in either program evaluation or differential diagnosis of particular skill competencies.

We need better operational definitions of career development skills (for example, self-assessment, career awareness, career decision making, job finding, work adjustment, and so on). We also need better means of diagnosing the discrete components of any given skill, such as decision making. It could be that an individual who is skilled in clarifying work-related values and generating alternatives has trouble assessing the degree to which various alternatives would provide desired benefits. We need to develop multiple indices of career development competence and specify the constructs those indices are based on. Ultimately, the goal should be the utilization of a multiple-measures approach providing concurrent validity in assessing the full range of career development skills.

PROMOTING CAREER EDUCATION

Assessment has many motives. For example, evaluators may collect data to comply with a law, for advocacy purposes, to serve as a catalyst for change, to guide program or curriculum improvement, or to comply with a contingency for continued funding. In this volume, we have mainly discussed assessment designed to promote formative evaluation of group instruction and the differential diagnosis of individual career development skills.

However, as noted by many contributors to this volume, the inherent worth of career education and career development programs is no longer accepted on faith. Drastic cuts in education budgets prompted by both federal policies and state and local taxpayer initiatives are resulting in the elimination of "nonessential" programs, staff, and services. Some view career education as a peripheral, nonvital part of the public education enterprise. Today many practitioners and advocates of career development find themselves in the unfamiliar and disheartening role of selling their product. However unappealing this role might be, it is an essential one.

How, exactly, should career education be promoted or sold? Several major strategies seem plausible. Career education can be sold on the basis of (1) the *success model* (showing that career education works); (2) the *importance model* (showing that its objectives are worthwhile); or (3) the *involvement model* (showing that it has captured the enthusiasm and interest of influential people).

The involvement model has a potentially dangerous, Catch-22-type drawback. Some might argue that if many people are enthusiastic about career education, the enterprise does not need the additional support of federal dollars. On the other hand, if there is little demonstrable enthusiasm, federal officials might claim that projects probably would not be continued after federal support had been terminated, and therefore should not be funded initially. Thus, the involvement model would probably fail to work as a central strategy.

We favor the success model, which encompasses the empiricism and methodological rigor many of us have been trained to pursue as evaluators, educators, and counselors. We believe that the success-model strategy no longer represents merely a compelling alternative point of view. Rather, demonstrated success in delivering the promises of career education objectives has become a practical necessity.

Granted, it may seem unfair or even illogical that the basic academic disciplines are not required to provide evidence of their long-term or "ultimate" effectiveness. Because of their widely recognized and long-standing importance, support for these disciplines is easily won. Career education does not enjoy such a posture. The importance model carried career education through its inception period. How could anyone expect demonstrable success from a new concept? However, in an era of shrinking financial support for educational programs, only core curricula and those with proven track records can hope to survive.

CAREER DEVELOPMENT OUTCOMES

- Career development outcomes should be sampled more extensively.

Should career education be evaluated by the extent to which people "learn skills" or "get jobs"? From the educator's point of view, learning skills is sufficient. From a political point of view, the acid test is whether the people trained in career education programs are actually able to get themselves employed successfully. However, one can get a job without being particularly proficient at a number of skills; furthermore, one can learn a number of skills without necessarily being successful in obtaining employment. Both criteria as well as many others are needed to gain a well-rounded picture of what happens as a result of career education.

Asked another way, should career education be evaluated on the basis of short-term, intermediate, or long-term objectives? Most studies use short-term outcomes because they are easiest to collect and least expensive, and the attrition of subjects is a less serious problem than with the other options. Most career education interventions are relatively weak and might not be expected to show massive, enduring effects, especially considering all the other powerful influences on human behavior over the years. Again, some would point out that better established disciplines such as English and mathematics are not required to demonstrate that teaching in those subjects has long-term effects. It is assumed that if short-term effects can be demonstrated, long-term effects are at least possible. However, if the short-term effects cannot be demonstrated, the longer term effects will probably not be seen either.

There are really at least two domains to consider when speaking of career development outcomes: institutional (schools) and vocational (work settings). The career development of adults in work settings is too often ignored. Most research has focused on immediate (usually "in-school") outcomes, and to a lesser extent on fairly remote outcomes, usually assessed in terms of job-satisfaction surveys. More emphasis should be placed on using intermediate criteria to assess the effects of career education programs. Given the increasing rates of novelty and transience in our labor force, we need to teach and measure career transition and work-adjustment skills. As employers in certain industries become increasingly concerned about problems of employee attrition, tools will be needed to measure the efficacy of programs designed to alleviate various causes of the problem.

- Progress in career education should be assessed in terms of both process goals and learner outcomes.

Laurel Oliver (1979) has written an excellent article reviewing outcome measurement in career counseling research and has offered some recommendations for future research and evaluation. She has stressed the use of multiple-outcome criteria, multiple measures of the same criterion, specific as well as global measures, and the need to define constructs more precisely. We also agree with Oliver's advocacy of validating instruments from previous research, reporting the validity and reliability data generated by career assessment instruments, and using objective and nonreactive measures wherever possible.

In thinking about what types of criterion measures are most appropriate for assessing career education programs, we need to review the full range of objectives. Some of these objectives are clearly terminal, or "end-product," types of behaviors, such as obtaining satisfactory employment. Other desired outcomes include increased awareness of career opportunities, increased confidence in one's decision-making ability, and job-adjustment and advancement skills. Such goals are often stated as learner outcomes by federal, state, and local educators. In this volume, the chapters by Borow, Hulsart and Burton, Finch, Bonnet, and Brickell all reflect an emphasis on measuring learner outcomes in assessing career education progress.

Attention to the process goals of career education is equally important. Chapter 10, by Owens and Haenn, on assessing the degree of implementation of programs is a good example of what we mean by measuring process goals. In other words, we should be paying attention to the degree to which the intended teaching and learning processes advocated by career development specialists actually occur. Owens' and Haenn's chapter describes instruments that assess the implementation of curricula and instructional processes, but we also need instruments that assess learning processes. Such learning processes include such critical career development activities as generating vocational alternatives, seeking occupational information, and using a personally meaningful model for making career-related decisions—for example, choosing school subjects, majors, and job-training opportunities.

It is conceivable that instruments will be developed to measure both process goals and learner outcomes. The Career Decision Simulation (CDS), described by Krumboltz, Hamel, and Scherba in chapter 9, potentially allows one to evaluate a career decision according to each decider's own specified value preferences, and to relate the numerical "goodness" of the choice to quantitative measures of behaviors (such as information-seeking) used to make the decision. The CDS yields a cumulative, sequential record of all information used to make a simulated career choice. Thus, the CDS provides researchers not only with outcome scores but also with data from which inferences can be made about a subject's decision-making procedure or style. It is possible to gather information about both decision-making processes and outcomes and see how these data correlate for individuals exposed to different instructional treatments. This rich store of "process" data has yet to be investigated thoroughly.

- The scope and specificity of career education objectives should be expanded.

IDENTIFYING GAPS

Any comprehensive review of existing career development and career education measures will reveal some unfortunate gaps in the assessment and evaluation framework. To clarify the problem, one could envision a two-dimensional grid consisting of program goals (for example, career-awareness, decision-making and employment-seeking skills) listed down the side, and assessment methods or domains (for example, performance, knowledge, attitude, affect) listed across the top. Many of the cells created by this grid would be empty. Almost all of our present instruments would fall into the knowledge and attitude columns.

This simple grid-system analysis helps demonstrate the lack of instruments for measuring some of the most crucial career development outcomes. The reasons for the gaps seem clear. Performance and affective variables are quite difficult to measure. It is much easier to assess an individual's knowledge of a concept or process than his or her mastery or implementation of that concept or process. The same could be said about assessing attitudes and beliefs. We are left without answers to a whole series of critical questions that take the form of "If individuals know about X or have the 'correct' attitude toward X, can they successfully perform X?"

Alternative assessment formats, especially in the performance domain, such as those described by Finch in chapter 8, are badly needed. But we also need to measure some very basic and practical phenomena that may help predict occupational success and satisfaction. For example, how clearly can students articulate their career goals and specify the steps necessary to attain them? How accurately can students appraise their own career-related strengths and weaknesses? What evidence would suggest that present workers are engaging in activities to promote desired career growth and development? Researchers and evaluators should be encouraged to develop sound instruments that will tap into these unmeasured variables. Such measures would greatly strengthen our battery of assessment devices.

ENTREPRENEURSHIP SKILLS

The desire to own one's own business is widely prevalent, but the obstacles to achieving it are many. The high failure rate of new businesses suggests that either the skills required for the successful operation of a business are not well known or the decision to inaugurate a particular enterprise is often ill founded. In either case some educational interventions might be useful.

Organizations such as Junior Achievement have successfully involved some young people in entrepreneurship. The National Center for Research in Vocational Education at Ohio State University has made available a Program for Acquiring Competency in Entrepreneurship (PACE), which includes eighteen modules for individualized student use plus teachers' guides. Topics include factors that contribute to the success and failure of small businesses, development of a business plan, location, legal issues, government regulations, types of ownership, financing, managing, accounting, selling, and public relations.

Although efforts have been made to train entrepreneurs, we know very little about the effectiveness of such training. What are the personal skills, attitudes, and interests that contribute to the success or failure of a new business? What types of training activities would be useful in helping people decide whether or not to begin a new business? What kinds of diagnostic instruments would be helpful in pinpointing individuals likely to succeed or fail? If certain deficits can be identified, which of them are most amenable to remedial training? Perhaps it is relatively easy to teach accounting skills but quite difficult to teach salesmanship. Is a training package in its totality able to increase the success rate of potential entrepreneurs? What components of a training package contribute most significantly to the success of graduates? What teaching methods are most appropriate? To what extent is a practicum experience desirable? How can practicum experiences be designed to promote more reasonable generalizations and fewer overgeneralizations?

AVOCATIONAL ACTIVITIES

Donald Super (1979) has severely critized the career education movement for failing to define the fundamental concept on which it rests, namely the word *career.* His analysis of the uses of the term reveals seven major definitions. In a most useful exercise in conceptual clarifying, he defines a number of key terms used in the career development literature. *Career* was defined as

> the sequence of major positions occupied by a person throughout his preoccupational, occupational, and postoccupational life; includes work-related roles such as those of student, employee, and pensioner, together with complementary avocational, familial and civic roles.

It is important to note that avocational, familial, and civic roles are included in Super's definition of career. Such a broad definition is useful in calling attention to the ways in which a variety of activities may be used to achieve personal goals.

In our society, people may be unable to satisfy their own interests and values primarily through their occupational activities, ideal though that might be. If all people could be employed in the occupations that they ideally preferred regardless of the economic need for those occupations, we might well have millions of movie stars but relatively few bus drivers. But occupational activities are only one way of satisfying personal needs. Those people who thoroughly enjoy performing for and entertaining other people might feel permanently frustrated if they were unable to secure an acting job, the number of which remains severely limited. However, avocational activities provide a way to satisfy this need in a variety of ways. Those interested can organize amateur theatrical groups or make home movies and show them to their friends and relatives. Relatively inexpensive video equipment provides yet another medium for displaying performing talents. Music lessons provide recital opportunities. Audio and video tape recorders allow every performer to have at least an audience of one. So it becomes possible for a person to work forty hours a week in an activity that may not necessarily be a first choice among interests but still satisfy one's interests through avocational pursuits.

Career counselors, in their efforts to help people find a career that satisfies all their interests, values, and talents, may find it difficult to help people achieve realistic goals if they use a narrow definition of *career.* However, by supplementing occupational activities with avocational activities, an individual might reasonably well satisfy his or her major needs and values.

Owens and Haenn, in chapter 10, describe ways to assess the implementation of a career education program. Among the competencies they mention are the ability to "maintain good physical health and make effective use of leisure time." But we need ways to assess how specific activities within the broad category of leisure-time pursuits might satisfy individual needs not otherwise satisfied by occupational activities. What are the patterns that people use to blend the two? How can instruments be designed to measure not just occupational satisfaction but the total quality of life derived from the balance of all activities? How can counselors best intervene in individuals' lives to promote integration of avocational and occupational activities? What would be the long-term effects of a concerted effort to help individuals integrate avocational activities into their career plans?

MAKING DEEDS CONSISTENT WITH WORDS

In the first chapter of this volume Bailey listed the nine original learner outcomes for career education adopted by the Office of Education in 1974. This list, with the addition of one objective, continues to be the official goal statement of the nation's career education efforts. A recent paper by Anita Mitchell (1980) points out some of the problems encountered when evaluators try to measure these objectives at the local level.

Mitchell's review suggests that several of the basic Office of Career Education (OCE) objectives have been largely ignored by evaluators and program developers across many settings. She contends that such oversights have resulted in a restriction of the focus of the movement to such outcomes as career awareness, self-knowledge, and decision making. On the other hand, almost no evidence has been gathered on targeted outcomes such as the improvement of basic academic skills and work habits, using leisure time productively, or developing an awareness of how to change career directions. Mitchell points out a sobering irony. The very public, legislators and business people, whose support for career education is so desperately needed tend to be most concerned about those outcomes for which very little evidence has been gathered.

Perhaps even more relevant to the present volume is Mitchell's observation that evaluators have failed to define the specific skills implied under each of the ten learner objectives. Only when the general goal statements have been translated into precise behavioral, cognitive, and affective outcomes can standardized instruments be developed and effective comparison studies be conducted. In reviewing the current status and future needs of each of the ten OCE objectives, Mitchell presents an alternative set of specific, concrete subobjectives that probably better represents the intentions reflected in the major objectives. Her suggestions seem most sensible and represent the kind of strategy needed to make rapid gains in evaluating career development outcomes.

METHODOLOGY

- Experimental assessment procedures based on flexible item banks keyed to specific objectives should be compared with more conventional standardized tests.

Unlike most well-established subject-matter fields, not all the objectives of career education, which cover a wide range, are necessarily subscribed to by practitioners in different settings. In evaluating the outcomes of any particular school's career education program, it makes little sense to include measures of irrelevant objectives. Ideally, teachers and administrators in any given program might be able to select evaluation procedures and test questions that specifically measure the objectives toward which they are teaching. The construction of item domains as advocated by Shoemaker in chapter 6 would enable tests to be tailored to specific objectives within a "skills framework." The current practice, however, is for a teacher to administer a prepackaged standardized test that measures a set of objectives considered by some test publisher to be desirable. The grouping of objectives may help somewhat in this regard. For example, the College Board's Career Skills Assessment Program makes available separate subtests that can be administered independently, but even within each of these subtests a large number of different objectives are measured.

There are two major objections to item banks: (1) their high cost, and (2) the difficulty in developing norms. The cost problem is undoubtedly the most serious. Who would want to develop a large number of sophisticated test items keyed to multiple career education objectives for many age levels and then make them available to others to weave into self-designed achievement tests? Probably no one who had to pay for such an effort would choose to do so. Publishers of standardized tests would not look kindly upon the cannibalization of their sophisticated products. Of course, teachers can always tell students, "Respond only to Questions 1, 12, 27, and 36 and skip the others." Or tests can be scored only for items of interest. However, administrative problems become considerable under such circumstances. A cooperative effort supported by a professional association or the federal government would be required to develop a sufficiently large number of items that would be available in the public domain to measure career education outcomes.

The norming problem is easier to solve. In the first place, the need for national norms is not all that clear and may even be undesirable, as Bonnet points out in chapter 11. It matters little whether a given classroom scores above or below a median based upon a national sample. If such statistics were required and items had been tried out on a national sample, norms could be estimated mathematically from the specific item statistics. The sum of the difficulty levels of each individual item would estimate the median for the test as a whole.

Before such a national effort could be launched, however, small scale studies would be needed to test the feasibility of the idea. To what extent would teachers make use of an item bank if it were available? How could an item bank be structured to enhance its usefulness? What experience has been gained from the use of other item banks? For example, what about the textbook test items that are often included in instructors' manuals? What precisely would be the relative cost of these approaches, particularly considering the cost of administrator and student time? Administering an hour-long examination when a fifteen-minute examination would do wastes forty-five minutes of every pupil's time—time the student could have spent learning something valuable. Some of the practical problems described by Bonnet in chapter 11 and Brickell in chapter 12 could be solved more readily if a flexible bank of items were available.

However, we will not be able to tell for sure whether such benefits would accrue until we try out the idea.

- Researchers should concentrate their resources on well-designed studies based on small representative samples.

Evaluation has become the watchword in education. Some writers have advocated that every educational activity should be a research study and every research study an educational activity. While it is difficult to quarrel with this noble sentiment in the abstract, some practical realities are involved.

If research studies are to produce unambiguous answers to important questions, they must be carefully designed with an eye to protecting their internal and external validity. As Cole pointed out in chapter 3, research costs are high and funds are limited. Studies must make efficient use of limited resources. A large sample size does not necessarily result in a better research study. Large samples may not necessarily be representative of any defined population. The time, money, and energy required to collect data from a larger sample may be spent needlessly. Researchers can easily lose control of data-collection procedures and thus wind up with inaccurate data. Finally, money may not be available to follow up on nonrespondents. It is far better to concentrate energies on obtaining complete data from a randomly identified representative sample than to attempt to achieve a total enumeration.

In no way are we attempting to minimize the importance of evaluating the impact of career education interventions on all the students involved. Such feedback is desirable both for the students themselves and for their teachers and administrators. But such evaluations cannot answer important research questions. They cannot tell us whether the curriculum used was better than an alternative curriculum. They cannot identify the relative contributions of teachers, classrooms, settings, materials, and methods. A clear delineation is necessary between evaluation studies that give feedback to participants and research studies that answer questions of general interest. For example, Stenner and Rohlf in chapter 4 and Westbrook in chapter 5 have shown how difficult it is for researchers to clarify constructs such as "career maturity" and develop uncontaminated measures of such constructs. It is equally difficult to identify the components of career education interventions that really make a difference. Thoughtfully designed studies on small representative samples can begin to give us economical answers to our questions.

A FINAL WORD

As we contemplate the numerous challenges facing the effort to assess career development, it is important to acknowledge that any kind of evaluation effort takes place in a larger cultural context. Annual budget appropriations determine the amount of tax dollars to be allocated for program development, research, and evaluation. And, of course, the quality of any one person's or one group's career development outcomes will be only as high as that of the curriculum materials and learning experiences provided by teachers, counselors, and the community at large. The decline in public school enrollments and subsequent cuts in staff and school programs pose a threat to the progress enjoyed by career education during the past decade. Thus, we must find ways of gaining community support, involvement, and cooperation. To do so, we badly need evidence of the benefits of career development training. Further program and curriculum development will probably await the verdict of the assessment and evaluation efforts described and urged in this volume.

REFERENCES

HOYT, K. B. *An introduction to career education: A policy paper of the U.S. Office of Education.* Washington, D.C.: U.S. Office of Education, 1975.

HOYT, K. B. Testimony prepared for presentation before the Subcommittee on Elementary, Secondary, and Vocational Education. U.S. House of Representatives, February 9, 1977.

MITCHELL, A. *Measuring career education objectives: Current status and future directions.* Los Alamitos, Calif. Southwest Regional Laboratory for Educational Research and Development, 1980.

OLIVER, L. W. Outcome measurement in career counseling research. *Journal of Counseling Psychology,* 1979, *26* (3), 217–226.

SHOEMAKER, J. S. Measuring career education outcomes: A federal perspective. Paper prepared for the annual meeting of the American Educational Research Association in Toronto, Canada, March 1978.

SUPER, D. E. The babble that is Babel: A basic glossary for career education. *Journal of Career Education,* 1979, *5,* 156–167.

SUPER, D. E., and HALL, D. T. Career development: Exploration and planning. *Annual Review of Psychology,* 1978, *29,* 333—372.

APPENDIX

Despite the youth of the career education movement, a surprisingly large number of assessment instruments have been developed to measure its outcomes. The basic assumptions underlying these different measures differ widely. In preparing this list of currently available assessment measures, Lynda Mitchell has selected those that can be used to assess program outcomes. She has generally omitted the types of measures that are used for individual career selection unless such instruments might also be used for program assessment. Each measure reviewed is classified and described briefly.

Obviously, the information in this appendix will become rapidly outdated as prices change, new instruments are developed, and old instruments go out of print. However, we believe that this listing gives up-to-date, concrete, operational evidence of the more abstract principles discussed in this text.

Career education measures

LYNDA K. MITCHELL
California State University at Los Angeles

This appendix describes the best currently available measures of the needs, processes, and outcomes of career education programs. The reviews are grouped in alphabetical order by title under the following seven categories:

1. Needs assessment
2. Batteries to assess ongoing career education programs
3. Attitudes toward work
4. Knowledge about occupations
5. Career decision making
6. Process measures
7. Follow-up measures

The purpose of career education is to enable the individual to make wise decisions concerning the choice of his or her eventual career, and to function effectively in that career. Thus, a career education program should expand an individual's knowledge of careers and their unique characteristics, teach decision-making and entry processes, and develop skills in self-evaluation, employment seeking, and work effectiveness. The measures reviewed here could be used to assess the extent to which any given career education program is educating the individual in one or more of these areas.

In the description of each measure, information is provided on its purpose and intended population; the number, name, and purpose of submeasures; the number of items; the type of items (for example, multiple-choice, true/false); the time needed to administer the measure; the response mode for the measure (for example, verbal, paper-and-pencil); and how the measure is to be scored. Additional information that may be of use to the reader, including other categories in which the measures are applicable, is provided at the end of each review.

Needs assessment

TITLE: *Community College Occupational Programs Evaluation System* (COPES) and
                  Student Accountability Model (SAM)

AUTHORS: Sponsored by the Chancellor's Office of the California Community Colleges in
                  collaboration with California community college personnel; coordinated by
                  COPES Service Center. Primary supervisor of COPES and SAM is William
                  Morris. SAM *Operations Manual* written by William Morris and Ben K. Gold.

DATE: System materials developed 1972.
                  COPES Guide, revised 1978.
                  SAM Operations Manual, February 1977; revised September 1978.

ORDER FROM: ERIC Clearinghouse on Adult, Career and Vocational Education, The National
                  Center for Research in Vocational Education, Ohio State University, 1960
                  Kenny Road, Columbus, Ohio 43210 (COPES, ED 162079; SAM *Operations
                  Manual,* ED 135443). For information, contact Dr. William Morris, Evaluation
                  Specialist in Program Evaluation and Approval; COPES Service Center, Chan-
                  cellor's Office, California Community Colleges, 1238 S Street, Sacramento,
                  California 95814.

257

PRICE: Free to community colleges and some state agencies for community colleges. Through the ERIC Clearinghouse on Adult, Career and Vocational Education: *COPES*—paper, $7.82; microfiche, $.83. *SAM Operations Manual*—paper, $6.32; microfiche, $.83 (add postage to all prices).

DESCRIPTION

The *Community College Occupational Programs Evaluation System (COPES)* is designed to enable community colleges to evaluate the goals, objectives, processes, and resources of their occupational programs. The materials composing *COPES* include a set of seven questionnaires that are distributed to the persons involved in occupational education at the community college.

Form 1 is completed by the college president and consists of two parts: Part A asks for basic factual information about the college and Part B elicits qualitative and quantitative ratings of program standards. Part B consists of thirty-nine items—two essays and thirty-seven five-item rating scales (for example, availability of appropriate supplies, rated from poor to excellent).

Form 2 is a faculty appraisal of specific occupational programs which is completed by full-time occupational instructors. The format is the same as Form 1. Form 3 is to be completed by administrators and counselors and has the same format as Forms 1 and 2.

Forms 4 and 5 are to be completed by part-time faculty and students, respectively. They consist of 11 five-item rating scales and are essentially a short version of Forms 1, 2, and 3. Forms 6 and 7 are for California community colleges exclusively and are completed by personnel involved in the COPES system there.

No time limit is given for individual forms, but fifteen to thirty minutes should be sufficient. Scoring is done by computer for California community colleges but may be done by hand in other areas.

The *Student Accountability Model (SAM)* accompanies COPES, and is designed to provide follow-up information on students after they leave occupational programs. *SAM* consists of a step-by-step program for designing a follow-up study, and includes several suggested questionnaires, which may be individually compiled by the administering colleges. The questionnaires are designed for both students and employers and obtain information about suitability of employment, working hours, problems with employees, and other pertinent data. The format of the questions is either multiple-choice or rating scale. The questionnaires may be designed to be administered in as short a period as five minutes or as long as thirty. Scoring is done as with *COPES*.

RELIABILITY: Reliability was established in 1973–1974 for the entire *COPES* system and ranged from .44 to .76. No information was provided on the reliability of *SAM*.

VALIDITY: System validity has been established through user feedback and validation visits by trained personnel.

ADDITIONAL
INFORMATION: The *Copes* and *SAM* materials include extensive guides for data analysis of all measures, the design of studies to evaluate programs, and suggested explanatory letters for participants. They also include complete information on the development of *COPES* and *SAM*.

OTHER
APPLICABLE
CATEGORIES: Process Measures, Follow-up Measures

TITLE: *Texas Career Education Measurement Series (TCEMS)*

AUTHOR: Texas Education Agency and Partners in Career Education (Elvis J. Arterburg,

Project Director; project sponsors include Dallas and Fort Worth Independent School Districts and Educator Service Centers for Regions X and XI, respectively)

DATE: 1977

ORDER FROM: I(T) WORK(S), Inc., 1204 Rio Grande, Denton, Texas 76201

PRICE: Not indicated

DESCRIPTION

The *Texas Career Education Measurement Series (TCEMS)* consists of a battery of sixty-three paper-and-pencil instruments and a general survey test. The sixty-three Basic Learner Outcome Tests (broken down from the original sixteen category tests) are designed to measure student development within nine career education categories. These categories are career planning and decision making, career and occupational information, job acquisition and retention, attitudes and appreciation for career success, skills in human relationships for careers, self-investigation and evaluation for career success, personal/work/societal responsibilities, economic factors influencing career opportunity, and education/career opportunity relationships. The sixty-three outcome tests each consist of from three to twenty-eight dichotomous or multiple-choice items. The general survey test, consisting of forty-five dichotomous or multiple-choice items, should be used to diagnose general areas of strengths and weaknesses of student development in career education. General student need areas can then be identified where administration of one or more of the sixty-three outcome tests or selected items from the tests can provide a more specific diagnosis of student performance.

These tests are designed for secondary students, and it is expected that five to twenty minutes should be sufficient for the administration of any one of the sixty-three tests. However, since this is a needs-assessment series, more time should be allotted if necessary so that the students may complete all the items. Scoring can be done by hand or machine. Two booklets describe the procedures to be followed for each type of scoring. The *User's Guide* gives various suggestions for using the survey and category tests and describes the printout of results received when these tests are machine scored. *Directions for Handscoring* gives detailed directions and provides reproduceable answer sheets for the survey and category tests.

RELIABILITY: No data are provided for individual tests. However, for the entire series, over 37 percent of the items had internal consistency reliabilities (Kuder-Richardson Formula 20) over .50.

VALIDITY: Validity information was not provided for individual tests. The entire series, however, was reviewed by students and professional personnel for content validity. The developers also tested the "cultural validity" of the tests to determine if ethnic origin or sex influenced student response.

ADDITIONAL INFORMATION: Besides the basic survey and outcome tests and the *User's Guide* and *Directions for Handscoring* mentioned above, several additional booklets are available with the series. The *Administrator's Manual, Basic Learner Outcomes for Career Education* describes the objectives on which the series was based. The *User's Guide for Basic Learner Outcome Tests* describes the use of those objectives. A *Student Needs Assessment* describes the overall plan and purpose of the series. A *Handicapped Student Needs Assessment* describes the use of the series for handicapped, and a *Report of the Assessment in Career Education* gives further statistical information on the tests.

TITLE:	*Wisconsin Career Education Needs Assessment and Survey of Resources Handbook*
AUTHORS:	Robert S. Meyer and Arlys E. Gessner
DATE:	1977
ORDER FROM:	Supervisor of Career Education, Wisconsin Department of Public Instruction, 126 Langdon Street, Madison, Wisconsin 53702
PRICE:	Free

DESCRIPTION

The *Wisconsin Career Education Needs Assessment and Survey of Resources Handbook* contains twenty-one paper-and-pencil measures designed to assess the career education needs of the preschool through retirement-age population. They were designed for the project to develop a Wisconsisn State Plan for Career Education. Three types of forms are included in the handbook. Forms PI-Q-60 through PI-Q-64, and PI-Q-69 through PI-Q-76 are needs-assessment instruments intended for the following populations:

PI-Q-60	Early childhood educators
PI-Q-61	Middle childhood (2nd – 3rd grade students)
PI-Q-62	Late childhood (4 – 5 – 6th grade students)
PI-Q-63	Early adolescence (7 – 8 – 9th grade students)
PI-Q-64	Adolescence (10 – 11 – 12th grade students)
PI-Q-69	Retired persons
PI-Q-70	Parents
PI-Q-71	Adults
PI-Q-72	Teachers
PI-Q-73	Counselors
PI-Q-74	Administrators
PI-Q-75	Special education teachers
PI-Q-76	Secondary special education teachers

Forms A, B, C, and D in the handbook are combined needs-assessment and survey-of-resources instruments intended for the following populations:

Form A	State government and agencies
Form B	Teacher and counselor training institutions
Form C	State educational associations
Form D	Occupational and civic support groups

Forms PI-Q-65 through PI-Q-68 are survey-of-resources instruments intended for the following populations:

PI-Q-65	Educational agencies
PI-Q-66	Cooperative educational service agencies
PI-Q-67	Colleges and universities
PI-Q-68	Vocational and technical educators

Each form contains about eighteen items and takes approximately fifteen minutes to complete. The forms may be administered separately or as a package, and are intended to be self-administered. A cover letter is provided for each form.

Items on the forms are rated on a five-point scale. An example from the student survey follows:

	No Need	Undecided	Little Need	Moderate Need	High Need
I need:					
1. Help in discovering what is important to me.	1	2	3	4	5

Items are similarly constructed for other populations in terms of "our students need. . . ."

Responses can be hand or machine scored on optically scanned response sheets available from Center for Vocational, Technical and Adult Education (CVTAE), University of Wisconsin-Stout, Menomonie, Wisconsin 54751. Data processing is available from CVTAE for both options.

RELIABILITY: Reliability has a .80 – .90 range.

VALIDITY: An informal content validity study was done on feedback from the pilot test. Participants indicated the measures were useful for career education. In terms of concurrent validity, users reported that the outcomes of the measures agreed with their other career education information.

ADDITIONAL
INFORMATION: Suggestions for modification of measures and local adaptation are given in the handbook along with suggestions for summarizing the data in a meaningful form.

Batteries to assess ongoing career education programs

TITLE:	*Assessment of Career Development (ACD)*	
AUTHOR:	The American College Testing Program, Research and Development Division	
DATE:	1974	
ORDER FROM:	Houghton Mifflin Test Department, PO Box 1970, Iowa City, Iowa 52240	
PRICE:	Student Test Booklets, Form C (reusable), package of 35	$13.95
	Answer sheets, pkg. of 35	4.35
	Test Administrator's Manual of Instructions Introducing the Assessment of Career Development, package of 35	4.95
	Handbook: *User's Guide and Report of Research*	1.95
	Supplement 1 to the handbook: *A Guide for Increasing Student Career Development*	.84
	Examination Kit	3.60
	Basic Scoring Service, per student (minimum charge, $39.00 per shipment)	.78
	Alternate Basic Scoring Service, per student (minimum charge, $48.00 per shipment)	.96

DESCRIPTION

The *Assessment of Career Development (ACD)* was designed to (1) obtain information needed in developing effective guidance programs tailored to student needs, (2) assess the outcomes of career guidance programs, and (3) obtain student reactions to their career guidance experiences.

The *ACD* is a paper-and-pencil test consisting of six units: job knowledge, preferred job characteristics, career plans, career-planning activities, career-planning knowledge, and exploratory job experiences. These six units elicit information concerning how much students know about occupations and career planning, what they have done about career exploration, what kinds of help they are looking for, and what effect the school's career development programs have had on them.

The test was designed for grades 8 – 11, and can be administered in one 135 – minute session or three 45 – minute sessions. There are 283 items in all. Items are multiple choice, matching, rating scales, checklist, or dichotomous choice. The test must be machine scored by Houghton Mifflin.

RELIABILITY:	Internal consistency (split-half reliability coefficients) are reported for grades 8, 9, and 11 on all the subscales of the test. Reliabilities ranged from .61 to .93, but were mostly in the .70 – .85 range.
VALIDITY:	Content validity should be determined at local sites.
ADDITIONAL INFORMATION:	In the handbook, the *User's Guide and Report of Research,* information is provided on the rationale and construction of the *ACD,* national norms, and further statistical properties of the test.
OTHER APPLICABLE CATEGORIES:	Needs Assessment, Process Measures, Career Decision Making, Knowledge about Occupations, Attitudes toward Work

---

TITLE:	*Career Education Cognitive Questionnaire (CECQ):* Grades 1 –3, Grades 4 –6, Grades 7 –9, Grades 10 –12
AUTHOR:	Minnesota Research Coordinating Unit for Vocational Education
DATE:	1975
ORDER FROM:	Minnesota Research Coordinating Unit for Vocational Education, University of Minnesota, Minneapolis, Minnesota 55455
PRICE:	CECQ Grades 1 –3 (each test contains 10 answer sheets) $3.00

CECQ Grades 1 –3 (each test contains 10 answer sheets)	$3.00
CECQ Grades 4 –6	.50
CECQ Grades 7 –9	.50
Optical Scan Answer Sheets (inserts for 1–3 tests)	.05
Optical Scan Answer Sheet (4 –6 and 7 –9)	.05
Administrative Manual and Technical Report	1.00
Scoring Key 1 –3	.30
Scoring Key 4 –6	.30
Scoring Key 7 –9	.30
Specimen Set (includes entire answer key, *Administrative Manual and Technical Report*)	6.00

DESCRIPTION

The *Career Education Cognitive Questionnaire (CECQ)* was developed to measure how much children know about concepts relating to the world of work. It assesses knowledge about industry, occupational levels, ability requirements, needs, working conditions, career-decision processes, and employment trends. All tests are paper-and-pencil and are designed to be administered in thirty to forty-five minutes. The *CECQ* 1 −3 consists of twenty-nine test items that utilize illustrations of workers and working conditions, and is designed to be read to the students. The *CECQ* 4−6 contains fifty-four multiple-choice and matching items. The *CECQ* 7 −9 and 10−12 contain fifty-five to sixty multiple-choice items. Answer sheets may be electronically or hand scored.

Test items represent blue-collar and white-collar occupations equally, and display males in prominently female occupations and vice versa.

Analysis of mean scores for each grade level showed students' scores increasing significantly with increase in grade level, which indicates that the tests are capable of measuring vocational maturity.

RELIABILITY: Test-retest reliabilities (Pearson product moment correlation) ranged from a low of .836 for seventh grade to a high of .969 for third grade.

VALIDITY: Face and content validity were attested to be five in-service teachers at each grade level. Complete discussion of validity and reliability data are provided in the *Administrative Manual and Technical Report.*

OTHER APPLICABLE CATEGORIES: Career Decision Making, Knowledge about Occupations.

TITLE: *Career Skills Assessment Program (CSAP)* (Experimental Edition)

AUTHOR: The College Board

DATE: 1977

ORDER FROM: Career Skills Assessment Program of the College Board, PO Box 2839, Princeton, New Jersey 08541

PRICE:

Starter Set (package of 25) exercise booklets, response sheets, and guides	$25.00 per content area
Exercise booklets (reusable), package of 25	13.50 per content area
Response sheets and guides,set of 25	13.50 per content area
Support materials	
Implementing the Career Skills Assessment Program	2.75
Sound Filmstrip Kit	48.50
Sample Set	5.00
Scoring and summary reports (minimum order: 100 response sheets per content area)	.33 per response sheet

DESCRIPTION

The *Career Skills Assessment Program (CSAP)* was developed to assess student competency in the areas considered to be most central to successful career development, and to provide students with guidance and insight into career planning and decision making. Thus, the measures were designed for both program assessment and self-assessment, and for the assessment of both needs and outcomes.

Six objective-based measures were included in the *CSAP*:

Self-Evaluation and Development Skills
Career Awareness Skills
Career Decision-Making Skills
Employment-Seeking Skills
Work Effectiveness Skills
Personal Economics Skills

The measures are designed to be used in any order or at any time. Teachers and counselors may administer one, several, or all six measures, depending on the structure of programs or the individual needs of students.

The Self-Evaluation and Development Skills measure assesses self-knowledge in the area of career planning, with an emphasis on personal values, interests, strengths, and weaknesses. The Career Awareness Skills measure assesses knowledge about opportunities in work, education, and leisure. The Work Effectiveness Skills measure is concerned with problems of interpersonal relations, value conflicts, supervision, work habits, and work attitudes on the job. The remaining measures, Career Decision-Making Skills, Employment-Seeking Skills, and Personal Economics Skills are self-explanatory.

Intended populations for use of the measures include high school students and adults in continuing-education settings such as community colleges, vocational institutes, and some four-year colleges.

Each measure consists of sixty to seventy multiple-choice questions and is designed to be administered in forty-five to sixty minutes. The response sheets can be self-scored by the students, and a self-instructional guide is provided with each response sheet to give immediate feedback to the students on their performance. The guide also discusses the skills involved in the content area being studied, including activities, materials, and resources that can be used to strengthen skills, and provides explanations for the preferred response for each question.

The completed measures may be sent to the College Board for machine processing. The College Board will return along with the individual scores of students, an Item Response Report, a Skill Summary Report, a Profile Report, and a Frequency Distribution Report for the entire set of scores.

RELIABILITY: Reliability data are based on representative students in grades 10, 11, and 12 in five states: Georgia, Maryland, Minnesota, New Jersey, and Ohio. Internal consistency computed by Kuder-Richardson Formula 20 ranged from .85 to .93, for the various measures.

VALIDITY: Information concerning content, construct, and criterion-related validity is presented in *Implementing the Career Skills Assessment Program: A Handbook for Effective Program Use*. Content validity has been judged adequate by content specialists, curriculum developers, and practitioners in the fields covered by the measures. Studies to assess construct and criterion-related validity are currently under way.

ADDITIONAL INFORMATION: Measures require seventh-grade reading proficiency. The user's guide, *Implementing the Career Skills Assessment Program*, provides extensive information on interpreting scoring results, statistical characteristics of the measures, and planning, organizing, and administering the assessment activities.

OTHER APPLICABLE CATEGORIES: Career Decision Making, Knowledge about Occupations, Attitudes toward Work, Needs Assessment

TITLE:	*National Assessment of Educational Progress Career and Occupational Development (COD): Released Exercises from the 1973–74 Assessment*
AUTHOR:	National Assessment of Educational Progress (NAEP)
DATE:	1975
ORDER FROM:	National Assessment of Educational Progress, Administration Office, 1860 Lincoln Street, Suite 300, Denver, Colorado 80295
PRICE:	$22.40 per set plus postage and handling (price includes the pertinent objectives booklet)

DESCRIPTION

National Assessment of Educational Progress developed these exercises to survey the educational attainment of 9–, 13–, and 17–year-olds and adults in the area of occupational development. The exercises are objective-based and assess learning in the areas of career decision making, career and occupational abilities, skills useful in the world of work, effective work habits, and attitudes toward work.

There are sixty-one exercises, ten of which are administered to only one age level. The remainder are administered to one or more age levels. The exercises are administered either in group sessions (about twelve students per session) or in a one-to-one interview situation. It is expected that the counselor or administrator will custom-design his or her own exercise package from the sixty-one available exercises, depending on local need.

The exercises are either in multiple-choice or open-ended format and are all paper-and-pencil. An example of an open-ended item for 13- and 17-year-olds and adults is:

Give six reasons why some people who are willing to work find it hard to get a good job.

A typical multiple-choice format is:

A. Have you ever taken any courses such as correspondence courses, on-the-job training, or adult education courses?

◯ Yes (Go to B)
◯ No (End the exercise)
◯ I don't know (End the exercise)
◯ No response (End the exercise)

Scoring keys are provided with the exercises so that open-ended answers may be classified or quantified. Multiple-choice answers may be hand or machine scored. Administration time varies depending on age level and number of exercises administered. Some open-ended exercises have no time limit, while some multiple-choice exercises are limited to thirty seconds. Instructions presented with the exercise package give detailed breakdowns on the amount of time needed for each exercise.

RELIABILITY:	No data presented.
VALIDITY:	Content validity was judged adequate by a group of experts.
ADDITIONAL INFORMATION:	The objectives of this measure are summarized by Shoemaker in chapter 6 (Table 6–2), and more details on the development of the test are provided by Hulsart and Burton in chapter 7. The exercise package provides national norms

for the exercises contained in the COD set. Results are expressed in terms of percentage of students in the nation responding correctly to each exercise during the assessment conducted in the 1973–1974 school year.

OTHER APPLICABLE CATEGORIES:	Career Decision Making, Attitudes toward Work, Knowledge about Occupations

---

TITLE:	*Project M.A.T.C.H. Career Education Program Tests*
AUTHOR:	Norman W. Steinaker
DATE:	1976
ORDER FROM:	Mr. Darvel Allred, Director, Project M.A.T.C.H., Ontario-Montclair School Districts, 950 West "D" Street, PO Box 313, Ontario, California 91761
PRICE:	Grades K–1, $1.55 per copy; set of 35, $5.70; set of 100, $17.00 Grades 2–3, $1.95 per copy; set of 35, $7.35; set of 100, $22.00 Grades 4–6, $2.25 per copy; set of 35, $8.35; set of 100, $25.00 Grades 7–8, $2.45 per copy; set of 35, $10.00; set of 100, $30.00

DESCRIPTION

The *Project M.A.T.C.H. Career Education Program Tests* were designed to assess the career awareness of students from kindergarten to Grade 8. There are four paper-and-pencil tests, which are designed for Grades K–1, 2–3, 4–6, and 7–8.

Test K–1 consists of fifteen multiple-choice items primarily concerned with knowledge about occupations—for example,

If you were making cars you would work:
a. in a factory.
b. in a home.
c. on a farm.

Test 2–3 contains forty-one multiple-choice items covering personal values, knowledge about occupations, and personal economics. For example:

Most people choose their career because of
a. what they are told to do.
b. what they like to do.
c. where they live.

Test 4–6 consists of fifty multiple-choice items covering the entire spectrum of career awareness. Following is an example item from this test:

In order to operate in a community, a business must
a. have its own newspaper.
b. be open all the time.
c. meet all business and legal requirements.
d. employ its workers from the community of its location.

Test 7 −8 also covers all areas of career awareness and includes fifty-four items. Following is an example item from this test:

Take home pay refers to one's
a. gross income.
b. net income.
c. fringe benefits.
d. withholding.

No time limit is indicated for the tests. They are hand scored, and students may respond on the test booklet.

A paper entitled *Evidence of Effectiveness* is available for the tests, and gives further statistical characteristics of the tests.

RELIABILITY: Pearson *r* test-retest reliability ranged from .81 for 4−6 to .92 for K −1.

VALIDITY: Biserial *r* (mean) item-validity index ranged from .29 for 7 −8 to .40 for K −1.

**OTHER
APPLICABLE
CATEGORIES:**   Needs Assessment, Career Decision Making, Knowledge about Occupations, and Attitudes toward Work

---

TITLE: *Student Growth Assessment of Career Development Inventory,* Forms A, B, C, and D

AUTHOR: T. Antoinette Ryan

DATE: Instruments, Fall 1974; final report, June 1975

**FOR
INFORMATION
WRITE TO:**   Mrs. Joanne Katsuyama Swearingen, State Planner, Career Education, State of Hawaii Department of Education, 1270 Queen Emma Street, Room 902, Honolulu, Hawaii 96813

PRICE: Instruments are not ready for distribution at this time (see "Additional Information")

DESCRIPTION

The *Student Growth Assessment of Career Development Inventory* consists of four forms, A, B, C, and D for grades 3, 6, 9, and 12, respectively. This paper-and-pencil test was designed to measure students' knowledge in four career development areas: Self-Realization, Economic Efficiency, Social Relationships, and Civic Responsibility.

Each form is composed of one hundred questions, twenty-five of which are devoted to each of the four career development areas listed above. Items are dichotomous choice and multiple choice for Form A, and multiple choice for Forms B, C, and D. No time limit is given for administration, but administration of each instrument may be broken up into two or four sessions to prevent boredom or fatigue. All forms are hand scored, and scoring keys are provided.

An example item from Form A is

26. A person who bakes bread is called a chef.   TRUE   FALSE

An example item from Form B is

10. When deciding to do something it is important to know
    a) both the advantages and disadvantages of doing it
    b) the advantages of doing it
    c) the disadvantages of doing it
    d) neither the advantages nor disadvantages of doing it

An example item from Form C is

38. There are many different jobs in the society because
    a) there exist so many different needs
    b) people like to try different jobs
    c) the population is so large in this country
    d) there are so many different people in this country

An example item from Form D is

43. The worker hardest hit by unemployment is likely to be the
    a) semi-skilled worker
    b) craftsman
    c) professional person
    d) unskilled worker

RELIABILITY: Pre- and posttest reliabilities ranged from .56 to .80 for the four forms. Form A had reliabilities ranging from .72 to .75, Form B from .77 to .78, Form C from .56 to .59, and Form D from .58 to .80.

VALIDITY: Content validity was established by keying the inventories to the goals, sub-goals, and objectives of the Career Development Continuum. Criterion-related validity has not been determined. Construct validity was determined by obtaining the intercorrelations among the inventory subtests.

ADDITIONAL INFORMATION: A report of the development and evaluation of the four inventories was written, including an administrator's manual of instructions; however, copies for extensive distribution do not exist at this time. The State of Hawaii Department of Education is hoping to obtain enough federal funding in career education to be able to retest the *Student Growth Assessment* of *Career Development Inventory* for additional reliability and validity information. This will help lead the way to making the instruments publicly available in the near future.

OTHER APPLICABLE CATEGORIES: Needs Assessment, Knowledge about Occupations, Career Decision Making

Attitudes toward work

TITLE:	*Student Attitude Survey (SAS),* Form AC (revised edition)
AUTHOR:	Evaluative Research Associates, Inc.
DATE:	1974; revised 1979
ORDER FROM:	Evaluative Research Associates, Inc., 8444 Florissant Road, Suite 207, St. Louis, Missouri 63121

PRICE:

Booklets, package of 50	$12.50
Processing (district, building, class summaries), per student	.35
Individual profiles, per student	.07
Individual labels, per student	.07
(Minimum scoring order, $45.00)	

DESCRIPTION

The *Student Attitude Survey (SAS),* Form AC is designed to measure the attitudes of primary-grade children toward work, school, self, and others. The survey statements are verbally presented by the administrator, and students respond to the items by coloring in a smiling, neutral, or frowning face. There are four scales, one for each of the four categories listed above, and each scale contains fifteen statements. The survey takes about twenty minutes to administer and can be hand or machine scored. Computer scoring includes raw scores, percentile ranks, and T-scores. Output includes class, school building, and district summaries. Also, individual profiles can be provided as well as score labels.

RELIABILITY: The reliability correlations ranged from .77 to .86, using the alpha coefficient.

VALIDITY: The SAS, Form AC was developed from the former instruments named SAS, Form A and SAS, Form C. The items on the revised form consist of those items in Forms A and C which had .60 or higher item validities and were free of sex bias. The scales on the revised form show no significant grade-level differences for preschool through grade 5.

ADDITIONAL INFORMATION: A nationwide normative study on the SAS, Form AC has been completed. A junior high-level form of the SAS is currently being revised (Form BD).

Knowledge about occupations

TITLE:	*Occupational Awareness Inventory (OAI)*
AUTHOR:	Jon C. Marshall
DATE:	1980
ORDER FROM:	Evaluative Research Associates, Inc., 8444 Florissant Road, Suite 207, St. Louis, Missouri 63121

PRICE:

Occupational Awareness Inventory, each	$.65
NCS Answer Sheets, each	.06
Standard Scoring Routine, each	.35

DESCRIPTION

The *Occupational Awareness Inventory* (OAI) is a multiple-choice instrument designed for use with junior high school students who have been exposed to a career awareness program. It consists of forty-eight items that can be either hand or machine scored. The purpose of the OAI is to determine an individual's awareness of careers through testing his or her career information knowledge. The test items are based on job definitions, vocabulary, and similarities among job types.

RELIABILITY:	Internal consistency correlations (using an alpha coefficient) was determined to be .89.
VALIDITY:	Construct validity exists in that all items were drawn from the *Dictionary of Occupational Titles* and are representative of all fifteen career clusters. Only those items that demonstrated high internal validity on an earlier trial form were included in the final form.

TITLE:	*Occupations and Careers Information BOXSCORE,* Series A and B
AUTHORS:	S. Norman Feingold, Sol Swerdloff, Joseph E. Barber
DATE:	Series A, 1978; Series B, 1973
ORDER FROM:	Chronicle Guidance Publications, Inc., Moravia, New York 13118

PRICE:

	List	Net
Series AX, set of 25 plus *Teacher's Guidebook*	$5.00	$4.00
Series BX, set of 25 plus *Teacher's Guidebook*	5.00	4.00
Series A, single copy	.14	.11
Series B, single copy	.14	.11
Series A *Teacher's Guidebook*	3.10	2.50
Series B *Teacher's Guidebook*	3.10	2.50

DESCRIPTION

The *Occupations and Careers Information BOXSCORE* was designed to provide an objective measure of the level of students' knowledge about occupational information. The test is paper-and-pencil and designed for grades 7–12. Areas covered on the test include amounts of schooling needed, licensing requirements, relative salaries, and what it is like to work in different occupations.

Two forms of the test are available, Series A and Series B. The two forms are designed to be as nearly equal in difficulty as possible and to have nearly identical content coverage. The two forms may be administered as pre- and postmeasures.

Each form contains one hundred questions, which are either dichotomous or multiple choice. One fifty-minute class period should be sufficient for administration. Scoring is done by hand, and scoring keys are provided in the *Teacher's Guidebook*.

RELIABILITY:	No formal study has been done.
VALIDITY:	An informal criterion-referenced study was done, but no data are available. The instrument has never been standardized.
ADDITIONAL INFORMATION:	The content of *BOXSCORE* is related to items listed in guidelines for the *Preparation and Evaluation of Career Information Media.* The *Teacher's Guidebook* for each of the series includes suggestions for class discussion for each item.

TITLE:	*Orientation to Career Concepts (OCC) Series*
AUTHORS:	Barbara Fulton and Robert Tolsma
DATE:	1974

ORDER FROM: Evaluative Research Associates, Inc., 8444 Florissant Road, Suite 207, St. Louis, Missouri 63121

PRICE: Total OCC Series, package of 35 reusable test booklets $36.00
Any combination of 5 tests, package of 35   22.00
Any combination of 2 tests, package of 35   11.00
Any one test, package of 35   6.50
Answer sheets, package of 35   37.50

DESCRIPTION

The *Orientation to Career Concepts (OCC) Series* is designed to assess the knowledge of students in ten different aspects of the occupational world: work awareness (relating children's daily activities to adult work), worker activities, vocational vocabulary, absurdities (occupational incongruities), occupational similarities, occupational tools, work stories (relating hobbies, interests, and abilities to possible occupations), working conditions, occupational training, and workers' earnings. Each knowledge area is measured by a separate paper-and-pencil subtest. The subtests can be utilized for grades 3 – 12, depending on ability levels, but are primarily designed for grades 4 – 8.

Each subtest contains twenty items and takes approximately twenty minutes to administer. The subtests may be administered separately or as a battery. Items are in multiple-choice format, and the tests may be hand scored or machine scored. Data processing for the series is available through Evaluative Research Associates.

RELIABILITY: Reliability for this measure has been assessed for both inner city and suburban samples on each of the ten subtests. Reliabilities (alpha coefficient) generally ranged from .60 to .90, but were occasionally much lower for the earlier grades (for example, .145 for occupational training, fourth grade, urban sample.)

VALIDITY: Items on the OCC were validated against student responses on the *Career Concepts Inventory,* the *Dictionary of Occupational Titles,* and the *Occupational Outlook Handbook.*

**ADDITIONAL
INFORMATION:**   The user's manual, entitled *Career Education Strategies,* describes the construction and administration of the OCC Series, provides further data on the statistical properties of the series, and discusses both norm-referenced and criterion-referenced use of the series.

TITLE: *Planning Career Goals (PCG)*

AUTHOR: John C. Flanagan and Associates at American Institute for Research

DATE: 1975 and 1976

ORDER FROM: CTB/McGraw-Hill; Del Monte Research Park; Monterey, California 93940

PRICE: *Test Books* (package of 25 plus *Examiner's Manual* with Answer Key)
Complete Battery $55.00
Ability Measures   32.00
Interest Inventory   15.25
Information Measures   18.00

Examiner's Manual	2.50
Planning Your Career (student guide)	3.00
Career Handbook	9.00
Counselor's Handbook	3.00
PCG Career Planning Profiles, each	.30
Technical Bulletin No. 1	3.25
Examination Kit	5.50
Scoring Service	
Basic Service—Career Planning Report	(minimum order, $100.00)
Complete Battery, per student	1.05
Interest Inventory, per student	.65

(Optional scoring services are available. CompuScan Answer Forms and Scoring Stencils also available.)

DESCRIPTION

Planning Career Goals (PCG) is a battery of paper-and-pencil tests designed to assist guidance and counseling personnel in helping students in grades 8 – 12 make realistic long-term educational and career plans. PCG combines an interest inventory, career-information measures, ability measures, and a life-and-career-plans survey in a single testing system. The career-information measure is applicable to the evaluation of career-education programs, and thus is the only measure which will be described in detail.

The career-information measure contains 240 items that sample knowledge individuals would have acquired if they had studied about an occupation or participated in activities related to an occupation. Items are multiple-choice and the time allotted for completion is eighty minutes. Scoring can be done by hand or by CTB/McGraw-Hill. If scoring is done by CTB/McGraw-Hill, they will return computer-generated narratives of each individual's profile in addition to a group profile.

RELIABILITY: Reliability coefficients (split-half coefficients using Angoff Formula 16) ranged from .67 to .87.

VALIDITY: The measure of career information has been shown to have predictive validity by analyzing the data from five- and eleven-year follow-up studies. In addition, the comparison scores for the information measures are based on the comparisons of those in the occupations in a specific career group.

ADDITIONAL INFORMATION: All interpretations of this measure are based on Project TALENT. Additional materials which accompany the tests include the *Counselor's Handbook,* which provides advice for guiding student use of the *Career Handbook,* in which descriptions of the occupations and personal characteristics data for members of each occupation and career group are listed. Other ancillary materials are acetate stencils for hand-scoring, the *Technical Bulletin,* and the *Examiner's Manual,* which gives instructions for administration.

TITLE: *Short Occupational Knowledge Tests (SOKT)*

AUTHORS: Bruce A. Campbell and Suellen O. Johnson

DATE: 1970

ORDER FROM: Science Research Associates, Inc.; 155 North Wacker Drive; Chicago, Illinois 60606

PRICE:

	List	School
Test booklets (available only in packages of 25 nonreusable booklets)	$16.80	$12.60
Administration cassettes, each	20.00	15.00
Examiner's manual	2.20	1.65
Specimen set	11.14	8.35

DESCRIPTION

The *Short Occupational Knowledge Tests (SOKT)* measure job knowledge, content, and concepts in twelve occupations, and are designed to distinguish between knowledgeable workers and those with only a smattering of knowledge in a specific occupational area. The occupations represented are auto mechanics, bookkeeping, carpentry, drafting, electrical work, machine operating, office-machine operating, plumbing, secretarial work, tool-and-die making, truck driving, and welding. There is no time limit, but each test takes ten to fifteen minutes. The questions are presented in multiple-choice format, and each test has eighteen to twenty items, yielding a single score—pass, fail, or unclassifiable. An optional administration cassette is available from the publisher. Tests are hand scored.

RELIABILITY: Internal consistency correlations (Kuder-Richardson Formula 20) ranged from .63 for carpentry to .88 for auto mechanics. Alternate form correlations ranged from .68 for carpentry to .93 for auto mechanics.

VALIDITY: In experimental studies, the tests correctly discriminated between experts in an area and novices from 73 percent (for office-machine operators) to 88.8 percent (for plumbers) of the time.

ADDITIONAL INFORMATION: Information on test construction and administration procedures, and additional reliability and validity data are given in the examiner's manual.

Career decision making

TITLE:	*Career Maturity Inventory (CMI)*
AUTHOR:	John O. Crites
DATE:	1973 and 1978
ORDER FROM:	CTB/McGraw-Hill, Del Monte Research Park, Monterey, California 93940

PRICE:	Test Books (package of 35 plus *Administration and Use Manual* and Answer Key)	
	Attitude Scale, Screen Form A-2	$16.45
	Attitude Scale, Counseling Form B-1	16.45
	Competence Test	27.30
	Complete Inventory	38.00
	Specimen Set	5.50
	Answer sheets, package of 50	5.00
	Administration and Use Manual	2.50
	Theory and Research Handbook	· 3.25

DESCRIPTION

The *Career Maturity Inventory (CMI)* assesses students' attitudes and competencies related to career decision making. The CMI consists of two subtests, the Attitude Scale and the Competence Test. The Attitude Scale assesses the individual's maturity in five areas of decision making: involvement in the choice process, orientation toward work, independence in decision making, preferences for career-choice factors, and conceptions of the choice process. Two forms of the Attitude Scale are available. Screening Form A-2 provides only an overall measure of the five areas, and thus is most useful for screening or survey purposes. Counseling Form B-1 provides a separate score for each of the five areas, and thus can be used for counseling purposes.

Both Attitude Scales contain fifty items, which the respondent marks either true or false. Form A-2 takes about twenty minutes to complete; Form B-1 takes about thirty minutes.

The Competence Test is composed of five subtests: self-appraisal, occupational information, goal selection, planning, and problem solving. Items are multiple choice and each subtest takes about twenty-five minutes to administer. There are a total of one hundred questions for all the subtests. Both the Attitude Scales and the Competence Test can be hand scored or machine scored, and they may be administered separately or together. Several optional scoring reports are available from CTS/McGraw-Hill if responses are sent there for processing.

The recommended grade level for the CMI is 6 – 12, but other grade and age levels may be used, depending on ability levels.

RELIABILITY: Internal consistency reliability on the Attitude Scales was computed using Kuder-Richardson Formula 20. Reliability coefficients ranged from .65 for grade 9 to .84 for grade 6. Internal consistency coefficients for the Competence Test generally ranged from .70 to .90 for the five scales, across all grades. However, the problem-solving subtest tended to be lower, ranging from .58 for sixth-graders to .82 for eighth-graders.

VALIDITY: For the Attitude Scale, content was validated by ten counseling psychologists. Extensive data on criterion-related and construct validity are also available in the *Theory and Research Handbook*. Both were judged to be acceptable. Validity studies are just beginning on the Competence Test, and preliminary results are available in the *Theory and Research Handbook*. Although data must be interpreted cautiously, construct, content, and criterion-related validity appear adequate. Note, however, the reservations expressed by Westbrook in chapter 5.

ADDITIONAL
INFORMATION: The *Theory and Research Handbook* provides extensive discussion of the construction and theoretical rationale of the tests, and their statistical properties. The *Administration and Use Manual* provides extensive discussion of the interpretation of tests results.

TITLE: *Cognitive Vocational Maturity Test* (as described in the interim report, "The Construction and Validation of a Measure of Vocational Maturity," Center for Occupational Education Technical Paper No. 1, 1973, published by North Carolina State University at Raleigh)

AUTHOR: Bert W. Westbrook and Joseph W. Parry-Hill, Jr.

DATE: 1973

ORDER FROM: Journal Supplement Abstract Service, American Psychological Association, 1200 17th Street, N.W., Washington, D. C. 20036, specify (Ms. No. 968); or ERIC Clearinghouse on Adult, Career and Vocational Education, The National

Center for Research in Vocational Education, The Ohio State University, 1960 Kenny Road, Columbus, Ohio 43210 (ED 101145)

PRICE: From Journal Supplement Abstract Service: $6.00, prepaid. From ERIC Clearinghouse on Adult, Career and Vocational Education: paper (102 pages), $7.82; microfiche, $.83 (add postage to ERIC prices)

DESCRIPTION

The *Cognitive Vocational Maturity Test* is a paper-and-pencil test designed to assess knowledge of the characteristics and requirements of a broad spectrum of occupations. The test is designed to be administered to grades 6 – 9. Questions from six areas judged to be more relevant to the objectives of career-exploration programs are included in the test. The six areas are fields of work, job selection, work conditions, education required, attributes required, and duties. Each of the six areas includes a representative coverage of occupational categories, classified into eight occupational interest fields: service, business contact, organization, technology, outdoor, science, general culture, and arts and entertainment.

There are a total of 238 multiple-choice items on the test. The entire test is organized into two booklets, each designed to be administered in a forty-five-minute class period. Therefore, the entire test requires two forty-five-minute periods to administer. The test can be machine scored using the IBM 1230 Optical Marking Reader, or hand scored.

An example item is

88. Experience in 4-H clubs is most helpful for which one of the following occupations?
    a. Lumberjack
    b. Fisherman
    c. Sales clerk
    d. Farmer
    e. I don't know

RELIABILITY: Internal-consistency-reliability estimates (Kuder-Richardson Formula 20) were determined for grades 6 – 9 on each of the area subtests. Reliabilities were mostly in the .70s and .80s, ranging from .67 for "job selection"—ninth grade, to .90 for "duties"—seventh grade.

VALIDITY: Super's Indices of Vocational Maturity, Lohnes's Readiness for Vocational Planning Scales, and Crites's Construct of Vocational Maturity were used to establish content validity. Criterion-related validity data were obtained from a sample of 249 ninth-graders in North Carolina. Mean scores on all area subtests increased across grade levels, indicating that the test measures vocational maturity. Construct validity was studied by obtaining correlations between the test and a measure of mental ability, and by obtaining intercorrelations among area subtests.

ADDITIONAL INFORMATION: The *Cognitive Vocational Maturity Test* is not available as a commercial instrument at this time, but only as included in the report by Westbrook and Parry-Hill. Complete information on the statistical properties of the instrument is provided in the report as well as an examiner's manual accompanying the test; the latter describes the standard procedures to be followed for administration. For further information on the development and status of this instrument contact Dr. Bert W. Westbrook, Department of Psychology, School of Education, North Carolina State University at Raleigh, P. O. Box 5096, Raleigh, North Carolina 27607.

Process measures

DESCRIPTION

The *Career Education Opinion Surveys* assess the attitudes of students, parents, and community participants about the career education programs in which they are participating or involved. There is a different opinion survey for each group.

Each survey contains from fifteen to twenty items. Items are either in rating-scale or open-ended comment format. No time limit is given for administration, but ten to fifteen minutes per survey should be adequate. The surveys can be either handscored or machine scored by RBS, Inc. Following is a sample item from the *Student Opinion Survey:*

3. Would you say that the Career Education Program has helped you to form career plans?

Definitely No   *Definitely Yes*
1   2   3   4   5

A sample item from the *Parent Opinion Survey* is

2. Have you received enough information about your child's progress in the Career Education Program?

Definitely No   *Definitely Yes*
1   2   3   4   5

A sample item from the *Community Participant Survey* is

3. On the whole, would you say that your organization gains by participation in the Career Education Program?

Definitely No   *Definitely Yes*
1   2   3   4   5

RELIABILITY: Kuder-Richardson Formula 20 coefficients for the *Student* and *Parent Opinion Surveys* ranged from .93 to .99. Reliability for the *Community Participant Survey* is not indicated.

VALIDITY: Content validity was indicated by external reviews.

ADDITIONAL INFORMATION: Other information on psychometric properties can be found in the *RBS Career Education Instrument Service Guide.*

OTHER APPLICABLE CATEGORY: Follow-up Measures

TITLE: *Student Placement and Counseling Effort (S.P.A.C.E.)*

AUTHOR: Minnesota Research Coordinating Unit for Vocational Education

DATE: 1977

ORDER FROM: Minnesota Research and Development Center, B 12 Fraser Hall, University of Minnesota, Minneapolis, Minnesota 55455

PRICE: Free, as long as present supply lasts

DESCRIPTION

The Minnesota Research Coordinating Unit for Vocational Education has designed a series of questionnaires to determine the opinions of students, employers, parents, and faculty on local secondary school counseling and placement programs. The questionnaires were specifically designed to assess the impact of Project S.P.A.C.E. *(Student Placement and Counseling Effort),* but could be easily adapted to conform to local counseling and placement services.

The faculty questionnaire contains twenty-four check-off items and room for open-ended comments—for example;

> Please answer the following questions by checking YES, NO, or UNSURE.
> 1. Should high schools provide comprehensive career-
>   related services including placement assistance?   ___ ___ _____
>   YES   NO   UNSURE

The student questionnaire contains twelve items similar to the above example, and fifteen items that directly assess the students' experience with the counseling program—for example;

Who Provided the Service? (check one or more)	Services	How Useful Was the Service? (check only one)		
	The high school helped me:	very slightly	none	didn't use
☐ S.P.A.C.E. staff				
☐ Counseling staff	3. Plan what to do after leaving high school			
☐ Teaching staff				
☐ Other school staff				

There is also an alternate form of the student questionnaire that does not ask who provided the services. Finally, there is a high school follow-up questionnaire that assesses current employment levels and opinions about the counseling and placement services after the students have entered the work world.

The parent questionnaire is similar to the faculty questionnaire. The employer questionnaire contains eighteen Likert scale items, which ask questions similar to those in the faculty questionnaire and also assess satisfaction with employees who have participated in Project S.P.A.C.E.—for example:

> If any students referred have been hired please rate these persons on the additional factors.
>
> 6. Ability to perform the job.
>
> | above | | | | below | can't |
> |---|---|---|---|---|---|
> | average | a v e r a g e | | | average | say |
> | 1 | 2 | 3 | 4 | 5 | X |

No time limit is given for the questionnaires, but they should take a maximum of twenty minutes to complete. The questionnaires are hand scored.

RELIABILITY: No data available.

VALIDITY: No data available.

**ADDITIONAL
INFORMATION:**   The Minnesota Research Coordinating Unit for Vocational Education will provide a manual for students, *Finding Your Best Job: An Instructional Guide for*

Job-Seeking Skills, and a manual for placement staff, *Placement Assistance Services: Procedures Manual.*

OTHER
APPLICABLE
CATEGORIES: Needs Assessment, Follow-up Measures

Follow-up measures

TITLE:	*Minnesota Satisfaction Questionnaire (MSQ),* long and short forms
AUTHOR:	Work Adjustment Project, Industrial Relations Center, University of Minnesota. Manual written by David J. Weiss, Rene V. Dawis, George W. England, and Lloyd H. Lofquist.
DATE:	1967; long-form revised 1977 to remove sex bias
ORDER FROM:	Vocational Psychology Research, N620 Elliott Hall, University of Minnesota, 75 East River Road, Minneapolis, Minnesota 55455
PRICE:	Requests for purchase of the *MSQ* should include a description of the qualifications of the prospective user. The *MSQ* is available for use only under the supervision of qualified psychologists.

Long-form MSQ (1967, revision will be sent only if specifically requested; minimum order, 15 copies, add postage to all prices).

15 – 499 copies, each	.20
500 – 999 copies, each	.18
1000 or more copies, each	.16
Computer scoring, per individual (minimum, 20 copies)	.55

Short-form MSQ (minimum order, 30 copies, add postage to all prices)
30 – 499 copies, each   .10
500 – 999 copies, each   .09
1000 or more copies, each   .08
Computer scoring, per individual (minimum, 20 copies)   .35

DESCRIPTION

The *Minnesota Satisfaction Questionnaire (MSQ)* is designed to measure an employee's satisfaction with his or her job. Two forms of the questionnaire are available for administration: a long form, containing one hundred items, and a short form, containing twenty items.

The long-form *MSQ* measures job satisfaction by means of twenty-five-item rating scales and a twenty-item general job satisfaction scale. The scales are rated on a continuum from very dissatisfied to very satisfied. The twenty scales in the long form are Ability Utilization, Achievement, Activity, Advancement, Authority, Company Policies and Practices, Compensation, Co-workers, Creativity, Independence, Moral Values, Recognition, Responsibility, Security, Social Service, Social Status, Supervision-Human Relations, Supervision-Technical, Variety, and Working Conditions.

The short-form *MSQ* is based on twenty items of the long form that best represent each of the twenty scales.

No time limit is set for administration of either test but no longer than thirty minutes should be required. Scoring can be done by hand with the scoring keys provided. Computer scoring is also available from Vocational Psychology Research.

RELIABILITY: Hoyt reliability coefficients were determined for each of the twenty scales of the long form for twenty-seven normative groups. Reliabilities were mostly in the .70s, .80s, and .90s.

VALIDITY: Construct validity was determined from validation studies of the Minnesota Importance Questionnaire *(MIQ)*, based on Hoppock's Theory of Work Adjustment. The results indicated that the *MSQ* measured satisfaction in accordance with expectations from the Theory of Work Adjustment.

**ADDITIONAL
INFORMATION:**   The *Manual for the Minnesota Satisfaction Questionnaire* contains normative data for the scales, administration and scoring instructions, and information on the development and evaluation of the questionnaire.

TITLE: *Student and Employer Surveys, School District of Pontiac*

AUTHOR: School District of Pontiac, Michigan

DATE: 1974, 1975, 1976

ORDER FORM: Stuart Packard, Research and Evaluation Department, School District of the City of Pontiac, 44 State Street, Pontiac, Michigan 48053

PRICE: Free, unless demand is heavy; then, nominal charge for reproduction and handling

DESCRIPTION

The 1974 "Follow-up Survey of 1972 Graduates" was used as part of a USOE-funded study of cooperative education. Approximately thirty items asked 1972 Pontiac graduates to evaluate the contribution of their school experience to their occupational choices and placement.

The 1975 "Pontiac Area Employer" survey also was used in the USOE-funded study of cooperative education. Employers were asked to respond to sixteen items about the preparation for work of graduates of the Pontiac schools and the value of vocational education in that process. Following is an example item from the employer survey:

8. In general, how would you rate the job which the Pontiac Schools do in preparing people for work—would you say they do a very good job, a fair job or a poor job of training students?

Very good job	1
Fair job	2
Poor job	3

The 1976 survey of the senior class of 1976 was designed to gather initial information to be used as a basis for a longitudinal study (now terminated) of the class. The 1976 survey contains about 70 Likert and dichotomous-choice items to assess the students' future career plans, current attitudes, and opinions about the current high school counseling program. The following is an example:

How do you feel about the following statements?

	Agree Strongly	Agree	Disagree	Disagree Strongly	No Opinion
Good luck is more important than hard work for success	1	2	3	4	5

No time limit is given for the surveys, but they should take about thirty minutes to complete. The surveys are hand scored.

RELIABILITY: No attempts have been made to test the reliability of the survey instruments.

VALIDITY: No attempts have been made to test the validity of the survey instruments.

ADDITIONAL INFORMATION: Summaries of the preliminary results from these surveys in the School District of Pontiac are also available.

OTHER APPLICABLE CATEGORIES: Process Measures

Subject index

Author index

Adkins, W. R., 36
Ahmann, J. S., 152, 157
Algina, J. J., 120, 132
Allen, J. A., 6 – 7, 15
Ansell, E. M., 94, 110
Arcia, M., 67, 95, 96, 98, 99, 100, 101, 104, 111
Arterburg, E. J., 259
Asche, F. M., 150, 157
Astin, A. W., 25, 36
Ausubel, D. P., 31, 36

Bachrach, P. B., 24, 25, 29, 37
Bailey, L. J., 1, 2, 3, 4, 11, 15, 122, 123, 132, 150, 157, 239, 241, 248
Baker, R. F., 61, 62, 65
Baker, R. L., 74, 108
Baltes, P. B., 32, 33, 36
Barak, A., 110
Barber, J. E., 273

Becker-Haven, J. F., 35, 37
Berg, I., 228, 237
Blau, P. M., 34, 36
Bloom, B. S., 156, 157
Boardman, R., 162, 171
Bonnet, D. G., 13, 16, 106, 108, 174 – 75, 207, 244, 249
Boocock , S. S., 162, 171
Borow, H., 2, 39, 40, 175, 241, 244
Brennan, R. L., 62, 64
Brewer, J. M., 18, 36
Brickell, H. M., 175, 176, 214, 241, 244, 249
Brolin, D. E., 14, 15, 16
Brown, D., 94, 103, 110
Burnett, K. F., 35, 37
Burton, N. W., 114, 134, 175, 241, 244

Campbell, B. A., 275
Campbell, D. T., 94, 107, 108
Campbell, J. P., 53, 64

293

Please send me _____ copies of ASSESSING CAREER DEVELOPMENT by John D. Krumboltz and Daniel A. Hamel (eds.) @ $22.95 plus $1.50 for postage/handling. In California, add sales tax.
Enclosed is my check ☐, money order ☐, or credit card number (on reverse) ☐.

_____
NAME

_____
STREET

_____
CITY   STATE   ZIP

Please send me _____ copies of ASSESSING CAREER DEVELOPMENT by John D. Krumboltz and Daniel A. Hamel (eds.) @ $22.95 plus $1.50 for postage/handling. In California, add sales tax.
Enclosed is my check ☐, money order ☐, or credit card number (on reverse) ☐.

_____
NAME

_____
STREET

_____
CITY   STATE   ZIP

Please send me _____ copies of ASSESSING CAREER DEVELOPMENT by John D. Krumboltz and Daniel A. Hamel (eds.) @ $22.95 plus $1.50 for postage/handling. In California, add sales tax.
Enclosed is my check ☐, money order ☐, or credit card number (on reverse) ☐.

_____
NAME

_____
STREET

_____
CITY   STATE   ZIP

VISA or
MASTERCHARGE

CARD NUMBER

EXPIRATION DATE   SIGNATURE

Mail to: Box JK
                    Mayfield Publishing Company
                    285 Hamilton Avenue
                    Palo Alto, CA 94301

Allow 4 to 6 weeks for delivery.

VISA or
MASTERCHARGE

CARD NUMBER

EXPIRATION DATE   SIGNATURE

Mail to: Box JK
                    Mayfield Publishing Company
                    285 Hamilton Avenue
                    Palo Alto, CA 94301

Allow 4 to 6 weeks for delivery.

VISA or
MASTERCHARGE

CARD NUMBER

EXPIRATION DATE   SIGNATURE

Mail to: Box JK
                    Mayfield Publishing Company
                    285 Hamilton Avenue
                    Palo Alto, CA 94301

Allow 4 to 6 weeks for delivery.

4